Translated Texts for Historians

This series is designed to meet the needs of students of ancient and medieval history and others who wish to broaden their study by reading source material, but whose knowledge of Latin or Greek is not sufficient to allow them to do so in the original language. Many important Late Imperial and Dark Age texts are currently unavailable in translation and it is hoped that TTH will help to fill this gap and to complement the secondary literature in English which already exists. The series relates principally to the period 300–800 AD and includes Late Imperial, Greek, Byzantine and Syriac texts as well as source books illustrating a particular period or theme. Each volume is a self-contained scholarly translation with an introductory essay on the text and its author and notes on the text indicating major problems of interpretation, including textual difficulties.

Editorial Committee
Sebastian Brock, Oriental Institute, University of Oxford
Averil Cameron, Keble College, Oxford
Henry Chadwick, Oxford
John Davies, University of Liverpool
Carlotta Dionisotti, King's College, London
Peter Heather, University College, London
Mark Humphries, National University of Ireland, Maynooth
William E. Klingshirn, The Catholic University of America
Michael Lapidge, Clare College, Cambridge
Robert Markus, University of Nottingham
John Matthews, Yale University
Claudia Rapp, University of California, Los Angeles
Raymond Van Dam, University of Michigan
Michael Whitby, University of Warwick
Ian Wood, University of Leeds

General Editors
Gillian Clark, University of Bristol
Mary Whitby, University of Liverpool

D1600387

Front cover illustration: The Arch of Constantine, Rome, from a drawing in J.A. Dosio, *Urbis Romanae aedificiorum illustrium quae supersunt reliquiae* (Florence, 1569)

A full list of published titles in the Translated Texts for Historians series is available on request. The most recently published are shown below.

For full details of Translated Texts for Historians, including prices and ordering information, please write to the following:
All countries, except the USA and Canada: Liverpool University Press, 4 Cambridge Street, Liverpool, L69 7ZU, UK (*Tel* +44-[0]151-794 2233 *Fax* +44-[0]151-794 2235, Email J.M. Smith@liv.ac.uk, http://www.liverpool-unipress.co.uk). **USA and Canada:** University of Pennsylvania Press, 4200 Pine Street, Philadelphia, PA 19104-6097, USA (*Tel* +1-215-898-6264, *Fax* +1-215-898-0404).

Translated Texts for Historians
Volume 39

Constantine and Christendom

The Oration to the Saints
The Greek and Latin Accounts of the Discovery of the Cross
The Edict of Constantine to Pope Silvester

Translated with notes and introduction by
MARK EDWARDS

Liverpool
University
Press

First published 2003
Liverpool University Press
4 Cambridge Street
Liverpool, L69 7ZU

British Library Cataloguing-in-Publication Data
A British Library CIP Record is available.
ISBN 0-85323-648-8

Set in Times by
Koinonia, Manchester
Printed in the European Union by
Antony Rowe Ltd, Chippenham, Wilts

To Alexander, Lucian and Jacob

CONTENTS

ACKNOWLEDGEMENTS

Three scholars have been kind enough to read through the entire typescript of this volume. Mary Whitby's comments on the structure and content of the introduction have been invaluable, and her vigilance has enabled me to avoid many inconcinnities and errors in the translation of the *Oration to the Saints*. Averil Cameron offered suggestions on the bibliography, and helped me to give a clearer and more comprehensive account of the traditions surrounding Helena and the discovery of the Cross. In the course of correcting the inaccuracies and omissions in my notes to the *Donation*, Raymond Davis has greatly enhanced my exiguous knowledge of Rome and the Papacy in the eighth century. Michael Whitby and David Taylor have given permission for the use of the map at the end of *The Ecclesiastical History of Evagrius Scholasticus* (Liverpool University Press, 2000) as a prototype for the map of Constantine's empire in this volume; the map of Rome is based, with the permission of the author and cartographer, on the one at the end of Raymond Davis, *Lives of the Eighth-Century Popes* (Liverpool University Press, 1992). The map of Jerusalem is reproduced, with the permission of Oxford University Press, from *The Oxford Encyclopedia of Ancient Near Eastern Archaeology* (New York, 1997), vol. 3, p. 236. The cover design is based, with the permission and assistance of the library staff at Christ Church, Oxford, on a drawing in J.A. Dosio, *Urbis Romanae aedificiorum illustrium quae supersunt reliquiae* (Florence, 1569). I also owe a debt of gratitude to Robin Lane Fox, who introduced me to the *Oration* fifteen years ago, and to Christ Church for its continuing support of my research. My wife Mali has been my inspiration in this work, as in everything else.

July 2002   Christ Church, Oxford

INTRODUCTION

The documents presented to English readers in this volume are united by the name of Constantine, a well-known figure of whom we know too little. His reputation states that he was the man who made Christianity the official religion of the Roman Empire; it may therefore be surprising to many readers that historians in the modern age have wondered whether Constantine was a Christian, and that some (though not the majority) have returned a negative answer. The first text in this volume, the *Oration to the Saints*, is the only one that has a bearing on this question about the religion of the man himself; if it is authentic, there is no doubt that he at least intended to be a Christian. The other two pieces, legendary in content, are none the less of great interest to historians, for it may be said without paradox that mediaeval Christendom was shaped more by the acts attributed to Constantine than by any that he actually performed. Two versions of the *Discovery* (or *Invention*) *of the Holy Cross* are translated here, the Latin being the longer one while the Greek is now presumed to be the older. Whereas these are fictions, the *Donation of Constantine* is a fabrication, and no other work of this kind was so artfully exploited or so angrily derided in late mediaeval and renaissance Europe. I hope to show in my notes and introduction that both forgeries, the *Donation* and the *Invention of the Cross*, ought to command the admiration of historians and classicists today, not only because they imposed upon the world for so long, but also because as literary artefacts they are not devoid of subtlety or even innocent of scholarship.

The *Oration*, on the other hand, is defended here as a genuine work of Constantine. The reader should be advised that, while my view of its authenticity is shared by most historians in the English-speaking world, the date that I assign to it and my estimate of its motives are unusual enough to be called eccentric. The arguments below draw heavily from, and sometimes add a little to, the ones that I have advanced elsewhere in studies of a more technical character. In the case of the other two texts I have followed the views of other scholars, and even (where this was possible) a consensus, though, as will become apparent, I have introduced some corollaries and conjectures of my own. It has not always been possible to follow the common method of historians, by commencing with the 'background' then proceeding to the text. The reason is that in all three cases much or all of the background must be constructed from our reading of the text itself, and no dissociation of the content from the context is permissible. Moreover, another starting point must be chosen before we approach the texts, for all study of religion in late antiquity or the early middle ages demands preliminary reflection upon the usage of the word 'Christian'. For the purposes of this volume we must ask above all what factors might cause a detached historian to apply it or deny it to a man such as Constantine.

GENERAL THOUGHTS ON THE CHRISTIANITY OF CONSTANTINE

By reputation Constantine was the earliest Christian emperor, and a legion of facts can be enrolled in defence of this tradition. In 306, on proclaiming himself the emperor or Augustus of the west, he revoked the edicts against the Christians that had been enacted in 303 by the emperors Diocletian and Maximian. In 312 he entered Rome as the conqueror of Maxentius, his rival in the west, and almost at once began to act as arbiter between Catholics and Donatists in Africa. In 313 he joined Licinius, an aspirant to the eastern throne, in announcing the repeal of legislation against the Church through-out the Empire; in 314 he summoned a council of bishops at Arles in Gaul; in 321 he invaded the dominions of Licinius – now not only his co-regent but his son-in-law – on the pretext of delivering the Christians from oppression; having overthrown Licinius in 324, he presided over the first ecumenical council at Nicaea in 325. By this time it was generally believed (on his own report) that he had been converted by a sign from heaven shortly before his seizure of Rome. In 330 he built a new capital at Constantinople, the ancient Byzantium and modern Istanbul, where the erection of pagan altars was forbidden. This city remained the seat of Christian emperors, with barely an intermission, for 1100 years.

It is therefore not surprising that the question whether Constantine was a Christian is a new one; historians from Eusebius in his own century to Mommsen[1] in the nineteenth never thought it profitable to ask it. To judge a king by his words and not his deeds, though it may no longer be a pious obligation, remains for scholars an axiom of neutrality, an acknowledgement

---

1 Mommsen (1996), 448 declares the question 'immaterial', but adds that Constantine (whom he despises) was 'not the genius that Burckhardt would like to make him out to be'.

of the limits of inquiry. History leaves to God the intrigues of Rodrigo Borgia, the egotism of Henry VIII, the treachery of his rivals and their Catholic successors; to deny that they were Christians merely because they were bad Christians would be to misunderstand the usage of a time which applied that term to any person who was neither Turk nor Jew. Constantine, perhaps as bad a man as any of these, was also as loud as any of them in his profession of Christianity; on this point the aspersions of his pagan critics – Julian, Eunapius and Zosimus – lend angry confirmation to the praises of the Church. At first sight, then, it seems that the Swiss historian Jacob Burckhardt was guilty of a solecism against his own profession when he doubted the sincerity of the emperor in his strident masterpiece, *The Age of Constantine the Great*.[1]

For all that, Burckhardt's challenge was not misplaced. Constantine, in contrast to the majority of European sovereigns who came after him, had once espoused other gods and other practices than those of Christianity – had indeed been at least a nominal persecutor of the sect – and after his conversion he continued to allow a choice of religions to his subjects. Even his own professions seem equivocal, as his coins did not eschew the solar imagery that had previously betokened his allegiance to Apollo, and one of his statues in the new capital at Constantinople is believed by some to have taken Apollo Helios as its model.[2] When names of pagan deities disappeared from his panegyrics, they were not replaced by those of God or Christ.[3] His legislation is taken as a key to his beliefs, and yet it hallowed not the Sabbath or the Lord's day but the day of the sun, and seems to have tolerated public sacrifice while suppressing only private divination.[4] The subsidies to churches under Constantine were unprecedented, but his legislation openly winked at the rites of pagans even while it openly abused them.[5] Worst of all, the date and circumstances of his conversion were disputed in antiquity, but

1 Burckhardt (1880/1949).

2 Fowden (1991).

3 See Alföldi (1948), 69–71 on this evasion, and 55–60 on the assimilation of Christianity to the worship of the sun. On the latter topic see also Baynes (1931), 95–103, but contrast the objections of Smith (1997) to the common view of Constantius I (father of Constantine) as a solar monotheist.

4 On divination, especially with respect to the emperor's fortunes, see *Theodosian Code* 16.10.1. The law against all sacrifices reported by Eusebius, *Constantine* 2.45 is not found in the *Theodosian Code*, and would have rendered superfluous the prohibition of sacrifice in 341 under his sons Constantius and Constans (*Theodosian Code* 16.10.2).

5 See *Theodosian Code* 9.16.2, with the comment of Alföldi (1948), 77, and compare the tone of *Oration*, chapter 11.

even his Christian advocates agreed that he deferred his baptism to the eve of death.[1]

The ends of faith will always coexist with those of prudence and ambition in the piety of statesmen. But since the question 'What was Constantine if not a Christian?' is susceptible of an answer that we could not give in the case of Cromwell or Charlemagne, it is no anachronism to suggest that his religion was a mere façade, an instrument of policy. Perhaps the strongest argument against this thesis is that it is not clear what an emperor stood to gain by such a fraud. According to most estimates, the Christians at that time were a small community, especially in the west; and even if it were true (as it is not) that they made up in cohesion what they lacked in numbers, the same or more could be said of the equestrian and senatorial orders, which continued to supply the state with magistrates, and the pagan cults with priests, up to the fall of the Roman Empire. Even in the last years of the fourth century the Christians would appear to have made up only half of the Senate in Rome,[2] so why should Constantine set out to estrange this wealthy and compact élite? We might say that it was not the civil magistrates but the army that raised Constantine to the throne, and it is probable that soldiers evinced a preference for cults that were not tied to local monuments and hereditary priesthoods. But in that case, why forsake the vaguer monotheism or henotheism of his early years, and ask his troops to worship the feeble Galilean, rather than Mithras or the Unconquered Sun? In any case the earliest date that is plausibly assigned to his conversion is the day in 312 before he entered Rome and, after six years of fighting for his title, exchanged the rule of arms for that of law.

Modern scholarship therefore seldom echoes Burckhardt's judgment on the architect of Christendom.[3] On the other hand, one often meets the opinion that, although he was not a hypocrite, he was bound to wander into syncretism or at least into injudicious toleration, as he had only the most imperfect familiarity with the creed of his own religion. Sometimes this is stated *a priori*: Constantine, a mere soldier, could not have mastered doctrines that are now known only to theologians educated at certain universities. Two fallacies are embedded in this argument. As regards the

1 See Eusebius, *Constantine* 4.62–63, where Constantine avers that he had hoped to undergo baptism in the Jordan.

2 See Ambrose, Letters 17 and 18, urging the demolition of the Altar of Victory in 384 against the petition of the prefect Symmachus. It is clear that neither combatant lacked supporters in the Senate.

3 See especially now the animadversions of Drake (2000), 12–18.

obscurity of the doctrines, that is a twentieth-century perception, and there is evidence that lay Christians of the fourth century, like those of the seventeenth, were instructed in the minutest points of faith. As to the incapacity of Constantine, he was the son of an emperor, and we ought not to slight the intellect of a man who overcame the best commanders of his day, who when he died could claim to have enjoyed the longest tenure of the Empire since Augustus, and who, unlike most of his famous predecessors, contrived to leave the entire realm to his sons.

But why, it may be asked, if he was not still flirting with his old religion, did Constantine do so little to enforce the spread of Christianity? How is it that he left it to his sons to outlaw sacrifice, to Gratian to banish sacerdotal privilege, to the younger Theodosius to separate the pagans from their livelihoods, and to the laity of the fifth century to sack the most famous shrines?[1] A similar question might be put to any of his successors, for, notwithstanding the modern vogue for talking of a 'Christian persecution', the law was their only instrument, and they made no attempt to reciprocate the tortures that had been applied to the bodies of the faithful by the emperors and governors who preceded Constantine. Even if some temples fell with imperial connivance, others were protected by decree.[2] Some historians trace this lukewarm policy to the strength of paganism or the weakness of Christianity, but theories of this kind lose their plausibility when we waive the dubious premiss that a religion must be intolerant because it is exclusive. We inherit this belief from the epoch of the Reformation, when diversity offended the pretensions of the state. The rulers of the Constantinian Empire, if they listened to the churchmen who advised them, will have rated *philanthropia* or humanity second only to faith itself; and after all, those Christians who believe that they have a duty to be bigots have some difficulty in annotating Christ's injunctions against the use of force.

It is generally agreed that the date of his baptism does not compromise the veracity of Constantine: the sacrament was frequently postponed by those who feared, with some authority in the New Testament and ecclesi-

---

1 On the slow attrition of paganism through Christian legislation see Salzman (1993).

2 See *Theodosian Code* 16.10.18–20. The buildings were preserved to be given over to better purposes, but Christian eruptions against them (see e.g. Marinus, *Proclus* 15 and 28) suffice to prove that they were still regarded as pagan centres. In Gaza, where the pagans were a truculent majority even in the late fourth century, magistrates connived at the survival of idolatrous practices in the shrine of Marnas, the local Zeus (Mark the Deacon, *Life of Porphyry of Gaza* 28).

astical teaching, that sins committed after it might be inexpiable.[1] Nor should we assume that the unbaptized would necessarily be ignorant, for the rite was often preceded by a series of catechetical discourses. Those who had yet to receive these, if they were literate, could discover all that was requisite to salvation in the Bible, in commentaries and homilies, in encyclicals and apologetic texts. We know of one apology by a contemporary of Constantine, the treatise of Arnobius *Against the Nations*, which was written by a Christian still awaiting his baptism.[2] Evidently, therefore, there is nothing in our knowledge of Constantine or of the Church that he adorned which would forbid us to regard him as the author of the first document translated in this volume, a defence of Christianity which is commonly entitled the *Oration to the Saints*.

THE APOLOGETIC TRADITION BEFORE CONSTANTINE

Some prefatory remarks are necessary to the reading of the *Oration*. Whether or not it was an ancient custom, it appears to be a law of modern scholarship that every Greek or Latin text must be assigned to a genre. No genre can be plausibly suggested for the oration except that of 'apologetic': this adjectival noun, first coined by Christians to define a species of literature, derives from the verb *apologein*, which means to offer a defence in court.[3] But whereas one who delivers an 'apology' (*apologia*) has only a single client in view, most commonly himself, the defendant in 'apologetic' is not an individual but a cause or an intellectual tradition. The works of the earliest Christian apologists retain a forensic colour, since, at a time when Christianity is unlawful, they undertake to show that the charges laid against the new religion are false, and that the policy of the magistrates is offensive to Roman principles of justice. In the second century it is common form to address a pagan magistrate, most usually the emperor, but all the surviving treatises are too long, too hortatory and too copious in argument to have

1 See e.g. Heb. 10.26.
2 For an unusual conjecture as to the date and occasion of this work, see Edwards (1999a), 198–99.
3 See further Price (1999), 115–16; Frede (1999), 225–31. The working definition of apologetic adopted by the editors of this volume (p. 1) is that it is 'the defence of a cause or party supposed to be of paramount importance to the speaker'. It was Constantine's contemporaries Lactantius and Eusebius who first made lists of apologetic writings on behalf of Christianity, and, while apologetic was thus established as a branch of ecclesiastical literature, it may reasonably be doubted whether comparable traditions ever emerged among Jews or pagans.

been designed to temper the severity of one man. Every Christian litigant takes it upon himself not merely to prove that he and his co-religionists are innocent, but to retaliate the jibes on the accusers: it is they, and not the Christians, who are atheists, murderers, fornicators and worshippers of imaginary gods.

There is no frontier between apologetic and polemic, for anyone on trial before a jury would do well in his *apologia* to carry the battle back to his opponents through derision, innuendo, hostile questioning and counter-accusation. In the most celebrated of all apologies – the speech that Plato puts into the mouth of the philosopher Socrates at his trial before an Athenian jury in 399 BC – there is also a foreshadowing of the genre that philosophers called protreptic, as Socrates attempts to convince his judges that his conscientious ignorance is a better path to wisdom than their unreflective knowledge. But in a private apology these elements of polemic or protreptic are subservient to the object of acquitting the defendant; in Christian apologetic, on the other hand, they often swell to engross all but a fraction of the text. The authors were, by their own account, rhetoricians and philosophers, who will have been aware that oratory was conventionally divided into three modes: the forensic for use in court, the symbouleutic or deliberative which was suited to political assemblies, and the epideictic or theatrical, which during the second century was the stock-in-trade of itinerant performers known as sophists.[1] Once again the boundaries are not rigid, for no-one could have hoped to sway a judge or move the Senate if he failed to round his periods, to adorn his diction with the occasional metaphor, to divide his speech according to rule and to end it with a memorable flourish. If one wrote, as the Christians did, with a purpose, one must also write for show, and their works bear a variety of titles which bespeak a variety of styles and motives. Aristides (as we hear[2]) wrote an *Apology* to Hadrian (c. 140 AD), Justin perhaps two *Apologies* to the Antonines (c. 160), Athenagoras an *Embassy* to Marcus Antoninus (c. 170), Tatian an *Oration to the Greeks* (who include the Romans, c. 170), Theophilus a long treatise *To Autolycus* (c. 180), Clement of Alexandria a *Protrepticus* (c. 190) and Tertullian an *Apologeticus* or *Apologeticum* to the Roman magistrates (197), together with a treatise *To the Nations*. Tertullian

1 For a circumspect application of rhetorical categories to the Greek apologists see Young (1999), 82–90.

2 Eusebius, *Church History* 4.3.3. Two versions of the *Apology* survive, one in Syriac and one in Greek, together with further fragments of the Greek. The discrepancies are so grave that one despairs of recreating the Greek original.

sowed a crop of neologisms – among them the noun *Romanitas* and the titular usage of *Apologeticus*[1] – in a style that defied the canons of Latinity; by contrast his fellow African Minucius Felix essayed a dextrous imitation of Ciceronian dialogue in his *Octavius* (?c. 170), which is adversarial but not forensic, and is plainly calculated not to appease but to beguile, and hence convert, the learned ear.

By the third century, Christians felt secure enough and erudite enough to address their harangues to intellectual critics rather than to their temporal overlords. Origen's eight books *Against Celsus* (?248), far exceeding the work of any previous apologist in learning and prolixity, belong to the category of remonstrations with the dead that had already amused the orators and philosophers of the second century. Origen was surpassed in his turn after fifty years by Eusebius, who maintained in his *Preparation for the Gospel* (c. 310) that the best thoughts of the Greeks exposed the vanity of idols and corroborated the teachings of the Church. Eusebius is the first author to possess an inventory of the Greek apologists;[2] at about the same time the African Lactantius reviewed the labours of his countrymen with ostentatious eloquence, not making any secret of his desire to outdo them in the seven books of his *Divine Institutes* (c. 310).[3] A portion of this work is dedicated to the young Constantine, and, like the *Preparation for the Gospel*, it does not contain any reference to a current persecution. The same is true of Arnobius' seven books *Against the Nations* (c. 295 or c. 325), which were written not to blunt the sword of a magistrate but to prove to senior churchmen that his conversion was sincere.[4] Apologetic had now become an art that one might cultivate with no pretence of seeking a pagan audience – a point that must be taken into account when one inquires into the date, occasion, authorship and initial destination of the *Oration to the Saints*.

We must concede, for example, that the *Oration* is addressed to a Christian audience at a time when persecution was remembered but not feared. Nevertheless, so long as it shares the character of works that were composed in a different era, the passing of the tyrants does not preclude the use of the

---

1 On the title see Price (1999), 115–16.

2 See *Church History* 4.3.1 (Quadratus), 4.3.3 (Aristides), 4.8.3 (Justin), 4.26.1 (Melito, Apollinarius), 5.17.5 (Miltiades). The last three and Quadratus are only names to us. Frede (1999), 227–28 observes that only petitions to the emperor are recognised by Eusebius as apologies, a fact that explains the absence of Theophilus and Tatian, though not that of Melito. See Frede (1999), 228 on references to Tertullian in the *Church History*.

3 See *Divine Institutes* 5.1, with the remarks of Edwards (1999a), 203–04.

4 Jerome, *On Illustrious Men* 80.

term 'apologetic'. Again, the speaker purports to be an emperor who has repealed the legislation against the Christians and tolerates only the inconspicuous practice of pagan rites; it follows that the Christians no longer had so much need of a protector, but not that Christianity no longer had any need of an intellectual defence. Again we might imagine that a Christian among Christians would not be required to vindicate his character; the example of Arnobius corrects us, and even if the sovereign could not be forced, he might think it expedient to include his own apology in an apologetic exercise on behalf of his newborn faith. Finally, it is true that when the pagans were in the ascendant, the majority of those who took up the pen in the cause of Christendom were Greeks; we should not infer, however, that the present speech is more likely to have been written in that language, as the Latins become more prominent, and more verbose, in the epoch when apologetic writing served primarily to embellish the reputation of the Christian orator.

THE *ORATION TO THE SAINTS*: CONTENT, AUTHENTICITY AND OCCASION

The *Oration to the Saints* appears as the fifth book[1] in Eusebius' biographical panegyric *On the Life of Constantine*. In the main body of this work he alludes to the speech by a slightly different title:

> The king therefore presented the written text of his words in the Roman tongue, and the interpreters whose task it was translated it into the Greek language. As a specimen of the translations, and so that no-one may imagine that my testimony to his speeches is a boast, I shall append immediately after the present work the one that he himself entitled "About the Assembly of the Saints", having dedicated this writing to the Church of God. (*Life of Constantine* 4.32).

If all 26 chapters were recited on the original occasion, the speech will have taken about two hours to deliver.[2] The orator commences by declaring that it is now the date of the Passion.[3] After this his discourse falls into three

---

1 See the final sentence of the translation in this volume.

2 The following synopsis is borrowed, with slight changes, from Edwards (1999b), 253–54.

3 I would take this to mean Good Friday, against Hall (1998), 96, though I agree that such a date would be incompatible with an allocution to an assembly composed of bishops, who would be celebrating Easter in their own churches. As Barnes (2001), 34 now agrees, there is no reason to assume that Constantine was addressing such an audience.

parts. The first (Chapters 2–10) puts the case for monotheism: the pagan gods, with their diverse births and characters, cannot maintain the concord of the universe, and their immoralities prove that they are either living demons or dead mortals. The notion that the world exists by chance is indefensible, as an almighty and benevolent creator would be needed to appease the eternal conflict of the elements. Plato had an inkling of the truth, but no philosopher has understood how the sum of things is governed by the Father through the offices of his Son.

Next (in Chapters 11–19) he extols the voluntary abasement of the Son in his incarnation. A god in human form, replete with virtue and inalienable wisdom, Christ has opened up the path to heaven by his teaching. Having manifested his philanthropy by his willingness to suffer, he imitates his Father's magnanimity by waiving his revenge for a certain interval, during which he enlightens every nation with the brilliance of his resurrected glory. His life and vindication were foretold by the Hebrew prophets, but the most persuasive arguments for pagans are a Sibylline acrostic which predicts the Day of Judgment and the Fourth Eclogue of Virgil, which celebrates the birth of an unnamed infant as the prelude to a returning age of gold.

Finally (Chapters 20–26) the speaker declares his personal adherence to the Saviour. He apostrophizes Decius, Valerian and Aurelian, the three persecuting emperors of the third century, and cites himself as a witness to the calamitous effects of the great persecution initiated by his predecessor Diocletian in 303. He claims that those successors of Diocletian who have perished most ingloriously were those who had compounded their defiance of the imperial constitution with the oppression of the Church. He ends with the praise of Christ, whose wise and merciful dominion he will never cease to acknowledge and proclaim.

Authenticity

Suspicion that the sermon is a forgery by Eusebius[1] is easily rebutted. First, no intimate knowledge of its contents is suggested by his approximation to the present title: what did he understand by an 'Oration *about* the Assembly of the Saints'? Second, no other work of his fluent pen reveals that he was capable of quoting a line from Virgil, whose Fourth Eclogue is almost a second scripture to our speaker. Third, the speech implies that pagan sacrifice is lawful, while Eusebius is the one witness who expressly credits

---

1 Or even that he has tampered with it, as Davies (1991) contends.

Constantine with a general prohibition of such rites. Fourth, the speaker intimates with regret that he was not raised in the knowledge of the true God; Eusebius states that Constantine returned to the 'religion of his father' in adopting monotheism. Finally, the theology of the *Oration*, as it is set out in the tenth chapter, conceives the second person of the Trinity, Jesus Christ, as an emanation from the Godhead, the uttered speech or *logos prophorikos* of the Father who issues from his immanent thought or *logos endiathetos*. Eusebius rejected this analogy, which seemed to him to contradict the scriptures and to compromise the indivisibility of God.[1]

Eusebius once excluded, the authorship could almost be awarded by default to Constantine, but in addition the character of the speech itself tells heavily in favour of his claim. As a forgery it could not have been published in the emperor's lifetime; if it were a showpiece, like the *Apology for Socrates* by Libanius, to entertain a subsequent generation, we should not expect it to ape the loud yet flaccid style of Constantine's own letters and legislation. Such an impersonation would be unparalleled, in Greek at least, except in the case of figures such as Plato or Demosthenes, whose works continued to be perused as literature. On this theory, therefore, the undistinguished Greek of the *Oration* would imply that it was written with the purpose of deception, and for an audience that remembered the ostensible author well enough to recognise verisimilitude in the imitation of him. But since the piece does nothing either to denigrate Constantine or to assist his hagiographers, the motives of the hypothetical forger are impossible to divine.

It seems, moreover, obvious that the speech was intended for a Latin audience; what orator would woo the Greeks with a commentary on Virgil, while omitting all mention of their native poets?[2] The evidence for Greek translation, let alone Greek exegesis, of Virgil before the accession of Constantine is nugatory; as for the only specimen of Greek verse in the oration, an acrostic from what is now the Eighth Sibylline oracle, that too was better known to Latin authors, such as Augustine and Lactantius, than to the Greek apologists. The purpose of adducing it is to show that a pagan seeress had proclaimed the final judgment and identified the judge as 'Jesus Christ, Son of God, Saviour'; yet on the rare occasions when the Greeks made use of Sibylline testimonia,[3] the aim was not to lift the seal of history

---

1 For references and bibliography, see Edwards (1995), with Edwards (1999b), 260–61 on the usage of the term *logos*.

2 Baldwin (1976) adduces the speech as evidence of a Greek translation of Virgil, but observes that extant papyri of Greek translations date from the fourth to the sixth centuries.

3 See Justin, *1Apology* 20.1 and 44.12; Athenagoras, *Embassy* 30.1.

but to prove the timeless attributes of God. It is true that a recitation of the lines in their original tongue would be difficult for western ears to follow; but this is no objection, as the acrostic would almost certainly be lost on any audience, Greek or Roman, at first hearing. If the full Greek text was incorporated into the published Latin version of the speech, it will not have been impenetrable, and may even have been familiar, to a readership whom Lactantius had already plied with untranslated fragments of the poem.

Equally congenial to a western author and his western audience is the theological tenor of the *Oration*. In the tenth chapter, part of the ecclesiastical teaching on the Trinity is expressed in words purporting to be Plato's, though in fact they seem to originate with Numenius, a second-century Platonist who was quarried by both Greek and Latin Christians of this period.[1] Christ becomes, by analogy at least,[2] a second God, subservient to the Father, and then, as we have seen, the *logos prophorikos*, the audible word engendered in the intellect. Eusebius was not the only easterner who disliked this interpretation of the term *logos*, as we meet it in the first verse of John's Gospel; Origen, the great scholar of the third century, had argued in his commentary on this Gospel that if Christ were merely the Father's speech he would not possess the *hypostasis*, the determinate being, that is proper to the Son of God.[3] Nevertheless this had been the common tenet of Greek and Latin Christianity up to Origen's day; in the west, where it was stamped by the authority of Tertullian,[4] it survived with little change into the reign of Constantine. In the east it held its own for a season in Alexandria, but its principal exponent, Marcellus of Ancyra, was adjudged to be a heretic at council after council, and punished by deposition from his bishopric. One great prelate, however, gave him shelter and had the hardihood to pronounce him orthodox – Bishop Julius of Rome.[5]

This dispute arose in the wake of the more notorious controversy that takes its name from Arius. The question that now came before the Church was whether Christ, like every being who was dependent on the Father, should be numbered among his creatures, or whether his relation to the Father was a unique one, which might be described as natural and defined as

---

1 See my notes to this chapter on Numenius, Chalcidius and Platonism.

2 And I would say indeed only by analogy, against Barnes (2001), 35. See further my annotations to this paragraph in the speech.

3 *Commentary on John* 1.25–26. Cf. Irenaeus, *Against Heresies* 2.12.5 on the Valentinian usage of the term 'immanent' (*endiathetos*).

4 *Against Praxeas* 5.

5 On Marcellus and Julius see now Kinzig and Vinzent (1999).

an identity of substance. The obstinacy of Arius, an Alexandrian presbyter who upheld the first opinion, precipitated the council of Nicaea in 325. It did not resolve the struggle, but it introduced the watchword *homoousios* ('consubstantial') into a creed that was later deemed to be ecumenical and binding on the clergy. Historians have often tried to ascertain which side in the war was taken by our orator. If he is convicted of an error, the inference may be that he is more likely to be Constantine, since emperors (unlike historians) cannot distinguish orthodoxy from heresy; conversely it may be argued that a monarch who was out to rule the Empire in alliance with the bishops would refrain from holding views that contradicted the prevalent doctrine of the Church. Some claims to have detected a lapse are specious – the *Oration* does indeed subordinate the Son to the Father, but not all subordination is heretical; others are quite fallacious – to say that Christ was born once from the Father and once from Mary is traditional and orthodox, and was possibly unpalatable to Arius.[1] In any case, deviations from the temporary consensus at Nicaea have no bearing on the provenance, date or purpose of this sermon if, as I suspect, it merely expounds the faith, as yet untested and untroubled, that was taught to all neophytes in the Latin west.

Dogma is not the linchpin of our speaker's case, as might be guessed from his appeal to Plato. That is not to say that he has no interest in theology. From time to time he apostrophizes dead or living pagans, and this gives to his speech the familiar marks of an apology, a tract designed to exculpate the Christians from the calumny and ridicule of outsiders. Accordingly his first, most prominent topic after the preface is not the Trinity but the unity of the Godhead – a platitude of course for all apologetic works and martyrologies, but reinvigorated in the first quarter of the fourth century, when Lactantius, Athanasius and our orator all buttressed it with an argument from the unity of the world. If there were not one God, they ask in unison, who would temper the harmony of the elements and prevent the world from falling into ruin under the counterplay of forces? In this they had been anticipated, not by earlier Christians but by Aristotle, who reinforced the lesson with Homer's maxim, 'the rule of many is not good; let there be a single ruler'.[2] In Homer this was the reasoning of a warrior, and the Church had little use for it until it found a Christian at the summit of political authority. Our speaker sees this perfectly when in the final chapter he declares himself the servant of the Almighty, leaving us to infer that if the Almighty has appointed

---

1 See Edwards (1995).
2 Aristotle, *Metaphysics* 1076a, citing *Iliad* 2.204.

only one servant (as he did in Jewish prophecy),[1] he will not leave even part of his world to a second viceroy. This might be the position of an autocrat or of one who shared his power but was an aspirant to autocratic rule; in either case, we must admit that the author writes very pertinently in the character of Constantine, if indeed he is not Constantine himself.

Once the speech is read as a manifesto of ambition, not merely a defence of Christianity, we can put aside the objection that the scribbling of apologies is no task for an emperor, as he has the power to countermand the polemics and persecutions which inspired all previous writing of this nature. On the contrary, while a forger would have no motive, this emperor would have had almost too many for composing such a piece. Whether he was joint ruler or sole ruler at the time of its delivery, he had to persuade this peaceable congregation of his right to rule by conquest, and of God's desire that the Empire should be governed from an undivided throne. As a newborn layman, who had previously condoned Diocletian's measures against the Church, he might wish to submit a personal confession of the kind that is exemplified in his own lifetime by Arnobius' seven books *Against the Nations*. As an emperor, on the other hand, he had mastered a vein of bombast that had almost become a literary genre in this epoch of royal loquacity, as every sovereign strove to impress his own religious view on the preamble to an edict for the enforcement or repeal of persecution. The result is what we have before us – a tract in favour of theocratic monarchy, mimicking the edicts of the tyrant Maximinus, which had urged that it was only ancestral piety, with its many rites, that ensured continuing peace among the gods.[2] Now that we have Eusebius, we can hardly miss the echo; in his own day, who but Constantine would have noticed, let alone thought of it?

---

1 Isa. 42.1, 49.6, 52.13; but perhaps most relevant to Constantine is 45.1 (the elevation of Cyrus).

2 The rescript to Tyre in 312, preserved by Eusebius, *Church History* 9.7.3–14 maintains that the world is governed by the providence of gods whose power is attested by their works and that the unity of all things is sustained by the hegemony of Zeus (9.7.3, 4 and 7). The existence of these gods is undeniable to anyone of intelligence (9.7.8) and the city to which this letter is directed has good reason to be sensible of their favours (9.7.3–4). The evidence of Eusebius is confirmed by two inscriptions to other cities which are discussed by Mitchell (1988), 108–10; as Corcoran (1996), 149–51 observes, the document is a rescript only in form, for the chorus of identical petitions which it purports to answer can only have been concerted by the emperor. Although the resultant text evinces so many similarities to Constantine's oration, I am not aware of anyone who maintains that Maximinus was too shallow or too unlettered to have drafted it himself.

The occasion

Any rhetorical exercise purports to be directed to a certain occasion and a certain audience. Sometimes this profession is fictitious and it is frequently the case that the original circumstances are obscured in the preparation of a publishable text. Nevertheless, in the absence of any countervailing evidence, it is reasonable to suppose that the *Oration* was intended for delivery, though perhaps in a shorter version that would not outstrip the patience and erudition of the listeners. If after all it is spurious, we must assume that the one who forged the contents with such industry would have taken pains to counterfeit a plausible situation. Inquiries into the date and destination of the speech have drained more pens than the question of authorship, from which of course they cannot be divorced.

As an illustration of the last point we may take the argument pressed by Richard Hanson against the ascription of the speech to Constantine.[1] Like many other scholars he chooses Antioch as a setting, and he finds that he can thus make sense of the otherwise gratuitous mention of Daphne, a maiden who was turned into a laurel tree to save her from being ravished by Apollo. Daphne was the name of Apollo's sanctuary near Antioch; in the time of Emperor Julian it was occupied by the bones of the martyr Babylas and the miraculous frustration of the Apostate's attempt to profane the relics was remembered as one of the great humiliations of his lamentable reign. Thus the allusion ceases to appear trifling, and virginity is no longer the only reason for the juxtaposition of Daphne and the Sibyl; unfortunately the light that history sheds upon this passage discloses also that its author must have lived at least a generation after Constantine. A single sally therefore threatens to bear both date and authorship away from the conservatives. In reply they could skirmish with the plea that readers of Ovid would recall Daphne as the first victim of Apollo, and that her name would thus suffice to furnish Constantine with a pretext for his defection from that god to a nobler patron.[2] It would, however, be a better strategy to argue that large questions are not decided by a paragraph, and that this one can be fought to an issue only on the broad ground that is offered by the whole body of the speech.

It is in two chapters, the twenty-second and the twenty-fifth, that we come upon historical 'facts', if such a name can be given to the invidious reminiscences of two dead men, both emperors and persecutors of recent

1 Hanson (1973).
2 See my notes to Chapter 18.

notoriety, whom the speaker does not feel that he needs to name. One, who held the reins in his 'dearest city', had seduced many with his promises – though not, it seems, the Christians, who had greeted the conqueror's advent with an immediate and spontaneous demonstration. The other had succeeded Diocletian in the command of the Roman army, until God had punished the vices of both leaders with the destruction of their troops.[1] Once these figures have been identified, we shall have a *terminus post quem* for the *Oration*, and some notion of the purposed time and place of its delivery. A span of barely fifteen years lies open to conjecture, but one so dense with usurpations, wars, alliances, conquests and auspicious deaths that half a dozen opinions could be espoused, and not all scholars have avoided serial marriages.

The flock of names decreases with the years.[2] Galerius, the ruler of the east and senior figure in a college of five emperors, expired in 311 after revoking the persecution that he and Diocletian had commenced in 303. To his signature on this palinode were added those of Licinius, nominal emperor or Augustus of the west since 308, and of Constantine, who in 306 had illegally proclaimed himself the heir to his father Constantius and since then had remained the actual suzerain of Gaul and Britain. The edict of repeal[3] does not contain the name of Maximinus, an unrepentant persecutor who would have been the legitimate successor to Galerius in the east had he not tried to forestall his rivals by a premature coronation in 310. Also missing, and probably not solicited, is the signature of Maxentius, son of the former emperor Maximian, who had been since 306 the ruler, or tyrant as others styled him, of Italy and Africa. After the death of Galerius, Licinius turned his arms against Maximinus, while Constantine advanced upon Maxentius in Rome. In 312 Maxentius died at the battle of the Milvian

---

1 The assertion of Barnes (2001), 28 that this figure can be no other than Licinius depends on the unjustified assumption that the 'good-for-nothing' was overcome by Constantine himself. In proposing Nicomedia in 321 as the theatre for this oration, Barnes does not anticipate my arguments here, and his newest theory is vulnerable to all the same objections that I advance against Piganiol, Lane Fox and the earlier thoughts of Barnes himself.

2 The principal sources for the following summary are the Latin panegyrics, Lactantius, *On the Deaths of the Persecutors*, Eusebius, *Church History* 8–10 and Eusebius, *Constantine* 1. Apart from the exact dates and the motives of the agents, little is disputed, and Barnes (1981), 3–80 remains an excellent essay in the creation of continuous narrative from polemical fragments.

3 Though the Latin text of the so-called palinode is given at Lactantius, *Pers.* 34, the names of the signatories appear only at Eusebius, *Church History* 8.17.

Bridge, on the eve of which it is said that Constantine became a Christian.[1] In 313 Maximinus succumbed to Licinius, and the Empire was then peaceably if not amicably divided between the latter and Constantine. Constantine snatched Serdica from Licinius in 316 under pretext of defending Roman territory from invasion. War broke out in earnest in 321, and Licinius enacted stringent laws against the Christians. In 324 he was driven from his capital and after his suicide in 325 the Roman Empire, for the first time in over forty years, became the property of a single man.

Can these names be matched with the anonymous intimations of the speech? If we take Galerius as the tyrant who had seduced the 'dearest city', it is most likely to be Serdica, the place of his death, and the date would perhaps be 316, in the aftermath of Constantine's occupation, or (as Barnes suggested later) 321,[2] when new hostilities made it profitable to rouse old memories of the persecution. The unworthy captain of Diocletian's host would be Maximinus, for only he could be said to have inherited the soldiery of the east. If, instead of naming the tyrant first we endeavour to locate the city, Antioch has been the most favoured choice,[3] as a metropolis whose wealth would make it dear to any emperor, and whose diligent support of Maximinus up to 313 entailed that it would not be gained without copious flattery for a Christian ruler. The difficulty is that if Maximinus is now identified as the tyrant of the dearest city, the general who mislaid Diocletian's army must be his conqueror Licinius, whose fall in 324 is thus being juxtaposed with that of Maximinus in 313. Advocates of this theory have proposed that the *Oration* was delivered at the Council of Antioch in 325, though records of this meeting are both scanty and uncertain, while no report of Constantine's attendance is preserved.[4]

Nicomedia, Diocletian's former seat and the capital of Bithynia, has been favoured in recent years by Barnes and Bleckmann, the former dating

1 Lactantius, *Pers.* 44.5. Eusebius, *Constantine* 1.28 does not give a location or date for the vision, which differs in some details from the one made famous by the Latin author. Lactantius is supported by Philostorgius, *Church History* 1.7 and Gelasius, *Church History* 1.3–4, but not, according to Elliott (1992), by Constantine's own utterances, which imply that even his western conquests were undertaken at the behest of God. It is possible that Constantine means that he did God's work without knowing it, just as Cyrus of Persia never heard the prophet saluting him as the servant of the lord at Isa. 45.1.

2 See Barnes (1976a) and (1981), 323.

3 De Decker (1978), 85; Lane Fox (1986); Hanson (1973), though contesting the authenticity of the work.

4 For the evidence relating to the council see Chadwick (1958).

it to 321 and the latter to 327.[1] Others advance an argument for Byzantium, the last stronghold of Licinius and the future seat of the Constantinian government;[2] by a parallel reading, on his own premises, of passages in the *Oration* and in Lactantius, Piganiol arrives at a date between 321 and 324, and opts for Thessalonica in 323, inferring the presence of Constantine at Easter from the Theodosian Code.[3] The authors who advance these theories tend to rest the whole argument on one or two particulars, offering neither a comprehensive analysis of the speech nor a satisfactory account of the occasion. By contrast, Harold Drake's study of the question is distinguished by its rigorous interrogation of everything in the text that might be redolent of past events or present circumstances.[4] His argument alights at Rome, which I also believe to have been at least the intended theatre for the emperor's performance. If I am right to think that each of the following points lends weight to this hypothesis, or at least dispels an objection to it, the cumulative probability must be reckoned very strong:

1. If Constantine composed the *Oration* it must have been in Latin, since Eusebius, who neglects no opportunity to flatter him, reveals that he had no competence in the formal use of any other tongue.[5] Those who contest this inference have argued that the speaker's exegesis of the Fourth Eclogue is at odds with the Latin text and presupposes his own Greek rendering of it. These arguments have been met, and even if they were stronger they would surely be outweighed by the consideration that only a Latin audience would defer to a Latin poet. I have argued in my notes[6] that we can always trace the comments to the Latin, and that the worst of the misquotations could have been committed only by a person who knew tracts of Virgil's poetry by heart.

---

1 See Bleckmann (1997), Barnes (2001), with Eusebius, *Constantine* 3.50 on Constantine's donations to the city. None the less there is no proof that he professed such an affection for that city as he claims to feel in the present speech, and he never occupied it as his capital.

2 See especially Mazzarino (1974).

3 Piganiol (1932).

4 Drake (1985b). While this article seems to me to imply an early date at least for the kernel of the speech, neither in this discussion nor at (2000), 292–305 will Drake consent to fix the occasion, and at (2000), 294 he suggests that 'the most important characteristic of this speech may be its timelessness'. No doubt; and the same or more could be said of almost any work by Cicero, St Paul or Edmund Burke, but that does not mean that they do not have a date.

5 *Constantine* 4.32, on which see Edwards (1999b), 255.

6 See Chapter 19, with Edwards (1999b), 259.

2. All claims to have discerned an Arian tenor in the speech are, as I have shown above, ill-founded; the probity of Eusebius as an editor, on the other hand, is proved by his having left intact some passages that contradict his own more studied and more precarious teachings. The theory that Lactantius was the author is now discarded, but the numerous parallels that can be adduced between his writings and the speech do at least illuminate the source of its theology, which (as I have explained above) is simply the orthodoxy of the west.

3. The city addressed is one for which the speaker has a special and (as he seems to think) notorious affection.[1] No doubt he had strong feelings for Jerusalem, the Holy City, for Serdica, his 'second Rome', for Byzantium, the site of his future capital, and even perhaps for Antioch, the metropolis of the Orient; but none of this is said to have aroused in him the compassionate indignation which, according to his panegyrists, was the sole reason for his march on Rome. Even Eusebius, careless and laconic as he is on western matters, has a long account of Constantine's celebration of this conquest. He testifies at the same time to a popular demonstration in his favour, very like the one that our orator attributes to his audience and the panegyrists of Constantine to all the Italian cities, but especially to Rome.

4. Eusebius adds that Constantine cemented his enthronement in the capital by parading a splendid figure of the Cross.[2] According to Lactantius, this symbol had been the army's sign of victory in the battle for the city; what subsequent occasion is more likely to have prompted the addition of a stanza spelling out the Greek word *Stauros* (Cross) to the Sibylline acrostic which dominates the centre of this speech?

5. Whatever the name of Daphne meant to Constantine, his sibyl is not the mouthpiece of a small shrine close to Antioch. To him she is at all times the Cumaean prophetess who inspired the Fourth Eclogue, and even when he is quoting lines attributed to the Sibyl of Erythrae, he tells us on the authority of Cicero that she made her home in Italy. This would be frigid learning in a Greek author, and a patriotic commonplace in a Latin one; to Constantine it was also a stroke of policy, for the Sibylline Books, acquired eight hundred years ago by Rome's last king, were frequently consulted by the Senate, and had been opened for the last time by Maxentius on the eve of his fatal battle.

1 See my notes to Chapters 22 and 25.
2 Eusebius, *Constantine* 1.40.2.

Rather than inform the resentful pagans of the city that their oracle was mistaken, Constantine more prudently invites them to conclude that she was on the Christian side.

6. The name of Rome appears within a few lines of the emperor's compliment to his 'dearest city'. I take this as evidence in favour of a Roman venue rather than, as others would, against it. Constantine had no reason to dilute an encomium of a proud Greek city with a reference to another which at that time would almost certainly have been reckoned its superior; nor would the unification of the east under his sway have been promoted by the admission that at one time he had not enjoyed the undivided loyalty of Rome. To say this in Rome was only to tell the audience what it knew already, possibly with an undertone of menace or reproach. As for the inelegance of attaching first a sobriquet then a name to a single subject in the same paragraph, I have pointed out elsewhere that a Gallic orator did not think it so artless.[1] And there is purpose in the variation: the blandishments are reserved for those who have lent support to Constantine, while the malcontents are neither led nor driven, but simply nudged into a colourless aside.

7. The tyrant of Chapter 22 will be Maximinus if the scene is Antioch, and Maxentius if it is Rome. In the former case the date of the speech is 325; in the latter any date after 312 can be maintained. While the people of Antioch would have little chance of deciphering an allusion to Maximinus twelve years after his death and the intervening downfall of Licinius, the *Oration* could have been designed for Rome without any fear that time and circumstance would have dimmed the notoriety of Maxentius. A delivery long after the event would be conceivable, for the panegyrics on Constantine assisted recollection and at any date the presence of the conqueror in Rome would have been a catalyst to memory. But, though so much may be said for the sake of argument, it is obvious that the speech would have been still less of an enigma to its audience if the occasion were so early, and the events of which it reminded them so recent, that there had been no opportunity to forget.[2]

---

1 Edwards (1999b), 266, citing *LP* 10(2)1.1 and 2.1.

2 Baynes (1931), 56, opining that Licinius is not the object of either of these allusions, concludes that the speech would not have been delivered by Constantine after 323. He suspects in any case that much of it is inauthentic.

8. The general who wasted Diocletian's army in Chapter 25 had allies in the city that the speaker is now addressing. Galerius, Maxentius, Maximinus and Licinius died successively in the space of fourteen years from 311 to 325. To make such a glancing reference to any of them more than a few months after his death would surely have imposed too great a tax upon the memory of an audience. The fallen despot cannot be Maxentius, who commanded armies only in the west, nor Licinius, who did not inherit Diocletian's troops except by conquest. He must therefore be either Galerius or Maximinus; but if he is Galerius, who died in 311, the *Oration* must have been composed before his evil destiny had been eclipsed by the downfall of Maxentius in 312 and of Maximinus in 313. Rome is the only city of note that fell to Constantine within this period; and if the allusion is to Maximinus, Rome again is the only city that claimed the favour of Constantine while the memory of that villain was still green. The chapter heading states that Maximinus is the man denounced by Constantine; and shortly after Constantine entered Rome his skilful archivists were able to show the Christians that Maxentius had contracted an alliance with this notorious persecutor. The speech would make the best use of these facts if it was written in the wake of Licinius' victory over Maximinus in 313 and delivered to former subjects of Maxentius in Rome.

The early date implied by setting the speech in Rome may also be a clue to its immediate occasion. Having taken the city in 312, Constantine could never have been present there at Easter after 315, for in 316 he abandoned it for Serdica and after 324 he took up residence in the east. Even had he returned to Rome, he could not have convinced the inhabitants that it was still his 'dearest city'. Now in 313 a council of Italian and Gallic bishops under Roman guidance had condemned the incipient schism of the Donatists in Africa; the controversy raged on until the emperor, who had hoped that the Roman verdict would prevail, was forced to convene another session at Arles in Gaul in the summer of 314. In the Eastertide of the following year[1] we may imagine that there was discontent in Rome as well as Africa, yet Easter, as the letters of the Donatists seldom failed to urge, was a time when brethren ought to make their peace. The paschal season will have been a time to remind all Christians, and especially the saints in Rome, of the unity that God ordained for his Empire and his Church.

---

1 I choose 315 in preference to 314 because the itinerary of Constantine in the latter year does not allow for a visit to the capital at Easter: see Barnes (1982). Of course we cannot rule out the possibility that the speech was delivered by a surrogate.

HELENA, JERUSALEM AND THE DISCOVERY OF THE CROSS

Great men grow in stature as they recede in time, and the triumph of Christianity surrounded Constantine with a penumbra of vivid legend, wholesome anecdote and tendentious fabrication.[1] He was already a second Christ to Eusebius, who seems conscious that his report of the conversion, though attested by the emperor himself, is not the common one, and has been suspected by some modern historians of embellishing the humble termination of the reign.[2] Every continuator of Eusebius thought it necessary to write the story of Constantine afresh, and even a pagan found it in his heart to write a posthumous encomium;[3] but the rudiments of later panegyric had already been sketched by Constantine before he found a friend to record his life. While he was still a pagan he announced through his panegyrists that he was not a mere adventurer but the pious favourite of immortal masters; as a Christian he gave free rein to his ostentatious passion for the patronage and creation of sacred sites. The *Oration to the Saints* contains one reference to the cult of martyrs, two to the display of martial trophies[4] – firstfruits of a new age of ecclesiastical pomp, in which the clergy, though not ready to condone the use of images, united with the sovereign in promoting the veneration of sites and relics.[5]

In Judaea, according to Eusebius, he decorated the tomb of Christ and built a 'royal temple' to overlook the adjacent precinct.[6] Yet his projects in the Holy Land were eclipsed by those of Helena, his mother, who is canonized by Eusebius in the third book of his *Life of Constantine*. She was, he tells us, adored throughout the world for a combination of munificence and modesty; she was gracious to prisoners, liberal to soldiers, rich in pious works. Her enterprises included a church at Bethlehem and the Church of the Ascension in Jerusalem.[7] Little more is said of her by Eusebius, except

---

1 The flowering of these legends in Byzantium can be studied in Kazhdan (1987).

2 According to *Constantine* 3.64, Constantine died at Pentecost in his capital. Woods (1997), however, argues from other sources that he died in a wayside hostel and was thus prevented from carrying on a projected war against the Persians.

3 On Praxagoras see Lieu and Montserrat (1996), 7–8.

4 See Chapter 11 (p. 22 n. 1), 12 (p. 28 n. 8), 22 (p. 53 n. 8).

5 See Grigg (1977) on the 'cult without images'.

6 Eusebius, *Constantine* 3.36.1: for recent commentary see Cameron and Hall (1999), 287–91.

7 Eusebius, *Constantine* 3.44–47. Cameron and Hall (1999) note that Eusebius ignores her humble origin (attested by Ambrose, *On the Death of Theodosius* 42); they also record the dubious tradition that her birthplace was Drepanum.

that she was ushered into heaven at the age of eighty, already a companion of the angels. Perhaps there was little more to know, and consequently her life was even more hospitable to pious fiction than her son's. Pagan friends of Constantine affirm that she was the first wife of Constantius, raised up from low estate and soon discarded; his foes say that she was never more than the mistress of Constantius and do not forget to sneer.[1] Theodoret, in the fifth century, relates that she brought up Constantine as a Christian, but this claim is rebutted by the emperor's testimony[2] and by the circumambulation of Eusebius: 'So far had he made her Godfearing, though she had not been such before, that she seemed to have been a disciple of the common Saviour from the first'.[3] The date of 315 which is allotted to her conversion in a late Greek source would be implausible even if it were not accompanied by a fantastic legend, in which Helena tries to wean her son from Christianity to Judaism, but then becomes a Christian herself after a contest in which Pope Silvester betters the miracles of a dozen rabbis.[4] The dates offered by the two accounts translated in this volume are, if anything, still less credible, but these texts are chosen for their antiquity, not for their verisimilitude. They mark the first appearance of two factors which remain constant in every narrative of Helena's conversion: it follows that of Constantine and culminates in that miracle of ancient archaeology, the discovery (or as the Latin says, the invention) of the True Cross.

This relic first became a public trophy in the last quarter of the fourth century, when the bishopric of Jerusalem, hitherto as weak as it was ancient, was beginning to displace its northern neighbour Caesarea as the centre of Christianity in Palestine. After the Nicene council of 325, which made it second to Caesarea, it soon acquired the patriarchal status that was otherwise accorded only to Antioch, Rome and Alexandria.[5] As it became in consequence a favourite goal of pilgrimage, new rituals took shape to excite the awe and generosity of the visitors. Judaea had been the cradle of Christianity, and not even Rome, where Peter and Paul were buried, could

---

1 See *Origin of Constantine* 2 at Lieu and Montserrat (1996), 43 against Zosimus, *New History* 2.8; the Byzantine epitomator Zonaras, *Annals* 13.1.4 cannot decide.

2 See p. 20 n. 2 to *Oration* 11, against Theodoret, *Church History* 1.18.

3 Eusebius, *Constantine* 3.47.2, translated by Cameron and Hall (1999), 139, with notes at 295.

4 See Lieu and Montserrat (1996), 28, quoting Zonaras, George Syncellus and the so-called Opitz-*Vita*.

5 See Bright (1882), 22–24 on the canons of Nicaea (325), Chalcedon (451) and Nicaea II (787).

vie with it in the number and antiquity of its monuments. Least of all could Rome display an heirloom like the one that bewitched the eyes of credulous travellers to Jerusalem at Eastertide in the late fourth century:

> The bishop's chair is placed on Golgotha Behind the Cross (the cross there now), and he takes his seat. A table is placed before him with a cloth on it, the deacons stand around, and there is brought to him a gold and silver box containing the holy Wood of the Cross. It is opened and the Wood of the Cross and the title are taken out and placed on the table. As long as the holy Wood is on the table, the bishop sits with his hands resting on either end of it, and holds it down, and the deacons round him keep watch over it ... [A]ll the people, catechumens as well as faithful, come up one by one to the table. They stoop down over it, kiss the Wood and move on.[1]

The spectacle that Egeria witnessed might have been created for her benefit, so far as earlier records go: the silence of the Bordeaux pilgrim, as Gibbon notes in a famous aphorism, 'satisfies those who think', while it 'perplexes those who believe'.[2] It is possible, however, that the sceptical historian places too much faith in the candour of his sources. Even one who had seen the Cross might choose to say nothing of it if he feared that the ceremony was idolatrous, or if, being loyal to another see, he did not wish to acknowledge that Jerusalem had a claim upon the holiest altar in the Christian world. Both motives would be present, for example, in the writings of the historian Eusebius. He was bishop of Caesarea, which, as he proudly boasts, was also the home of the great theologian Origen and the martyr Pamphilus; like these predecessors he was a resolute iconoclast, regarding images of both gods and emperors as mere stones. It is possible that his silence belies his knowledge of the Cross; in view of the habitual incongruity between the texts that he cites and the deductions that he makes from them, it is possible too, as Harold Drake maintains, that he quotes a document which obliquely records the finding of the Cross in the excavation of the Holy Sepulchre. It is clear at least, on the evidence in Eusebius, that the ground was well dug up beside the city, and that the emperor announced the exhumation or erection of an artefact to which he gave the name *tropaia*

---

1 *Pilgrimage of Egeria* 37.1–2, trans. Wilkinson (1971), 136–37. On p. 3 Wilkinson dates the pilgrimage to the years between 381 and 384.

2 Gibbon (1929), II, 481 n.66; though on behalf of credulity one could urge that the pilgrim wrote in 333, while the church was completed only in 335. His work is translated by Wilkinson (1971), 153–63.

(spoils or trophy).[1] Drake's inference that this was the Cross is tenuous and disputed; perhaps it gains a little strength from the presence of other tendentious errors in Eusebius,[2] but how much weight does it lend to the tradition that attributes the discovery of the trophy to the mother of Constantine?

We might be less inclined to suspect that Helena's deed is fabulous were it not for the contemporaneous growth of another tale about the Cross, in which the heroine, Protonike, is patently fictitious.[3] As her legend now survives in Syriac and Armenian, Protonike is the wife of Emperor Claudius and a convert to the new faith. She excavates the Cross as an act of piety, but the Church has little time to display the trophy, as it is buried once more by Trajan and its site concealed by a temple of Aphrodite. This sequence of events would have a little more verisimilitude if Protonike were the consort not of Claudius but of Domitian, who died only two years before Trajan assumed the purple. And indeed there are traditions which allege that his persecution of the Church had been inspired by the discovery that his wife had an inclination to Christianity, and that he himself had interrogated the grandchildren of Jude, the brother of Christ.[4]

THE FINDING (OR INVENTION) OF THE TRUE CROSS

The two accounts of Helena's feat translated here are variants of the same narrative. Its wide dissemination in the ancient world is attested by the survival of two later and less barbarous Latin versions, together with a Syriac redaction which has recently been translated into English with a commentary by Han Drijvers and Jan Willem Drijvers.[5] The contest of priority between these texts is not easily determined, but Borgehammar

---

1 Drake (1985a), citing *Constantine* 3.34 at 93.18–20 Heikel. Elsewhere in *Constantine*, the term *tropaia* often denotes the Cross, though only in the singular: 21.16, 22.25, 76.12, 78.7 etc. The use of this term to signify the Cross dates back at least to Justin Martyr, *1Apology* 55.1.

2 E.g. his use of the appellation 'Church of the Holy Sepulchre', on which see Borgehammar (1991), 103–04. See also Stemberger (2000), 54–64 on the tendentiousness of Eusebius, especially his suppression of Macarius, whose name appears only in Constantine's letter at *Constantine* 3.31.

3 With Heid (1992), I incline to regard the legend as in origin independent of that of Helena, though its present form has certainty been shaped by a desire to outdo the version that was most current in Greek and Latin.

4 Eusebius, *Church History* 3.19. I feel that this hypothesis gains some strength from the fact that Judas is the name of the last Jewish bishop of Jerusalem, who died in the time of Hadrian, at Eusebius, *Church History* 4.5.4.

5 Father and son: Drijvers and Drijvers (1997).

argues that the Syriac must be dependent on the Latin.[1] In both, the story of Helena is prefaced by a fanciful narrative of her son's conversion; the Syriac, however, lacks the evidence of suture which can still be seen in the Latin. This, to judge by the rubric at the beginning, is a record of the *Adventus Sanctae Crucis*, the advent of the Holy Cross; but the subject indicated by the corresponding sentence at the end is not an *adventus* but an *inventio* or discovery, and this is also what we read in the title of the Greek text, which does not recount but presupposes Constantine's profession of belief. It is probable therefore that a composite document, created first in Latin, was translated into Syriac – though not without variations, as I indicate in my notes – while the Greek account remained uncontaminated. Is the Greek or the Latin then the earlier redaction of the *Inventio*? Answering in favour of the former, Borgehammar[2] has noted several places where the Latin has the air of a translation, the most notable being those where it has adopted a grammatical construction that would be more at home in Greek.

The outline of the tale in all three languages is as follows. The empress Helena, moved by her son's conversion and the Holy Spirit, makes her way to Jerusalem in search of the Holy Cross. Her plan is to interrogate the remnant of the Jewish population, but though they obey her summons, she fails to overcome a preconcerted vow of silence. She dismisses them with menaces, and they hold a second conference. One of their number, Judas, reveals that he knows the secret, which was entrusted to his father by his grandfather, a witness to both the crucifixion and Stephen's martyrdom. On no account, he says, is the queen to learn it; but under duress his countrymen surrender him to Helena, and after a week's imprisonment without rations he confesses that he knows where the Cross is buried. He is taken to the site and intones a prayer that is half a spell. Three crosses come to light, along with a loose inscription that had formerly identified one as that of 'Jesus of Nazareth, King of the Jews'. Helena is at a loss, but when providence sends a corpse to them, Judas promises that the True Cross will disclose itself by a miracle; each cross is applied in turn to the dead man, and the third brings him to life. Helena is now prompted by the Spirit to seek the nails of the crucifixion. These, once found, are used by Constantine to adorn the bridle of his horse, and thus fulfil the prophecy of Zechariah 14.20: 'On that day

---

1 Borgehammar (1991), 246–48, though his arguments are not identical with those that I advance in the present paragraph.

2 Borgehammar (1991), 237–39. I have commented on the most important of these infelicities in my annotations.

there shall be upon the bells of the horses, *Holiness unto the Lord*'. The Cross is laid in a silver chest by Helena, and Judas, now converted under the name of Kyriakos or the Lord's man, is appointed as bishop in the sanctuary. (No reference is made to Macarius, bishop of Jerusalem in Helena's time, though the elevation of Kyriakos is sanctioned anachronistically by 'Eusebius of Rome'). Helena dies soon after, but not before she has instituted a day on which all Christians are to commemorate her finding of the Cross.

This is the common matter of three narratives, none of which is truly primitive. For one thing, none of them is a strict translation of another: the Syriac revises the chronology of the Latin, and the obvious ineptitude of the Latin author cannot account for all his aberrations from the Greek. One riddle, which has not yet found a solution, is that in every version only two generations are supposed to have elapsed between the death of Christ and Helena's excursion to Jerusalem. Perhaps the best explanation is that the tale has been confused with one in which the archaeologist is the wife of a previous emperor – perhaps, as I suggested above, the unfortunate wife of Domitian. In the story of Protonike, the Jews oppose the recovery of the Cross, and their rebellion under Hadrian and the irrevocable diaspora that followed would suggest themselves to any Christian reader as an edifying pendant. The punishment of the Jews at the conclusion of the *Inventio* is an echo of the same calamity. At the same time it may allude to the annual feast of Purim, when the Jews gave thanks for the massacre of the Gentiles that was commemorated in the book of Esther; in the fourth century it was believed that they were mocking Christ by fashioning a gallows for an effigy of their enemy Hamann. Such a reminiscence would not have gone unnoticed in the age of Constantine, when Jews began to suffer under Christian supremacy. Constantine himself passed florid laws against voluntary and involuntary apostasy from the Church to Judaism, adopting for the first time in the history of Roman legislation against this people a tone that was not merely restrictive but polemical.[1] The Nicene council of 325 imposed a Christian patriarch on Judaea in opposition to the Jewish one[2] and while Eusebius taught that God had revoked his ancient covenant by permitting the

---

1 See *Theodosian Code* 16.8.1 and 16.8.5 against the punishment of apostates from Judaism; *Code* 16.8.22 and *Sirmondian Constitution* 4 on the enfranchisement of Christian slaves who were forcibly circumcised by Jews. Although Stemberger (2000), 43–47 argues that the laws are less inclement than is generally supposed, the rhetoric is colourfully vindictive, and Christians of the fourth century not only took up the rhetoric but married it to action.

2 Though, as Stemberger (2000), 238–39 shows, the Jewish patriarchate enjoyed legal privileges from the reign of Constantine.

destruction of the temple, Helena's buildings raised the Church to a visible altitude above its ruins. The *Inventio*, which portrays the Jews as leaderless malignants, is the voice of the Church triumphant and vindictive, its ambitions fanned by the Christian occupation of the throne.

Some time before the *Inventio* reached its present form, hostilities had been inflamed by Emperor Julian's plan to restore the Temple in 363. An earthquake and untimely death forestalled him, but self-aggrandisement at the expense of Israel now appeared as a sacred duty to the bishopric of Jerusalem. Not content with seeking out the bones of Stephen, the first of the Gentile martyrs,[1] it added Kyriakos, an imaginary convert from the Jews, to its list of bishops. He worked his share of miracles,[2] but his name does not appear in the earliest claims to the possession of the Cross. Of this we hear first in the *Catechetical Homilies* of Cyril of Jerusalem; his boasts were quickly followed by the salutations of bishops in other Greek cities – Gregory of Nyssa, John Chrysostom of Antioch and Cyril of Alexandria. For our first account of the discovery, however, we are indebted to a Latin prelate, Ambrose of Milan.[3] Writing an obituary of Emperor Theodosius I in 395, he says in a concise and allusive paragraph that Helena had excavated the hill of Golgotha, found there crosses lying in confusion and recognized that of the Saviour by its *titulus* or rubric, 'Jesus of Nazareth, King of the Jews'. He hastens to admonish us that she worshipped the king and not the wood itself – a sign that the Cross was famous enough to have become an object of superstition. He adds that she 'illuminated the Cross' (*crucem refulsit*) – a statement that could be understood only by those already acquainted with the legend – and that the Spirit moved her a second time to seek the nails with which Christ had been fastened to his gallows. Once found, these were inlaid in a crown (*diadema*) and presented with a rein (*frenum*) to Constantine; both these gifts he bequeathed to his successors with his faith.

Only a little later than this passage, and apparently independent of it, is one in the *Ecclesiastical History* of Rufinus, which relates that a statue of Venus (the Latin name for Aphrodite, goddess of love) had usurped the site and was taken away before the relics were disinterred.[4] His account is also

---

1 See Van Esbroek (1984), with Bradbury (1996).

2 See Luigi (1904, 1906) and Pegoulewsky (1921).

3 *On the Death of Theodosius* 43–47.

4 Rufinus, *Church History* 10.7–8. According to Jerome, Letter 58.3, there were two effigies, one of Jove and one of Venus. The original information comes directly from Eusebius, *Constantine* 3.26, but there the site is Heliopolis.

embellished by a miracle: the *titulus* in this version has become detached, and the bishop of Jerusalem, Macarius, advises the queen to test the power of each of the crosses in turn upon a paralytic woman who has been brought to them at that moment on a bier. When the third proves efficacious it is acknowledged as the True Cross; Helena builds a 'temple' as an act of thanks, and encloses the Cross itself in a silver chest. The nails (which seem to be part of the same discovery) are used by Constantine as decorations for his helmet and the bridle of his warhorse. In Paulinus of Nola,[1] who already speaks of a 'story of the Cross' (*historia crucis*), the chest is kept in Helena's church, which now acquires gold trappings, and the relic is exhibited once a year, as the prerogative of the bishop, to those who gather in the city on Good Friday. Paulinus, who says nothing of Macarius, appears to have been the first to state that Helena gleaned her knowledge from 'the most learned of the Jews'. Since Ambrose, Rufinus and Paulinus are near-contemporaries, they are witnesses to the currency of the legend in the west in the late fourth century, but cannot help us to plot successive phases in its growth. As men of letters they must be given credit for the invention and idiosyncrasy which even Christian palates now demanded as condiments to a twice-told tale.

The Greek ecclesiastical historians – Theodoret, Socrates, Sozomen[2] – form a junction with Eusebius by turning the statue into a pagan temple, the removal of which makes way for the Church of the Holy Sepulchre. Some argue that they offer us better history – or at least a better history of imposture – than Eusebius, whose tongue (it is alleged) was tied by jealousy once Macarius of Jerusalem had become his rival in Palestine and his opponent at Nicaea.[3] Be that as it may, they possess traditions that were almost certainly unknown to him. Sozomen has heard of a certain 'Jew living in the east', who ascertained the location of the Cross from 'paternal records'. The story that the Cross had revived a dead man he reports with circumspection, but he follows Socrates in applying Zechariah 14.20 to

---

1 Epistle 31 to Severus.

2 Socrates, *Church History* 1.17; Sozomen, *Church History* 21.1; Theodoret, *Church History* 1.17.

3 In canon 7 of the Nicene Council, at Jonkers (1954), 42, Aelia is accorded a place of honour after Caesarea, to be added to its own dignity; in fact it quickly overshadowed its neighbour in the eyes of Christendom. It may be assumed that Macarius and Eusebius were not of one mind in theology, as there is no record of opposition to Macarius from the orthodox. Nevertheless, in the list of subscribers to the Creed at Gelasius of Cyzicus, *Church History* 2.28.7, his name is coupled with that of the Caesarean, priority being accorded to Jerusalem.

Constantine's decoration of his reins with the nails of Christ. This text must already have been sewn into the legend in the late fourth century, when Jerome thought it worthy of his satire.[1] He was not, it should be said, an unbiased witness, but a sedulous foe to Bishop John of Jerusalem, who in 392 honoured Porphyry of Gaza with the post of Staurophylax, or custodian of the Cross.[2] When Cyril of Alexandria glossed the verse in Zechariah with an allusion to the treasures in Jerusalem,[3] he was evidently repeating what he took to be a common association. At the same time, he gave notice of the interests that defined his role in later controversy, when he urged that it would belie both Creed and gospel to deny that the Cross of Jesus was also that of God.

Thus from an aggregate of about ten writers, spanning the interval from the middle of the fourth century to the last decades of the fifth, we can put together a circumstantial and coherent narrative, which was circulating rather than evolving, though in detail it betrays the slight plasticity that characterizes even written tradition in this epoch of Church history. If we seek a name for the author, we cannot improve on Borgehammar's argument for Gelasius of Caesarea,[4] whose history was compiled around 360. Nor, for all the rivalry of the sees, can we imagine that the impulse to invention reached him from any other quarter than Jerusalem, for the tale brought fame and profit to that city and its origins coincided with the earliest exhibitions of the Cross. At the same time this survey of its antecedents shows that the *Inventio* has made two momentous changes. First, the blessed Macarius of Jerusalem gives way to Kyriakos, whose see is merely the sanctuary of which he is the warden. The corollary for him is an instantaneous transformation in mid-story, for he both knows more and fears less as a Christian saint than as a Jewish renegade. Second, the ecclesiastical primacy, even in Palestine and even in the Greek version, is awarded to a personage called 'Eusebius of Rome'. While this is not a fictitious appellation, the only man who bore it during this period lived too early to have seen Constantine's conversion, let alone to have acted as counsellor to Helena, whose journey to the Holy Land is treated in all our sources as a sequel to the council of Nicaea in 325.

---

1 *Commentary on Zechariah*, book 3, *ad loc.*

2 Mark the Deacon, *Life of Porphyry of Gaza* 10; see further Stemberger (2000), 59. On Jerome and John see Kelly (1975), 192–205.

3 *Commentary on Zechariah* 94, cited at Holder, p. 49.

4 Borgehammar (1991), 3–57. If this is in substance the narrative that now survives in Gelasius of Cyzicus, *Church History* 3.7.3–10, Macarius of Jerusalem had not merely an active role but the longest speech in the original romance. The Jews do not yet figure in this account, although a pagan statue does.

Unless the Syriac text is the original, and the Greek and Latin have misconstrued the word Rum[1] which denotes the Roman Empire rather than the city, we must conclude that the author of the *Inventio* had two objects – to chasten the pretensions of Jerusalem and to augment the dignity of the Roman see.

This would not be a rare combination of motives after the middle of the fourth century. Jerome, for example, having found nothing to content him from Jerusalem to Palestine, took refuge in the fiat of the Roman Pope Damasus from the interminable synods of the east.[2] Some westerners feared that Cyril of Jerusalem was an Arian, as he never affirmed that Christ was consubstantial with the Father; in their eyes the stature of Damasus will have risen when (although for different reasons) he declined to endorse the council of Constantinople in 381, where Cyril was acquitted.[3] The whole of the west had a grievance against Jerusalem after 415, when a synod under the bishop of that city found in favour of the arch-heretic Pelagius.[4] These considerations do not imply that the *Inventio* must have been composed in Latin; even an eastern bishopric might foster the authority of Rome to get the better of a disputant or rival, and even a western author might have cause to write in Greek. It should also be remembered that the Syriac and Latin texts are conflations of two narratives, an *Adventus* and an *Inventio*, which might be of different provenance – must be indeed, if the theory of a Greek origin for the *Inventio* is maintained. While it is quite conceivable that a Greek should wish Macarius out of the story and a Roman bishop into it, such an author was evidently not the creator of our Eusebius, for in the Greek *Inventio* nothing is said to introduce him or account for his intimacy with Helena. The most probable solution is that the *Adventus*, written in Latin, was a source for the Greek *Inventio*, and was used as a prolegomenon for that text when it assumed a Latin dress.

It remains to propose a date for the invention of Eusebius. For our *terminus ante quem* we are indebted to the Greek chronicler Agathangelos,

---

1 See Drijvers and Drijvers (1997). If it were permitted to us to toy with this hypothesis, I would suggest that the intended name was that of Hosius, the emperor's adviser and confessor in the later years of his reign. On the ease with which the names Hosius and Eusebius were confused in the Syriac script see Chadwick (1958), 297–98.

2 Jerome, *Letters* 16.2.2 and 17.2.2.

3 See Bright (1882), 92–96 on Roman opposition to the third canon of Constantinople which, by according the place of honour after Rome to Constantinople, implied that worldly stature was the measure of ecclesiastical rank.

4 See Merdinger (1997), 127 with n. 55.

who, writing about 460, attests the baptism of Constantine by Eusebius but says nothing of the Cross.[1] The decade after the council of Chalcedon in 451 was a propitious time for the distribution of Roman propaganda in the Greek world, for the council itself had fortified its doctrine of two natures in the person of Christ by canonizing a letter from Pope Leo, which had already been provided with a meticulous equivalent in Greek. If then we assume that Agathangelos is the earliest witness, and not merely the first one known to us, we need not suppose that the legend of Eusebius was created more than a generation earlier. The years between (say) 420 and 450 coincide with theological strife in Italy, Africa and the eastern provinces; in almost every controversy the bishop of Rome declared himself the arbiter, and pressed his claim by dwelling on the antiquity, the majesty and the long-acknowledged privileges of the apostolic see. It was in this spirit that the decrees of Pope Gelasius, at the beginning of the sixth century, commemorated Eusebius as the pope who had baptized the first Christian emperor and witnessed the discovery of the Cross. If we take this as evidence that the *Adventus* and the *Inventio* had already been fused in a Latin text, the Greek original of the *Inventio* can be assigned – with all the caveats that are usual in such matters – to the final quarter of the fifth century.

SILVESTER AND THE *DONATION OF CONSTANTINE*

Except for the chronology and the proper names, the narrative of Constantine's conversion in the Latin and Syriac prologues to the *Inventio* is the one told by Lactantius and Eusebius, which is generally agreed to be true in substance. All there record that Constantine was about to fight a battle, that in a dream the Cross was revealed to him as a sign of victory, that he took it as his emblem, won the battle and was reborn. Unchallenged in its own day, this tradition later acquired a rival, which, although it may have even been born as humorous fantasy, was adopted as good history by some pagans and was thought to deserve rebuttal by at least one Christian writer. In his satirical dialogue, the *Caesars*, Julian the Apostate asserts that Constantine put his son to death on a flimsy pretext, then, dismayed by his own atrocity, sought absolution from the pagan gods. All the priests refused him, except the Christians, who proclaim that every sin can be forgiven at no

---

1 Fowden (1994b), 160–62.

cost.[1] The libel was repeated in the *Chronicle* of Eunapius and the *New History* of Zosimus;[2] Garth Fowden makes the plausible conjecture that the most foolish yet most durable of all the Christian tales surrounding Constantine was devised as a rejoinder to these texts.[3] Nevertheless, the main object of the *Acts of the Blessed Silvester* as it now exists is evidently to glorify the papacy and to prove that the man who occupied the see in the reign of Constantine had the right to be called a saint. No scholarly edition of this document was available for translation in this volume,[4] but the gist of it is included in a translation of a later and still more influential figment, generally known in English as the *Donation of Constantine*.

The first half of this edict (after its sonorous preamble) is a pure romance in which the monarch relates the circumstances of his conversion. Paraphrasing the *Acts of the Blessed Silvester*, he recalls that as sole ruler he maintained the persecution with a high hand, and was punished by God with a leprosy that no medicines could cure. The Roman priests convinced him that he must make himself a potion from the blood of 2000 infants, but before he could initiate the massacre he was visited in a dream by the apostles Peter and Paul. They told him that his remedy lay in the hands of Pope Silvester, who was hiding in a cave with his priestly retinue. The cave was found, and Constantine perceived that a miracle had been vouchsafed to him when Silvester showed him perfect likenesses of the two apostles who had come to him in the night. He therefore allowed the pontiff to baptize him and confessed the Holy Trinity. After this testimony comes the *Donation*, in which the emperor, avowing his intention of transferring the seat of monarchy from Rome to Constantinople, grants to the pope the unrestricted sovereignty of all the western provinces, together with Judaea. He also

---

1 Julian, *Caesars* 336b; see Lieu and Montserrat (1996), 18 for this passage, and 13–17 on the contribution of Eunapius.

2 Zosimus, *New History* 2.29. On the tenor of his account of Constantine see Lieu and Montserrat (1996), 15–17; for discussion of his sources see Woods (2001), 109–14.

3 Fowden (1994), 163–66 suggests that after Eunapius and Julian provoked the composition of the *Acts*, they were parodied in turn by Zosimus.

4 Much of it is quoted in Pohlkamp (1988), and I have cited him liberally in the footnotes to the *Donation*. Lieu and Montserrat (1996), 27 review a number of Byzantine adaptations, in which the events described in the *Acts* supervene upon the vision of the Cross as this is recounted by Eusebius and Lactantius. The half-converted Constantine, still driven to persecution by his wife Maximiana, is now too squeamish to carry out the slaughter of the children. Silvester, both here and in the original *Acts*, is less pusillanimous, and even slays a dragon. In addition Lieu and Montserrat (1996), 144 n. 16 quote the testimony of Aldhelm, *On Virginity* 25 that Silvester was the one who prompted Constantine to shift his capital.

bestows a mitre, a diadem and purple raiment, though he admits that the faithful minister of Christ declines to wear them. These presents and the lands themselves are secured to the perpetual dominion of Silvester and his pontifical successors; anyone who commutes or counteracts the gift is threatened with the fires of hell; the official text of the edict is deposited and the date appended in the Roman style.

All informed opinion since Lorenzo Valla's treatise of 1440[1] has agreed that the *Donation* is a forgery. It falsifies the early career of Constantine, perpetuates an incredible account of his conversion and slights not only truth but probability when it makes him hand the fruits of a life of strategy and bloodshed to a cleric who had never swung a sword. Nowhere does the genuine legislation of Constantine show any knowledge of this document, and indeed it is never cited within five centuries of the date at which it purports to have been composed. Its radical defects are aggravated by a rash of anachronisms in geography, theology and diction; only the name of the emperor's fellow consul Gallicanus in the final sentence seems to aim at verisimilitude.[2] Yet whereas Valla, the humanist and reformer, was content to mingle proofs of the forger's ignorance and temerity with censorious parentheses on the avarice of popes, the historian in the modern age turns these blemishes into virtues by construing them as indices of the audience, date and motive of an author who was evidently wise in his generation. He was well aware, for instance, that a classical vocabulary would not be so impressive to contemporaries as one that echoed the tone of legislation since Justinian, the Constantine of the sixth century, who had rescued the Church from heresy and Italy from the Goths. Thus the word *divalia*, which would have been an archaism to Constantine, was restored to use in the *Digest* of Justinian, and applied to the imperial letters received from eastern emperors by some popes in the *Book of Pontiffs*. The Persian title satrap, which as Valla rightly says would have been incongruous in Roman legislation, was used of local governors in the same period by Germanic overlords.[3] The occurrence of these terms in the *Donation* is a small part of the evidence that leads scholars to assign it to the embryonic period of the Carolingian Empire. More cogent still is the silence of every witness before the ninth

---

1 The Emperor Otto III denounced the document even in the eleventh century: Maffei (1964), 15–16.

2 See my notes on the final paragraph.

3 For these observations see the relevant notes to the *Donation* in this volume.

century,[1] and most convincing of all the clear utility of this document to the Roman Church of the eighth in its endeavours to strike new covenants with the temporal powers in Italy and France.

In this age an extension of the lands that were governed by the Roman see went hand in hand with an enlargement of its spiritual pretensions. In public works and charities the popes displayed an opulence that dazzled their biographers and intimidated princes. Nevertheless their authority remained tenuous, and was strengthened by precarious alliances with two nations: the Franks, who had become Christians under Clovis in the sixth century, and the Lombards whose conversion at the turn of the seventh century was the crowning work of Gregory the Great.[2] The Lombards had made frequent benefactions to the Roman see in the hope of marrying secular hegemony with spiritual advantage; in the first half of the eighth century, however, they began to advance their own frontiers by preying on papal territories, and the duchies of Ravenna and Spoleto became the prizes of an oscillating war. In earlier times the popes would have sought protection from the emperor in Byzantium, whom they still professed to acknowledge as their sovereign; but the emperors of this period were iconoclasts, committed to the abolition of images in defiance of tradition and a great part of the clergy, and were therefore heretics in the eyes of Rome. Consequently a new league was cemented with the Frankish ruler Pepin, who was building both a dynasty and an empire on the ruins of the Merovingian monarchy. In 774 the Lombard kingdom fell, and Rome was honoured by the presence of the victor Charles, son of Pepin, whom we know as Charlemagne or Charles the Great.

Throughout the *Donation* traces of these events are all too visible. The pictures of Paul and Peter that Silvester shows to Constantine would have been mere curiosities to the traveller, and idols to the zealot of the fourth century,[3] but in the eighth such relics were indispensable phylacteries against iconoclasm. Pope after pope exhibits his devotion to them in the

---

1 See Migne (1844), 569–70 for a catalogue of witnesses; it is generally agreed that the earliest pope to cite the edict was Leo IX, in a hostile letter of 1054 to the patriarch of Constantinople Michael Cerularius. See Maffei (1964), 16–17, but note too the possibility that Hadrian I alludes to the *Donation* in a letter to Charlemagne in 778: *Codex Carolinus* 60, cited at Walter (1970), 171 n. 58.

2 On the Lombards and the papacy see Wallace-Hadrill (1967), 43–63 and Davis (1992) *passim*.

3 See Thümmel (1992) on the uniformity of the official voices in the fourth century; Grigg (1977) on the views of Constantine.

Book of Pontiffs. One of the principal aims of the *Donation* is to show that the Church of Rome owes no allegiance to Byzantium, since Constantine's migration left the western lands in the absolute possession of Silvester and his successors. Since the iconoclasts had claimed the right to appoint their own patriarchs,[1] the *Donation* hardly ever uses the titles pope and pontiff without the qualifying epithets 'universal' and 'supreme'. We may wonder whether Rome had as many churches in the pontificate of Silvester as the *Donation* implies;[2] the *Book of Pontiffs* lists them with their treasures in the biography of Silvester, the longest before the eighth century, and commends the restorations that were carried out in that century under a number of the popes. The scrupulous description of crowns and vestments in the document seems as meretricious to us as it did to Valla;[3] but in an age when wealth and ostentation were synonymous, the *Book of Pontiffs* seems determined not to rob the Church of a single fabric, let alone a jewelled Cross or a golden chalice, in its inventories of ecclesiastical treasures. The compilers who appear to have been contemporaries of Charlemagne recorded his munificence and spared no detail of the vivid pageants that preceded both his baptism by Pope Hadrian I and his reception of the imperial diadem from Leo III.[4] The mantle, tunic and diadem which Charlemagne paraded at this ceremony were all listed among the insignia that Constantine bestows on Pope Silvester in the *Donation*; the successors of Silvester in the eighth century transferred this regal garb from the heretics of Byzantium to an emperor who restored an orthodox and Roman government to the west.[5]

One precedent for the forgery that must not be overlooked is the Donation of Quierzy in 754, by which Pepin guaranteed to the pope the

---

1 See Herrin (1987), 340–43 on the forced resignation of Germanus of Constantinople under Leo the Isaurian.

2 See my notes on the Lateran, St Peter's and St Paul's.

3 Valla, *Donat.* 15.48–18.60 (pp. 42–53 Schwahn). The order of coronation in the tenth century already found it necessary to state that the gems on the crown were emblems of virtue: Elze (1960), 9.

4 See Einhard, *Life of Charlemagne* 23, Folz (1974) and the selected witnesses in Pullan (1971), 11–14. The precedent had already been set by Constantine and his posterity. See Bowersock (1986) on the inflation of regal and sacerdotal dignity in the fourth century; Dufraigne (1997), 73–83 and 250–325 on the Christian appropriation of the triumphal *adventus*.

5 This observation is pursued at length by Gregorovius (1971), 55–64, though at 73ff. he blames the rise of papal supremacy and the 'theocratic principle' on Charlemagne's weaker heirs.

enjoyment of his present territories.[1] It is also worthy of note that two successive pontiffs, the brothers Stephen II and Paul, both ostentatious devotees of images and (from time to time) of Pepin, were the offspring of a man named Constantine. That name became notorious when, after Paul's demise in 767, Constantine II, Duke of Toto, seized the papacy, and, though a layman, seems to have possessed it with the approval of his eastern namesake Constantine V. The Franks rejected Constantine II, and the *Book of Pontiffs* does not even recognize his tenure.[2] At the same time, the frequency with which the name of Constantine the Great was attached to ecclesiastical buildings of this era has been noticed by historians, and utterances attributed to this Constantine make up the longest of the twenty items in Pope Hadrian's collection of decrees.[3] Charlemagne himself took Constantine the Great as his model in portraiture.[4] If, then, the *Donation* was composed around 770,[5] when the Lombard realm was already dead or toppling and Byzantium was less powerful than the Franks, one of its objects will have been to show that any potentate who bore the name of Constantine could justify it only if, as pope, he stood in the true line from Silvester or, as emperor, he divided his prerogatives with the apostolic see.

Another aim – to build up the reputation of the Lateran, which had hitherto been overshadowed by St Peter's – is suggested by the greatest living authority on the *Donation*, W. Pohlkamp.[6] He also defends the author against the imputation of falsehood, urging that we should read his work as an essay in the recreation of history. We might say rather, an essay in the creation of a false historical memory, for it is clear enough that no-one appealed to the document in the centuries that followed unless they thought that it was, or at least pretended to be, a statute handed down by Constantine.

---

1 On the authenticity and authority of this grant see Davis (1992), 107–11. Halphen (1977), 20–23 maintains that the *Donation* inspired the ceremony at which the king prostrated himself before the pope, and therefore was already in existence by 754. Wallace-Hadrill (1967), 93 suggests, a little fancifully, that Stephen II produced the text to reinforce his position at the meeting.

2 See Davis (1992), 85–87.

3 See Hinschius (1863), 766.

4 See Walter (1970), 171 n. 59.

5 The view of Davis (1992), 110. Mirbt and Aland (1967), 107 give a date of 757–767 without further commentary. Folz (1974), 109–11 suggests that the *Donation* was intended to confirm the legitimacy of Pepin's grant of 754 – which surely supports my thesis that it represents the common interests of the Franks and Rome. For a review of theories old and new see Maffei (1964), 1–10.

6 Pohlkamp (1988).

The success of such deceptions is more easily explained if they occur at the behest of an authority that has power to silence doubt. Whether it was Rome, or Rome alone, that had the motive and the power to forge the *Donation* in the eighth century is, however, a different question. Although it served the interests of the papacy at the time, it is not a charter of absolute supremacy, for it indicates that a pontiff will prefer indigence to riches, and that whatever goods he may possess in this world come to him only from the hand of his temporal lord.[1] If the popes were ever to reclaim the crown that their modesty had ceded to Byzantium, it could only be to put it on the head of a worthier sovereign. We know of at least one occasion on which the crown overreached the papacy: in 774 the *Donation of Charlemagne* confirmed and amplified the terms of Pepin's donation, and thus secured the allegiance of the Roman see, but the promise of new estates was not made good at any time in the long reign of the donor.[2] In the later Middle Ages, the *Donation* was perhaps a double-edged sword in the hands of prelates who demanded not the friendship but the submission of worldly powers;[3] and it was useless to the popes of the Renaissance, in the century after Valla, when they were buffeted from different sides by the French king and the Holy Roman emperor – each in his way the heir of Charlemagne.

NOTE ON THE TEXTS AND TRANSLATIONS

The only available text of the *Oration to the Saints* is that of Heikel (1902). The Greek text of the *Inventio* used here is that of Holder (1899); for the Latin I have also used his edition, but with an eye to his apparatus and the critical text prepared by Borgehammar (1991). The majority of my notes are attached to the Latin, because it is the longer; I have annotated the Greek

---

1 This corollary does not suggest itself, e.g. to Ullmann (1965), 61, where it is argued that the document represents the emperor as holding power 'by sufferance' of the pontiff. None the less, the notes to the edition of Migne (1835), 569–70 record the speculation that it was forged by a Greek to show that the prerogatives of the Roman see were of merely human origin, and one scholar even claimed to have discovered the Greek exemplar (p. 579). On the Greek editions that came to light in the Renaissance see Fuhrmann (1968), 38–41. Even if a genuine Greek archetype existed, it would not prove that the forger worked in the east or wished to compromise the papacy, for, as Wallace-Hadrill (1967), 62 observes, Rome became an asylum for Byzantine malcontents under the Iconoclasts.

2 Davis (1992), 111–22 defends both the authenticity of the grant and the integrity of Charlemagne.

3 According to Walter (1970), 171–74, even Leo IX, and even in a picture at the Lateran, preferred to be shown receiving the crown directly from the apostles.

where there was no corresponding passage in the Latin, or where the language seemed to demand a comment. Texts of the *Donation* are all too numerous, and many will regret that I have followed the one reproduced in the Abbé Migne's *Patrologia Latina*.[1] This choice is not intended as a slight to the modern researches which have shown that this is not the most primitive version; it merely reflects my opinion that, when we have to do with a forgery, the archetype is of less historical interest than the version that has seduced the largest public. The Migne text is the one that has been most accessible for the last millennium, and consequently the one that a historian of the mediaeval period will most often have occasion to consult. In any case Migne's text diverges little from that of Fuhrmann, which has some claim to be the most original;[2] in my footnotes I have indicated the discrepancies, together with the reasons that have led the Church to give precedence to the reading in the *Patrologia*. I have, however, borrowed the division into chapters which Fuhrmann and other editors have found conducive to ease of reference and the relief of tedium. Like the other documents in this volume, the *Donation* is the work of a man whose style was too ambitious for his talents; except where I have pruned their solecisms or expanded abbreviations, I have endeavoured to produce an accurate crib for all these authors, retaining as many of their infelicities and extravagances as modern English idiom will bear.

1 More precisely Migne (1844), because it contains notes that are lacking in the edition of 1853. I have not detected any disagreement between the two.

2 See Fuhrmann (1968), 9–10, maintaining with Grauert (1882) the superiority of the 'Frankish' tradition against the defence of the 'Pseudo-Isidorian' redaction in Williams (1964). Both parties agree in dating the earliest version to the ninth century.

CONSTANTINE: THE ORATION TO THE SAINTS

Constantine Augustus,[1] to the assembly[2] of the saints.

1. The splendour that outshines day and the sun,[3] the prelude to the resurrection, the new composition of bodies which have travailed in times past, the sanction of the promise and the road that leads to eternal life,[4] the day of the passion[5] is here, O most beloved leaders, and all you other dear men. It is made blessed, also by the great multitude of worshippers and by the very God who is worshipped, declared as he is in oracles,[6] through the inner senses of each person and through the utterances of unceasing hymns.[7] As for you, all-mothering nature,[8] what did you ever before bring to

1 Though Lactantius, *Pers.* 24.9 confers the title Augustus on Constantine as soon as he proclaims himself successor to Constantius in 306, his permanent assumption of it is dated by Creed (1984), 105 n. 6 to some time after his marriage to Maximian's daughter Fausta on July 25 in 307. Barnes (1976a), 417 deduces from the absence of the title *Nikêtês* (Victor) that the speech was composed before Constantine's defeat of Licinius in 324. The title was employed in all his subsequent correspondence, except (as Lane Fox (1986), 779–80 notes) in a letter to King Sapor of Persia (Eusebius, *Constantine* 4.9). In that case, however, the omission may be explained as a prudent courtesy in writing to a sovereign of equal or greater power.

2 For *sullogos* as a Christian congregation see Origen, *Against Celsus* 3.51 etc. 'Saints', as in the New Testament, denotes all the living Christians in any congregation.

3 Cf. Constantine's letter to Alexandria at Eusebius, *Constantine* 3.67, and for the origin of the metaphor see John 9.5, Eph. 5.14 etc.

4 Combining Matt. 7.13–14 and parallels with e.g. John 6.68.

5 That is, it is Good Friday. It outshines the sun despite the darkness of Matt. 27.45 par.; it is the prelude to the resurrection because of Matt. 27.53. On Constantine's concern with the date of Easter see Eusebius, *Constantine* 3.18, and for another celebration of the Passion see *Constantine* 3.30.1.

6 Both those of the Jewish prophets and those of the Sibyl, on whom see Chapter 18.

7 As Heikel regards his own text as corrupt, I have given a sense that is closer to the emended version offered in the *apparatus criticus*. The precept that God should be worshipped both with the heart and with the voice is a biblical commonplace (Col. 3.16), though Origen, *First Principles* 1.1.9 etc. is the source of the notion of 'spiritual senses'.

8 Personified by contemporary Platonists as an artisan subordinate to Intellect: Plotinus, *Enneads* 3.8.4. On the inadequacy of naturalistic or 'physical' cosmologies see Irenaeus, *Against Heresies* 2.29; Clement of Alexandria, *Stromateis* 4.2. As an agent in God's service nature has her role at e.g. Clement, *Stromateis* 3.83 and Origen, *Against Celsus* 6.60.

perfection in the world to match this? What in short is your workmanship, if the cause of all is also the cause of your being? For this one fashioned your nature, since the order[1] of nature is life according to nature.[2] For there prevailed a quite incongruous state of affairs: no-one showed reverence to the God of all in the manner that befits him, and all things were believed to be held together not through providence[3] but at random without order or regulation. While among all nations the divine Spirit was announcing these tidings through prophets,[4] impious unrighteousness, far from rendering them obedience, withstood them with every kind of stratagem, calumniating the light of truth while it embraced the all too plausible claim of darkness.[5] Nor was even this achieved without force and savagery, especially the collusion of the policy of the rulers with the mindless onslaught of the vulgar populace.[6] Rather, indeed, it was this policy that instigated this untimely madness. For this reason, a life of this kind, oppressed for many generations, was a cause of the greatest evils to the people of the time.

But when, of a sudden, the Saviour made his brilliant sojourn, righteousness came into being in place of unrighteous works, and peace in place of the multitudinous wave;[7] and everything that the prophets had predicted came to pass. Therefore, lifted up high to his paternal hearth,[8] having compassed the

1 'Order' renders the Greek word *kosmos*, often translated 'world'. In the New Testament, it is used in contrast to *ktisis* to signify the realm of sin and bondage (John 3.16, 17.14 etc.).

2 A Stoic definition of virtue, already commended to Christians by Rom. 1.26.

3 Though parallels might be drawn with Plato, *Timaeus* 30a, or with Lactantius, *DI* 1.21.1, defence of providence is, as Bolhuis (1956), 26 remarks, a desideratum for any thinker who wishes to oppose the fatalism of the Stoics or the Epicurean derivation of all events from the random motion of atoms. It might be added that providence, in the sense of a disinterested vigilance for the welfare of his subjects, is also the characteristic of a good emperor, as Corcoran (1996), 147–48 observes, citing *Theodosian Code* 7.20.2.5–6.

4 Cf. Heb. 1.1 on the preparation of the Gospel in Israel; Justin, *First Apology* 43.12 on the inspiration of the Gentiles through the Sibyl and Hystaspes; Theophilus, *Autolycus* 9 and Clement, *Stromateis* 6.42 on the concurrent inspiration of Jews and Gentiles.

5 Cf. Eph. 3.18–21 for the antithesis between light and truth.

6 Perhaps an allusion to the death of Socrates, on which see Chapter 9. Chapter 25 asserts that the people of Diocletian's reign were better than their rulers, no doubt because Christianity had already shed its light upon the world.

7 Cf. Gen. 1.2, Ps. 69.1, Isa. 57.1, Rev. 21.1 and Theophilus, *Autolycus* 2. for the use of water as an image of the godless world.

8 The word *hestia*, also used by Constantine in his letter to Antiochenes (Eusebius, *Constantine* 3.60), combines the senses of 'altar' and 'hearth'. Its presence here may be inspired by the use of it elsewhere as an appellation for Jerusalem, e.g. at Eusebius, *Tricennial* 9. Or Constantine may have in mind the mysterious hearth which is said to remain unmoved at Plato, *Phaedrus* 247a.

inhabited world with the rays of awe and temperance, he established the Church on earth to be, as it were, a sacred temple of virtue, eternal, indestructible, in which the things due to God his most exalted Father and those proper to himself were reverently performed. What then did the raging wickedness[1] of the nations contrive after this? Its schemes were to oust the gracious works of Christ and destroy the Church which had been founded for the salvation of everyone, and it set up anew its own superstition,[2] so that once again strife, wars, battles, an intractable way of life and love of money (which is by nature germane to wickedness[3]) might sometimes charm by specious hopes and sometimes strike with fear. But let this [wickedness] lie, subdued by virtue as is right, torn apart and scattered by repentance.[4] Our task now is to say what pertains to the divine Word.[5]

2. Hear now Church,[6] you pilot intent on purity and virginity, you nurse of immature and ignorant youth, whose care is truth and love of humankind, whose ever-flowing springs exude the liquor of salvation. I pray you, listen favourably, you who worship God rightly[7] and are therefore dear to him, attending not to the diction but to the truth of what is said, not to me the speaker but to the reverence of my devotion.[8] For what profit would there be in words if the disposition of the speaker were left unexamined? If therefore

1 Cf. Ps. 2.1: 'Why do the heathen rage?'

2 Even before the Romans had begun to speak of Christianity as a *superstitio,* Christians had applied its Greek equivalent *deisidaimonia* to the religion of the Greeks: Acts 17.22.

3 Cf. 1 Tim. 6.10, Matt. 13.22 etc.

4 The word *metanoia* was used since apostolic times to denote the Christian's turning from his sins and from the world: Mark 1.15, Rom. 2.4, Acts 26.20 etc.

5 Here, as often in Christian prose, one is not sure whether *logos* should be construed as a common noun or as an epithet of Christ; cf. John 10.35, Heb. 4.12 and Origen, *Philokalia* 5.4 on Christ as the Word behind the 'many words' of scripture.

6 Perhaps combining the image of Noah's Ark (applied to the church at 1 Pet. 3.20, Origen, *Genesis Homily* 2.5 etc.) with that of the woman clothed with the sun at Rev. 12.1 (identified as the church by Methodius, *Symposium* 8.5). Lane Fox (1986), 631 observes that the word *ekklêsia* is inserted by Heikel, and conjectures that the pilot may have been not the congregation but its leader. Nevertheless, the whole congregation is addressed elsewhere in the second person singular.

7 Cf. John 4.24.

8 Real or feigned lack of eloquence could be turned to account in various ways, especially by a practised orator: see e.g. Antiphon, *The Murder of Herodes* 1.1 (on the authority of experience where the art of speech is wanting); Ovid, *Metamorphoses* 13.10 (on the superiority of deeds to words); Dio Chrysostom, *Oration* 32.39 (on the professional duplicity of sophists). Christians would remember the disclaimer of Paul at 1 Cor. 2.1–4.

I dare great things, I ascribe my daring to my implanted[1] love for the divine, since this represses even awe. I therefore recruit as allies those who understand the divine mysteries,[2] so that if any error befalls my words, you may be at hand to correct it,[3] not looking for exactitude of learning but accepting the faithfulness of the attempt. And may the greatest inspiration from the Father and his beneficent Son be present to me as I say whatever things it expresses and puts into my mind.[4] For if anyone without God's help pursues rhetorical skill, or any other supposes that he perfects his work adequately, both he and what he labours at are revealed to be unfruitful.[5] Yet no-one who has once enjoyed the divine inspiration ought to tremble or delay. Let us now therefore, eschewing a lengthy preamble, attempt to fulfil our aim.

3. The good to which all things aspire, the God who is for ever above all being, has no birth and therefore no beginning.[6] For he himself is the origin[7] of all that comes to be. And the one who received his beginning from him is united to him again, undergoing separation and union with him not in space[8] but intellectually. For it is not through any internal lesion in the Father's bowels[9] that the one begotten has come to be, as is naturally the case with things that come from seeds; rather it was by the dispensation of providence, which contrived that he was to be the governor of the sensible world and its inhabitants. Hence also comes the cause of being and life to all things which

1 Cf. James 1.21. In view of Constantine's account of his youth in Chapter 11, we cannot ascribe to him an 'innate' love of God.

2 For *mustêria* as the higher doctrines of the church see Mark 4.1; Ignatius, *Trallians* 2.3 etc. The word in the Latin original may also have been *mystêria*, as in Rufinus' rendering of Origen, *First Principles* 1.2.3.

3 A layman's plea, as in Origen, *First Principles* 1.6.4 etc.

4 For the prayer that God will guide his meditation cf. Ps. 19.14; for the claim to speak in the spirit of the Lord cf. 1 Cor. 7.40.

5 Cf. Ps. 127.1: 'except the Lord build the house they labour in vain'.

6 Constantine may not have been aware that his first two clauses marry Aristotle, *Nicomachean Ethics* 1094a with Plato, *Republic* 509b. The latter text is quoted in Plato's own words by Eusebius (*Ecclesiastical Theology* 1.7), who is therefore plainly not the translator of the present text. That God has no beginning is an axiom of Christian apologetic: Aristides, *Apology* 1 etc. For God as the supreme good see Alcinous, *Isagoge* 10; Clement of Alexandria, *Schoolmaster* 1.8 etc.

7 For the term *arkhê* cf. Rev. 21.6 and Origen, *Commentary on John* 1.16–19.

8 Cf. the argument of Athenagoras, *Embassy* 8, that polytheism would entail the occupation of different spaces by different gods which is self-evidently absurd.

9 By contrast Arius urged that the Father must suffer division or passion if he begets a son: Socrates, *Church History* 1.15.

are compassed in the world. Hence too come the soul and all senses and the organs through which significant information is imparted to the senses.

What then does the argument show? That there is one overseer for all existent things, and that everything is subjected to his sole rulership, both things in heaven and those on earth,[1] both natural objects and organic bodies.[2] For if there were not one but many authorities over these innumerable things, there would be share-outs and divisions of elements and [things told in] ancient myths;[3] envy and avarice, dominating according to their power, would mar the harmonious concord of the whole,[4] as many disposed in different ways of the shares allotted to each, and took no thought to maintain the whole world in the same state and according to the same principles. And who would know the Maker of the whole realm of being? Who would be first or last in prayers and litanies?[5] To whom could I pay especial worship without impiety to others?[6] Or perhaps if I had need of something for my livelihood, I would offer thanks to the one who aided me, but blamed the one who withstood? From whom would I have prayed to

1 For this phrase, indicating the subjection of the entire creation to Jesus, cf. Eph. 1.10, Phil. 2.10 etc.

2 This would mean a body endowed with organs, according to the majority of modern and ancient interpreters of Aristotle; cf. Chalcidius, *On the Timaeus* 258. It is possible, however, if the original was in Latin, that the Greek is a mistranslation of some phrase like *instrumento elementorum* at Tertullian, *Apology* 17.

3 On myths as incitements to immorality and false doctrine cf. 1 Tim. 4.7; Plato, *Republic* 391; Aristides, *Apology* 13.7 etc.

4 This reasoning can be traced to Aristotle, *Metaphysics* 12, 1076a, though it becomes especially frequent in Christian authors in the age of Constantine. See Edwards (1999b), 272, citing Lactantius, *DI* 1.3.18–19; Athanasius, *Against the Nations* 36–38; Eusebius, *Tricennial* 6. Aristotle quotes a line from Homer (*Iliad* 2.20.40), and the analogies between the rule of god and the earthly government of man had already been drawn by flatterers such as Dio Chrysostom in his Third Oration. The edicts of the persecutor Maximinus Daia had maintained that the gods do everything in harmony, while *Latin Panegyrics* 2(10).11 likens the joint rule of Maximian and Diocletian to the partnership of Jupiter and Hercules, who rule the world through lesser deities.

5 Early pagan hymns suggest that the worshipper made this choice, but Orphic poetry had already insisted that Zeus must be the first, the middle and the last, while Christians assigned these places in a rigid order to Father, Son and Holy Ghost. See Matt. 28.19; Justin, *1Apology* 13.3 etc.

6 To judge by *Latin Panegyrics* 11(3).3 the answer is Jupiter, who had recently been personified on earth by Diocletian, while his junior colleague Maximian played the role of Hercules. The author of this eulogy, like the author of 10(2), commends the more than fraternal amity of the emperors, no doubt because some had doubted whether a realm divided could remain at peace.

know the cause of the present calamity and thought fit to obtain relief? Let us imagine that we had received responses from oracles and prophecies, but that it was not in our power and these things were the province of another god: what pity would there be, what pity would there be, what providential oversight of God with regard to humanity? Unless indeed the one who was more philanthropically disposed ruled by violence over the one who had no relation to him. The result would be wrath, strife and vituperation, as each neither minded his own business nor was content, through avarice, with his booty; then finally the confusion of all things would follow. What then after this? Obviously the strife of things in heaven would devastate those under heaven and on earth; the procession of the seasons, the change of times and the enjoyment of the fruits that grow in accordance with the times would have disappeared, and so would day and the nightly rest that succeeds it. Enough now of these things and let us return once again to the irrefutable argument.[1]

4. Whatever has a beginning has also an end, and a temporal beginning is called coming to be.[2] But all things that come to be are corruptible and time effaces their form. How then could things that come of corruptible generation be immortal? The sort of opinion that goes the rounds among unthinking people is the belief that there is marriage and begetting among the gods.[3] But if those born are immortal, and they are perpetually being born, the race is bound to increase excessively. As this increase supervenes, what heaven, what earth has accommodated such a great swarm of supervenient gods? What is one to say of men who join heavenly siblings in fellowship by marriage, and reprimand adultery and incontinence? Let us say boldly that even their honours and their tributes from men have been compounded with overweening and impurity. For as it is, one who composes metrical hymns, or even puts together hymns without a metre,[4] and a statue-maker who

1 Or again 'Word', i.e. Christ. Cf. Justin, *1Apology* 5; Eusebius, *Tricennial* 15 (p. 245.19 Heikel).

2 A cardinal assumption of Greek philosophy, e.g. Aristotle, *On Coming to be and Passing away* and Plato, *Timaeus* 28a–b. Constantine appears to be unaware that the verb *gignesthai* ('come to be') was now employed by Platonists to signify ontological dependence without temporal beginning: see Dillon (1977), 243.

3 Though, as Bolhuis (1956), 29 observes, this too is a commonplace, it is likely enough that Constantine drew most of his commonplaces from Lactantius. This one occurs at *DI* 1.16.5–6.

4 The prose hymn is only scantily represented in the literature that survives from classical times. The chief examples are those of the second-century sophist Aelius Aristides, and the Emperor Julian's hymns to the Sun and the Mother of the Gods, which were composed a generation after the death of Constantine.

conceives some form in his intellect[1] fabricate an artificial plaything, and as it were forgetting in the meantime pays it pious homage as an immortal god, though he confesses that he, the father and maker of the statue, is mortal. And they themselves display the tombs and monuments of those gods,[2] and pay tribute to them in death with immortal honours, not knowing that what is truly blessed and incorruptible has no need of honour from those who are corruptible. For what is visible to the mind and apprehensible to the intellect neither desires a form by which it may be known nor submits to a shape such as an image or representation. But all these things occur for the sake of the dead, for they were human beings when they shared the life of the body.[3]

5. But why do I stain my tongue with polluted words, when my intention is to hymn the true god?[4] First indeed, I wish to cleanse my mouth, as though from bitterness, by the sacred drink.[5] Now the sacred drink pours from the ever-flowing spring of the God who is hymned among us, and my proper task is to hymn Christ through my way of life and the thanksgiving due to him from us in return for many great benefits.[6] This one, I say, established the beginnings of this entire world, and invented a constitution for human beings by legislating with his word,[7] then forthwith accommodated the newborn beings in a certain blessed and flowery place, rich in fruits of many kinds, wishing them at first to be untutored in good and evil,[8] but finally to give them the seat on earth that belongs only to the rational creature, and

1 Cf. Plotinus, *Enneads* 5.8.1, where the insight of the sculptor is commended, but not the translation of it into plastic form.

2 Cf. Tertullian, *Apology* 25; Athenagoras, *Embassy* 28 and 30, citing the Hellenistic poet Callimachus, *Hymn 1.* 8-9 on the grave of Zeus. Tit. 1.12 is a garbled echo of the same lines.

3 The theory of Euhemerus, that all gods were originally mortals, would be known to Latin speakers through the translation made by Ennius, the father of Latin poetry, and cited by Lactantius, *DI* 1.11–14. Cf. Eusebius, *Tricennial,* 13.

4 A variation on the pagan commonplace, 'why do I speak of an oak or a rock?', sometimes used as a preface to the reported words of a god: Hesiod, *Theogony* 35; Porphyry, *Plotinus* 22.

5 Cf. Origen, *Homily on Numbers* 28.10 (on the sweetening of the waters of Marah at Num. 33.8).

6 Here Constantine conforms to Origen's precept that Christ may receive thanksgiving and intercession, though not the adoration to which the Father alone is entitled. See, however, my note on the final paragraph of the speech.

7 Here and elsewhere Constantine plays on the fact that *logos* served both as an ordinary noun meaning 'reason' or 'utterance' and as the proper name of Christ in the Trinity.

8 Apart from Gen. 2.9 (on the plants of Eden) and 3.3 (on the prohibition of the tree of knowledge), this passage is also redolent of the flowery plain of truth at Plato, *Phaedrus* 248b, where souls have not yet felt the touch of evil (250c).

then indeed to unfold the knowledge of good and evil as befits rational creatures.[1] At that time[2] he bade the race to increase, so that the whole area enclosed within the circuit of the Ocean[3] might be inhabited. But as humankind multiplied in this way, and arts useful to life were discovered, the race of irrational creatures multiplied at an equal rate.[4] A certain special power of nature was found for each kind: in gentle creatures meekness and submissiveness to humans, in savage ones strength, swiftness and a sort of native intuition of the means of escaping dangers.[5] And by his legislation he enjoined on humans a certain care for gentle creatures, but a certain conflict with the savage ones.[6] And after this he formed the race of birds,[7] very great in number and diverse in nature and habits, outstanding in its variety of colours and endowed with an innate musical harmony. And having distinguished all the other things that the world holds in its embrace, and having defined a fixed rule of life for all these, he arranged the most perfect fulfilment of the whole.

6. The majority of people, however, in their stupidity make nature the cause of the ordering of all things, though some of them ascribe it to fate or

1 Apparently taking the view of Theophilus, *Autolycus* 2.25 and Irenaeus, *Against Heresies* 4.38–39, that knowledge of good and evil was only temporarily denied to Adam and Eve. There seems to be here no doctrine of the fall described in Genesis 2–3.

2 Exegetes of the fourth century laid stress on the 'difference of times' between the old covenant and the new: the former not only countenanced polygamy but failed to perceive the blessings of the celibate condition.

3 According to e.g. Homer, *Iliad* 14.301–02 (cited by Athenagoras, *Embassy* 18.3), this river encircles all the land of the world, and is also the origin of the gods.

4 Lovejoy and Boas (1935), 96 adduce Cicero, *Offices* 2.5, which ascribes to the Hellenistic thinker Dicaearchus the claim that beasts had sometimes become so populous as to exterminate the humans in their territory. But Constantine may be using the brutes as a symbol of vicious passions, as Theophilus does at *Autolycus* 17. In that case he is repeating the Roman platitude, exemplified in Lucretius, *On Nature* 5 and Seneca, *Letter* 90, that moral corruption always accompanies progress in the arts. It was characteristic of Hellenistic, rather than classical, thinkers to extol the primitive state, and characteristic of Romans, rather than Greeks, to dwell on the evils that attended the development of the arts.

5 Cf. Plato, *Protagoras* 320d; Pliny, *Natural History* 7 proem; Lactantius, *On the Workmanship of God* 2–3.

6 This distinction, manifestly lacking in the command to subdue all creatures at Gen. 1.28, is none the less presumed in the occasional exegesis of the dietary laws as parabolic injunctions to befriend the righteous and avoid the wicked: see e.g. *Barnabas* 10.3.

7 Genesis 20–25 suggests rather that God created first the creatures of the sea, then those of air, then those on land.

chance.[1] When they attribute to fate the capacity for these things, they do not even understand, when they use the name 'fate', that they are uttering a name but not indicating an activity or an underlying substance.[2] For what would fate be in itself if nature has given birth to everything? Or what would nature be thought to be, if the law of fate is not to be transgressed? But the very assertion that fate is a law reveals that every law is the work of the lawgiver.[3] Now fate, if it is a law, would be the invention of God; everything therefore is subject to God and nothing exempt from his power. And we accept that fate is, and is reckoned to be, the will of God, but how can righteousness, discretion and the other virtues be according to fate?[4] And whence come their contraries, unrighteousness and incontinence? For wickedness is from nature,[5] but not from fate, and virtue is the correction of character and manners. As to the lapses, or conversely the corrections, of the good and right will, however, which yield different results according to chance or fate, and everything that is just or apportioned to each according to his desert, how are these according to fate?[6] As to laws and exhortations to virtue and dissuasions from what is wrong and praises and censures and punishments and everything which either prompts us to virtue or leads us away from wickedness, how is this said to arise not from righteousness,

1 'Fate' may represent the Stoic position, attacked e.g. by Justin, *2Apology* 7; Hippolytus, *Refutation* 1.21.1–2; Eusebius, *Tricennial* 13. 'Chance' stands for the atomism of the Epicureans, on which see e.g. Theophilius, *Autolycus* 2.4 and Lactantius, *DI* 1.9–20. But since he is taking issue with the 'majority', Constantine must also have in mind the popular doctrines of astrology, attacked e.g. by Tatian, *Oration* 8–11.

2 According to Stobaeus, *Eclogues* 1.79.1–12, the great Stoic thinker Chrysippus styled fate sometimes a *logos*, sometimes a pneumatic substance (*ousia*). Both terms apply to Christ in Constantine's vocabulary.

3 On God as the author of the natural law see Psalm 19; Theophilus, *Autolycus* 5; Numenius, Fr. 13 Des Places, cited by Eusebius, *Gospel Preparation* 11.18.13–14.

4 The four cardinal virtues of philosophy after Plato are justice (*dikaiosunê*, here translated 'righteousness'); temperance, moderation or discretion (*sophrosunê*); wisdom (*sophia*); and courage (*andreia*).

5 That is, perhaps, from our corrupted nature, as Rom. 5.12–17 may imply. If so, this is the only indication that Constantine knew a doctrine of the fall.

6 This sentence seems to conflate the Stoic position, that the virtuous will is free and the only good, with the doctrine of Christianity and Plato that the gods reward our actions after death. The relation between providence and fate is a leading theme of Chalcidius' *On the Timaeus of Plato* (see p. 14 n. 4); at 176–77 he concludes that providence is the will of God which acts as the mind of the world, while fate is the system of natural law sustained by the world soul.

which is proper to God in his providence, but from fortune or chance?[1] For it depends on the manner of people's lives and their deserts; the plagues and dissensions, scarcity or abundance which attend them manifestly and openly declare, all but speaking, that such are the corollaries of our lives.

For creation[2] rejoices in righteous actions and rejects all impiety and welcomes the modest cast of mind. At the same time it abhors audacity and boastfulness that exceeds the condition of the living being. If the proofs of this, for the most part, are clear and lie before our eyes, they none the less shine forth more manifestly whenever, collecting ourselves inwardly and, as it were concentrating our minds,[3] we consider the cause of them within ourselves. For this reason I say we ought to live modestly and decently, not raising our thoughts above nature, and always reflecting on the constant presence to us of the God who oversees all that we do. The truth of the claim that all things arose from fortune and chance should be tested in this way also.[4] Heavens and the stars, earth and sea, fire and winds, water and air, the vicissitude of the seasons, the periodicity of winter and summer – should one be persuaded that all these arose without reason and just as it chanced to occur, rather than being fashioned? For some who have no minds say that human beings thought out most of these things because of their own needs,[5] nature supplying everything without stint. Grant that there is something reasonable in this opinion as applied to what is earthly and destructible: are the immortal and immutable things then also a human invention? For the progenitor of all these and their like, whatever is divorced from our senses and apprehensible by mind alone, is not the human being, a creature of matter, but the intellectual and eternal essence of God.

Yes indeed, the very principle of order is the work of providence, in that the day shines forth illuminated by the sun, and when it wanes night succeeds it, but having succeeded it is not left utterly dim because of the

---

1 Cf. Origen, *First Principles* 3.1.5. The argument was trite, as Alexander of Aphrodisias, *On Fate* 25–27 reveals.

2 The Greek word is *ousia*, 'being' or 'substance', but probably here rendering Latin *natura*.

3 A phrase that savours of Platonism: cf. Porphyry, *Plotinus* 8.21–23 and Plotinus, *Enneads* 1.4.9.

4 The following argument is reminiscent of Lactantius, *DI* 7.3.2.5, but also, as Bolhuis (1956), 29–30 shows, of many other passages.

5 No-one can have held such a preposterous tenet regarding the elements and the seasons; Constantine appears to have in mind the Euhemeristic theory that the gods of myth were originally the humans who invented such useful arts as writing, weaving and agriculture. On this cf. Lactantius, *DI* 1.14.

ballet of the stars.[1] What is one to say of the moon which is full when it stands in direct opposition to the sun, and grows slender on its approach to it at close quarters?[2] Does not this reveal the indwelling reason[3] and sagacity of God? The ready action of the sun's flame in maturing crops, the winds that blow to bring good climate, the refreshing rain and the harmony of all these, whereby all things are disposed with reason and order, and the eternal dispensation whereby the planets return to the same place at the due and expected times[4] – is it not manifest that God determines this, that the stars perform perfect service in obedience to the divine law? The altitude of the mountains and the hollow depths of the valleys and the evenness of the spreading plains – do these seem to exist without God's providence? Not only is the sight of these delightful, but the use is delightful also. The measures and intervals of water and earth, sufficing both for agriculture and for the importing of necessities from elsewhere – how do these not prove the accurate and calculated forethought of God? For the mountains contain water, then the smooth receives this and when it has irrigated itself sufficiently for recovery, discharges the rest into the sea, and the sea in turn passes it on to the Ocean. And shall we still dare to say that all this happens by chance and fortuitously? We have still to show what shape or form characterizes chance, which has no substance, either intelligible or sensible, but is just the noise of an insubstantial name buzzing about the ears.

7. For chance is in truth the name uttered by persons whose thoughts are haphazard and irrational[5] and who, failing themselves to comprehend the rationale, believe through the weakness of their comprehension that those

---

1 Cf. Ps. 147.4 on the creation of stars; Job 38.7 on their songs; Plato, *Timaeus* 40c for the stellar dance, translated *chorea* by Chalcidius, *On the Timaeus* 123. Markschies (2000), 5 styles this a pagan motif when he encounters it in the *Theophany* of Eusebius (c. 333), but cf. Origen, *On Prayer* 7.

2 A fact discovered as early as the fifth century, according to Heath (1913), 79–80, who cites the Christian author Hippolytus (*Refutation* 1.1.8) on Anaxagoras. Some authors (e.g. Lucretius, *Nature of Things* 5.575–6) continued to doubt the dependence of the moon's light on the sun.

3 The Greek is *endiathetos logos*, identified in Chapter 10 with Christ. For Christ as Wisdom see 1 Cor. 1.21–23, Heb. 1.3 (by implication), drawing on Prov. 8.22 and Wis. 7.25–26.

4 Cf. the emperor's reasoning at *Constantine* 2.57–58.

5 Cf. Eusebius, *Constantine* 2.56, where the context once again implies a contrast between the steadfastness of nature and the aberrations of the human mind.

things for which they cannot give an answer are irrationally ordered.[1] Nevertheless in the case of certain things the true comprehension of the truth about them lies in the depths; these are things that have a marvellous nature, as is the case with the nature of hot waters. For no-one has a ready account of the cause of such a great fire, and it is marvellous that when entirely surrounded by cold water, it does not depart from its native heat.[2] These phenomena, however, seem rather rare, and are easily enumerated throughout the inhabited world. My conviction is that they are intended to make the power of providence[3] become easily recognizable to humankind, declaring that the two most contrary natures, heat and cold, are filtered through one and the same root. Many and innumerable, therefore, are the contributions of the higher power to human comfort and enjoyment, and especially the fruit of the olive and the vine,[4] one of which conduces to the recovery of spirit and gladness, the other likewise to bodily enjoyment and therapy. An outstanding marvel also is the continual and inexhaustible flow of rivers by night and day, a symbol of everflowing and inexhaustible life.[5] Of equal weight is the alternation of night.

8. So let us make these statements as a confirmation that nothing occurs without mind or reason, and that reason and providence are God. It is he also who has decreed that the service of metals shall supply our needs. He deposited in due measure the nature of bronze and gold and the rest, decreeing that those which were to be widely and variously used should be furnished liberally, whereas those which were only for the purpose of ornament and liberality [he supplied] at once magnanimously[6] and sparingly, somewhere between parsimony and prodigality.[7] For if the same liberal

1 The Stoics would have agreed that chance is hidden cause: see Sambursky (1959), 56. Chalcidius, *On the Timaeus* 159 adopts the classic definition of chance (*fortuna*) as the unforeseen concurrence of two processes which in themselves are not extraordinary. See Chalcidius, ed. Waszink (1962) *ad loc.* for a collection of Platonic and Aristotelian antecedents.

2 Lane Fox (1986), 645 traces Constantine's interest in subterranean fires to Trier, citing *Latin Panegyrics* 6.22.2. But Seneca, *On Providence* 1 reveals the triteness of this example.

3 Constantine's writings are marked by a profound belief in the rule of providence: see e.g. *Constantine* 2.68, where he is once again addressing the Christian clergy.

4 Cf. Ps. 104.15 on wine and oil. Both ancient and modern authorities hold that the culture of vines and olives by the shores of the Mediterranean was coterminous with the spread of civilization: Sallares (1991), 32–33.

5 For the association of life with rivers cf. Ezek. 47.1, John 7.37–39, Rev. 22.1 etc.

6 Cf. Irenaeus, *Against Heresies* 4.39 on the *magnanimitas* of God, with my note on the recurrence of the term in Chapter 11.

7 Cf. Job 28.1–2 on God's concealment of metals.

provision were made of articles created only for ornament, avarice would prompt those who mine metals to despise the ones that are useful for agriculture, building and the construction of ships, such as iron and bronze; they would neglect to amass them, taking more thought for those that conduce to luxury and useless excess of wealth.[1] For this reason they say that the discovery of gold and silver is more difficult and laborious than that of other metals, so that the intensity of desire may be balanced by the intensity of labour. And how many other works of divine providence can be numbered in respect of all those things that it has liberally given to us, openly exhorting human lives to temperance and all the other virtues, and leading them away from untimely avarice. To trace the principle behind this is a superhuman task, for how could the intellect of the corrupt and feeble creature attain to the exact truth? How could it comprehend the pure will of God from the beginning?[2]

9. Therefore we must apply ourselves to what is possible and in accordance with our nature. For the inquiries that take place in disputations have a plausibility that leads most of us away from the truth about what exists. This has befallen many of the philosophers as they dabbled in words and the investigation of the nature of what exists. For whenever the greatness of the phenomena defeats their investigation they conceal the truth with certain tortuous procedures. The consequence is that, for all their vaunted wisdom, they hold contrary opinions and fight one another's doctrines even though they pretend to be wise.[3] Hence arise popular rioting and harsh judicial decisions from those in power, who believe that the ancestral custom is being destroyed.[4] Often the death of the philosophers themselves has ensued. For Socrates,[5] who exulted in dialectic and made the worse argument

---

1 Drake (2000), 281 accuses Constantine of overlooking the 'laws of supply and demand', which entail that precious metals derive their value from their rarity. But as Pindar, *Olympian* 1.1–2 reminds us, the ancients profess to love gold because it is beautiful and not because it is scarce.

2 Cf. Rom. 11.3–5, Ps. 3.7–8

3 Both Clement of Alexandria (*Stromateis* 5) and Lactantius (*DI* 3) had pressed this argument at some length.

4 The usual pretext for Roman measures against Christianity was defence of ancestral custom (*mos maiorum*). See e.g. the edict of Galerius in Lactantius, *Pers.* 34, and for the Christian response see Minucius Felix, *Octavius*; Origen, *Against Celsus* 1; Arnobius, *Against the Nations* passim.

5 Socrates (470–399 BC) was the tutor of Plato and a founder of the dialectic method in philosophy, which aims at the clarification of belief as a precondition for the discovery of truth. The claim that he made the worse argument the better is quoted from Aristophanes' *Clouds* by

the better and trifled on every subject with contradictory arguments, was put to death by the jealousy of his compatriots and fellow-citizens. Pythagoras, who professed to cultivate outstanding temperance and silence, has been convicted of falsehood.[1] For after his sojourn in Egypt, he declared to the Italians as a personal revelation to himself from God the things that at a time long before had been spoken by the prophets.[2]

And Plato himself,[3] who excelled all others in gentleness and first accustomed human intellects to revert from the sensible to the intelligible and the things that are always thus, the one who taught us to look up to things above, did well when he postulated the god above being, then made a second subordinate to this one,[4] dividing the two essences numerically,[5]

Diogenes Laertius, *Lives* 2.5. He was put to death on a charge of introducing new gods and corrupting the young; his death was represented in the *Apology* and *Phaedo* as a martyrdom, and Christian authors generally profess a high estimation for his character (Justin, *1Apology* 5; Tertullian, *Apology* 14 and *Martyrs* 4). Only Lactantius, *DI* 3.19–20 speaks as scornfully as Constantine.

1 Pythagoras of Samothrace was reputed to have lived around 500 BC and to have founded communities in southern Italy, whose members were committed to ardent friendship, vegetarianism and the liberation of the immortal soul. On the celebrated silence of his followers see Iamblichus, *On the Pythagorean Life* 199.

2 On the travels of Pythagoras see Porphyry, *Life of Pythagoras* 11, though it is usually Plato who is credited, on the weak authority of his own *Timaeus*, with plagiarism from Egyptian sources. The claim that all Greek philosophy was derived from the barbarians was entertained even by some classical authors, to the indignation of Diogenes Laertius, *Lives of the Philosophers*, preface.

3 For the claim that Plato anticipates the gospel see Justin, *1Apology* 8 and 60; for the view that his understanding was insufficient see Origen, *Against Celsus* 6.43 etc. On the use of Plato in the apologists, who admired above all his postulation of a unique and benevolent creator, see Daniélou (1961), 103–22. Lactantius (*DI* 3.20–21) and Arnobius (*Against the Nations* 2.11) are more hostile to the great philosopher than Constantine.

4 Following not so much Plato as Numenius, a disciple of both Plato and Pythagoras in the mid-second century AD, and a precursor of the Neoplatonists. See esp. Fragment 11 Des Places, which may have its origin in the spurious second epistle of Plato. If Constantine did not have first-hand knowledge of such passages (ours is in Eusebius, *Gospel Preparation* 11–12), there may have been Latin sources. The commentary of the Christian Chalcidius on the *Timaeus*, for example, is, as the edition of Waszink (1962) reveals, even more indebted to Numenius than his use of his name suggests. Waszink accepts the conventional date of c. 400 AD, but Dillon (1977), 401–08 and Barnes (1981) have argued that Chalcidius was a contemporary of Constantine, who dedicated his work to Bishop Hosius of Cordova. The frequency with which I draw on his commentary in my notes may add some weight to this position; nevertheless, some other writer would have to have been the intermediary for the doctrine of two gods, to which Chalcidius never alludes.

5 Cf. Justin, *Trypho* 129.5 on the differentiation of Father and Son.

while both shared one perfection and the essence of the second god[1] received its concrete existence[2] from the first. For the maker and governor of the universe is clearly sublime, while the other after him, in submission to his commandments, refers to him the cause of the constitution of all things.[3] According to the exact account[4] then, there would be one God who exercises care over all things and takes thought for them, having set all things in order by his Word. And the Word is himself God[5] and the child of God,[6] for how could anyone escape the greatest error, for how could anyone escape the greatest error if he gave any other name than the appellation 'child'? For the

1 Constantine does not apply the words 'second god' directly to Christ, but even if he did I could not agree with Barnes (2001) in detecting an Arian tendency in this passage. Barnes, who now dates the speech to 321, observes that the expression 'second god' was denounced as an Arianizing blasphemy by Marcellus of Ancyra, while Marcellus' principal adversary, Eusebius of Caesarea, makes use of cognate terms. But Marcellus, if we judge by frequency of condemnation, was the most intransigent heretic of his era, while Eusebius, whether heterodox or orthodox, declined to be an Arian, as he could not find scriptural warrant for the tenet that the Son was made 'from nothing'. For him at least the notion of Christ as 'second god' was authorized by Origen's *Against Celsus* 6.61, where Origen's aim is not to subordinate the Second Person of the Trinity to the First, but to defend the application of the title *theos* to both. The Nicene Council of 325 was likewise solicitous only to maintain that Christ is God (against the Arians) and that none the less he is different from the Father (against Marcellus); it made no attempt to determine whether one of them is superior in dignity to the other.

2 For *hypostasis* as the concrete expression of essence or *ousia*, see Porphyry, *Isagoge* 18.25.

3 Cf. Numenius, Fr. 12 Des Places (Eusebius, *Gospel Preparation* 12.18.6–10). The language of restoration is reminiscent of 1 Cor. 15.28 and Acts 3.21. On the orthodoxy of the present passage see Edwards (1995).

4 The word for 'account' is *logos*. It is not clear whether Constantine means to assert that this portion of Plato's teaching is true or to contrast its imperfections with the more accurate formulation offered by Christianity. On the Father's government of the world through Christ cf. Athenagoras, *Embassy* 10.4, following Prov. 8.22.

5 A clear affirmation of the position that was declared to be orthodox at the Nicene Council of 325. It was only in 327 that Arius consented to call Christ God in the confession that he submitted to Constantine. Unlike the emperor, he was prepared to apply the term 'creature' to Christ, as he denied that he was Son in any sense that made him the product of the Father's nature rather than his will.

6 The Greek uses *pais* ('boy') rather than the more usual *huios* ('son'). Although Acts 4.27 and 4.30 could be cited as a precedent, Ison (1987) suggests that the phrase alludes to the honorific nomenclature of emperors in the age of Constantine. The formula *Deus et Dei filius* appears in Tertullian, *Apology* 21 and *Hermogenes* 18. In the latter it is coupled with the title *verbum* ('Word'), with an allusion to, or even an erroneous Latin version of, John 1.1.

father of all[1] would rightly also be called the father of his own Word.[2] So far then Plato was wise; but in what follows he is found[3] to err from the truth, introducing a host of gods and assigning a form to each, which became a pretext for greater error among the most unreasoning people, who did not look towards the providence of the Most High, but worshipped images of [the gods] which had been transformed into human types and those of other creatures.[4] The result is that a nature and discipline which were excellent and worthy of highest praise, mixed with such shortcomings, are in an impure and defective state.

But the same man seems to have taken himself in hand and corrected his errors, where he manifestly asserts that God has breathed into us his own Word,[5] clearly showing that the spirit of God is a rational soul[6] and at the

1 Although it savours of *Timaeus* 28c, this phrase is also warranted by Rom. 11.36 and perhaps by Eph. 5.6, though there it may mean only that God is the father of all believers. Daniélou (1961) offers good reasons for supposing that the Greek apologists knew *Timaeus* 28c from a florilegium, and it was certainly under Plato's influence that early Christians began to see God as the father of the world, not merely of his adopted nations, Israel and the Church. But Rist (1981), 158 is probably right to argue that a more cautious speaker, after the Nicene Council of 325 at least, would have taken pains to avoid the implication of this passage, that Christ belongs to the Father in the same way as his creatures.

2 Perhaps a punning allusion to Plato, *Symposium* 177d, where the same phrase means simply 'author of the account or argument'. The passage implies that Christ is styled the logos because he stands in the same relation to the Father as a spoken word to the one who utters it. Origen, *First Principles* 1.24–26 rejected this position, maintaining that the title is conferred on Christ as the architect and governor of the ordered universe. Arius appears to have embraced the same view, to judge by the position of the word *logos* in his confession of 327.

3 If Constantine is alluding to the account of the lesser gods which follows that of the creation at *Timaeus* 40d–41a, he would seem to be acquainted with the dialogue from some other source than a florilegium. The translation of Cicero would have been available to him; so perhaps would that of Chalcidius, on whom see p. 14 n. 4 above.

4 A standard topic of Jewish and Christian invective, from Isaiah 45 to Tertullian's *On Idolatry*. Though Plato himself had neither endorsed nor condemned the use of images, Porphyry's *On Statues* (known to us from Eusebius) justified the worship of the divine through the material intermediaries appointed by tradition.

5 Conflating Gen. 2.7 with *Timaeus* 90a, and, in the manner of Tatian (*Oration* 7) and Lactantius (*DI* 4.6), making no verbal distinction between the Spirit and the Word.

6 Curiously ignoring the distinction, already drawn by Tatian, *Oration* 12, between the soul and the spirit more sublime than soul. Perhaps he has in mind Gen. 2.7 again, where Adam is said to have become a rational soul when God breathed into his nostrils; he may also know that Origen spoke of Christ as the soul of God at *First Principles* 2.8.5. Alternatively, he may be indicating that the rational soul of Christ himself was identical with the Spirit, a doctrine not without precedent in Rome: see Heine (1998) on the role of the Spirit in the Christology of the Roman bishops, c. 200 AD. It would, however, be unsafe to hold the speaker to an exact

same time dividing all things into two kinds, the intelligible and the sensible, one <simple and immaterial>,[1] the other compounded from the structure of the body, and one apprehensible to the mind, the other opinable with opinion and sensation.[2] Thus what partakes of the Holy Spirit, as being uncompounded and indissoluble, is eternal and has been allotted eternal life, whereas the sensible, in every way dissoluble on the principle by which it arose, has no share in eternal life. And, remarkably, he goes on to teach that those who have lived well, obviously the souls of holy and good men, after their departure from the body, are sanctified in the most beautiful parts of heaven.[3] Now this also is useful to life; for who, without believing him and expecting the same good fortune, will practise the best life, righteousness and discretion, and reject evil? And in keeping with these statements he imposes on the souls of the wicked a wandering like that of people carried about in a shipwreck in the streams of Acheron and Pyriphlegethon.[4]

10. There are, however, some whose intellects are so impaired that, when they encounter these very facts, they are not converted and feel no dread, but despise and ridicule them as though they were hearing invented fables.[5] And while they praise the versatility of expression, they reject the doctrine as a hard one, they believe in poetic fables and they spread their trite and lying words throughout the whole Greek and the whole barbarian world.[6] For the

---

interpretation of his words when Latin theology of his day applied the term *spiritus*, with little discrimination, to the substance of the Godhead, the Third Person of the Trinity and the incorporeal nature of Christ himself; see e.g. Lactantius, *DI* 4.6.1 on Christ as spirit.

1 Following Heikel's supplementation of the lacuna. For the distinction between the noetic and the sensible, cf. Plato, *Timaeus* 27d. Biblical thought is content to contrast the visible and transient with the unseen and eternal: 2 Cor. 4.18.

2 Cf. Plato, *Republic* 477c–478e.

3 Cf. Plato, *Gorgias* 524a, *Phaedrus* 247–48.

4 Cf. Plato, *Phaedo* 111c–114c, especially 111e and 113d, which use images of sailing (and in the first case may allude to the shipwreck of Odysseus between Scylla and Charybdis). Acheron and Pyriphlegethon were rivers of the underworld in Greek mythology; Pyriphlegethon is mentioned among the poets' fables by Tertullian, *Apology* 47.

5 Though episodes of the Gospels were often likened to pagan myths (Justin, *Trypho* 67; Tertullian, *Apology* 21 etc.; Lactantius, *DI* 1.9; Arnobius, *Against the Nations* 1.54), the doctrine of the afterlife appears to have been ignored in philosophical polemic. Had the Latin poet Lucretius lived a century later, his ridicule of infernal terrors (*On Nature* 1.102–30) could have been aimed at Christians as well as at his poetic predecessors.

6 Not that the author himself divides the world into Greeks and barbarians, but that fabulous tales begin among the Greeks; cf. Lactantius, *DI* 1.18 and Arnobius, *Against the Nations* 5.24.

poets[1] say that children of the gods, human beings, judge souls after death, hymning their judgments and legal decisions, and setting overseers over the departed. The same poets[2] set forth battles of the demons[3] and certain warlike practices, and speak of their fatal decrees, declaring that some are harsh by nature, others indifferent to their tutelage of humankind, and certain others malign. And they put them on stage,[4] grieving over the slaughter of their own children, as though incapable of aiding, not just strangers, but even those dearest to them. And they represent them as subject to human passions,[5] singing their wars and wounds, their joys and griefs.[6]

And what they say is worthy of belief.[7] For if it is by divine inspiration that they address themselves to poetry, it is proper to trust them and believe what they proclaim in their raptures.[8] Yet they tell of the sufferings of gods and demons. These sufferings of theirs then are absolutely true. But someone will say that it is possible for poets to lie,[9] since it is the property of poetry to charm[10] the souls of hearers, whereas truth is the case where what is spoken of is no different from what it is said to be. Let it therefore be the property of poetry sometimes to snatch away the truth; nevertheless those who lie do not

---

1 See e.g. Homer, *Odyssey* 11.568, cited at *Apology* 41a etc. In view of the following note, however, it is possible that Constantine found this lore in the Orphic poetry which is cited more often than Homer in such Christian apologists as Tatian and Athenagoras.

2 The most obvious candidates here are the Orphic poets and Empedocles (Fr. 115 DK etc.). See Origen, *Against Celsus* 6.42 on the archaic mythographer Pherecydes.

3 The word *daimôn* signified in pagan usage a being intermediate between gods and men, whether evil or benign; Constantine takes up the word in its Christian sense, which was always pejorative.

4 Cf. Augustine, *City of God* 2.13. The seminal attack on tragedy as a form of art is Plato, *Republic* 377 and 395–96, closely followed in the fourth century by such Christians as Basil of Caesarea (*On Reading Greek Literature* 4), though neither Aristotle nor the Neoplatonists held the same position.

5 The impassibility of God, i.e. his immunity to all extraneous influences, is an axiom of Christian as of Platonic thought. As Lactantius, *On the Anger of God*, was at pains to show, it does not exclude such voluntary dispositions as benevolence and philanthropy, of which more is said below. On the sufferings of the gods see Tertullian, *Apology* 14–15.

6 The worship of warlike deities breeds strife on earth, as Chapters 22 and 25 will demonstrate.

7 Plato, *Timaeus* 40d strikes the same note of irony; cf. Lactantius, *DI* 1.11.23.

8 See Plato, *Ion* and *Phaedrus* 245a–b on the 'enthusiasm' of the poets; *Laws* 682a draws the corollary that Homer speaks the truth.

9 A privilege already claimed by Hesiod, or his Muses, at *Theogony* 27.

10 Poetry is commonly represented as a species of enchantment (*goêteia*): Plato, *Republic* 383a etc.

lie without purpose. For they either do this for some profit and advantage, or conscious of some evil practice in themselves, they dissemble because of the penalty imposed by the laws.[1] For it was possible for them, in my opinion, not to spread lying and impious reports about the higher nature in contradiction of the truth.

11. If therefore anyone knows that he is unworthy of the good life because he has lived in licence and disorder, if he changes and looks to God, the eye of his soul being purified, and becomes a stranger to his former base course of life, receiving God's healing,[2] he will live for all eternity. And it is fitting to give thanks on this account to the God who has saved him and saves all.[3] And they would be saved with fewer pains if they accepted the healing of their souls with pure faith and did not vacillate, like people who sometimes entrust themselves to medications and turn away, but endured with noble fortitude the remedy of righteousness, discretion and the rest.[4] Let us for our part strive to fill the uninitiated[5] with the good hope[6] that is in such words, calling God to our aid in the endeavour. For it is no small work to have turned to piety the souls of those who hear us, should they happen to be good, and if they be evil and ignorant, to lead them to the opposite course, rendering them profitable instead of good for nothing.[7] Rejoicing indeed in these same endeavours, and thinking it the work of a good man to hymn the

1 Alluding again to the persecution of freethinkers by the Athenians and Romans.

2 Christ was regularly described as a physician (Mark 2.17; Ignatius, *Eph.* 7.2 etc.), but here there may be also an ironic recollection of Lucretius, *On the Nature of Things* 1.936–50, where Lucretius undertakes to administer the drug of poetry to those who are deceived by the puerile teaching of the poets.

3 Not a confession of universalism, but an echo of the Pauline doctrine (1 Cor. 15.22, Rom. 5.18) that Christ died for the salvation of all humanity.

4 Another enumeration of the cardinal virtues, faith perhaps standing in the place of wisdom as at Heb. 11.3.

5 Greek *amuêtos*, meaning one who is not admitted to the mysteries (see note to Chapter 2). Constantine's son Constantius used the term to signify those who were not baptized (Theodoret, *Church History* 3.3), but Constantine cannot mean this, as he was not himself baptized at the time of speaking. Notwithstanding the precedent of Tertullian, *To the Nations* 1.7, Latin Christianity preferred the term *sacramentum*, and only after Constantine did legislation begin to discriminate between the 'mysteries' of the faith and pagan cults (*Theodosian Code* 10.8.19 etc.).

6 On faith as a source of hope amid tribulation cf. Constantine at Eusebius, *Constantine* 2.26.1.

7 Perhaps a reminiscence of Philemon 11, though if so it was not detected by the Greek translator.

Saviour, I dismiss all that the base sway of fortune[1] imposed on my unfortunate predicament, reckoning repentance the most efficacious salvation. I fervently wish that this revelation had been granted to me long ago,[2] if indeed the man is blessed who has been brought up from infancy[3] gladdened in the knowledge of things divine and in the beauty of virtue. And let this be said with moderation, for even if, as people say, it is not from earliest youth or from the cradle that the good are wise,[4] it is none the less a welcome thing if they achieve wisdom even in the prime of youth.

In me, however, no human education ever gave me assistance, but God is the source of whatever gifts of character or conduct are of good report among people of understanding.[5] I possess, and as it were hold before every vicious expedient that the evil one contrives, no weak shield,[6] but the knowledge of what pleases God. So choosing from this what is profitable to the present argument I shall hymn the Father of all.[7] And do you come to assist my zeal for holiness, Christ saviour of all, and set in order my description of your virtue, leading the way in solemn speech. And let no-one expect to hear my words and vocables adorned with any cunning;[8] for well I

---

1 As Plutarch, *On the Fortune of Alexander* and *On the Fortune of the Romans*, reminds us, conquerors have always been apt to see themselves as the favourites of fortune. By contrast the private person in antiquity often regarded himself as the plaything of a cruel mistress, and a religious conversion might be represented, as by Apuleius, *Metamorphoses* 11, as an escape from her dominion to that of a more benign and potent deity. Though Fortune resumed her throne in the Middle Ages, a more careful theologian of the Constantinian era would have taken heed of authors such as Origen, *Against Celsus* 8.65 and refused to surrender even the lives of pagans to any overseer but God.

2 Notwithstanding the memorable piety of his mother Helena during his reign, and the laxity of his father Constantius in enforcing Diocletian's edict (Eusebius, *Constantine* 2.49.1 etc.), Constantine does not seem to have been raised a Christian. Eusebius, *Tricennial* 9 avers that he was self-taught before entering Rome under the sign of the Cross. At *Constantine* 1.17 he makes Constantius a monotheist, though Smith (1997) finds little evidence of the 'solar monotheism' that is commonly ascribed to Constantius by modern scholars. It is not clear what Eusebius means by saying at *Constantine* 1.27 that Constantine had elected to return to his paternal god; if this were the god of Christians, how could Constantine have been still unacquainted with the cross at *Constantine* 1.32?

3 Cf. 2 Tim. 3.15.

4 The implication of e.g. Wis. 7.1ff.

5 Cf. Gal. 1.1 on the origin of Paul's apostolate.

6 At Eph. 6.16 Christians are exhorted to oppose the wicked with the shield of faith. But Constantine may also be alluding to the occasion when he ordered that the cross should be inscribed on the shields of his troops.

7 See Chapter 1 and the concluding prayer to Christ.

8 Cf. 2 Cor. 2.1 for another disclaimer of eloquence, with my note on Chapter 2.

know that people of intelligence abhor the abandoned ranting that aims only at pleasure, when the speakers are more concerned with applause than with discretion in speech.

Now there are some thoughtless and impious people who say that our Christ[1] was punished by justice and that the cause of life to those who live was himself deprived of life.[2] It is no marvel that people who have once dared to act impiously should not be afraid to hide their wickedness, but it passes all foolishness that they seem to have persuaded themselves that the indestructible God has been vanquished by human beings, or that savagery could have prevailed over love of humankind.[3] Instead they should reflect that that which is magnanimous[4] and long-suffering cannot be turned aside by insult or robbed of its natural rigour by abuse; rather that nature always <prevails>,[5] breaking the savagery of its attackers through the counsel of its reason and magnanimity.

For God, in his love of humankind, elected to wipe out unrighteousness and to exalt propriety and righteousness. For this reason, having gathered together the wisest of men,[6] he set out the supremely fine and profitable doctrine that the good and happy should emulate his own providential care for the world. What greater good could anyone name than this, that God should give a crown to righteousness and make those worthy of his education resemble himself, so that as goodness was distributed to all people, well-

1 'Our' may imply that the veneration of Christ is the distinguishing mark of Christians (cf. Aristides, *Apology* 15.1), or stress that (in contrast with pagan deities and the Jahweh of the Jews) he is not only the Lord but the Saviour of his people (cf. Titus 2.13, Ignatius, *Ephesians* proem etc.).

2 Justin, *1Apology* 30 and Arnobius, *Against the Nations* 1.51 record that Christ was charged by some with sorcery, a capital offence.

3 Rendering *philanthrôpia*, an ideal of Stoic philosophers and Hellenistic monarchs, which was transferred to God by Justin, *1Apology* 10 and Origen, *Homilies on Ezekiel* 1.1 and 6.10. See Osborne (1994), 164–84 on philanthropy as an attribute of God; Eusebius, *Constantine* 2.53 on Constantine's profession of the same virtue. Drake (2000), 384–92 shows that the vocabulary of Hellenistic literature on the good king is pervasive in Eusebius' panegyric on Constantine.

4 The Greek word *megalopsukhia* implies at Aristotle, *Ethics* 1123b a proper estimate of one's merits, but is used in Christian literature to signify generosity (Chrysostom, Homily 19.4 on 2 Corinthians) and is attributed in this sense to Constantine himself by Eusebius, *Constantine* 2.2. God the Father is credited with *magnanimitas* in the Latin translation of Irenaeus, *Against Heresies* 4.39.

5 As Heikel notes, at least one word is missing.

6 Meaning the apostles, perhaps the children of wisdom at Matt. 11.19, notwithstanding their lack of education (Acts 5.13).

being should abound for humankind to all eternity? This is the solemn victory, this the greatest work and the rule of discretion that brings harmony to all peoples. And the victory-tokens of all these we give to you with blessings, O Saviour of all.[1] But as for you, wicked and abominable blasphemy, puffed up with lying statements and declarations, you deceive infants, persuade boys and such men as follow boyish habits,[2] leading them away from the worship of the true God[3] and setting up factitious statues for their prayers and homage, so that having been deceived they await the wages[4] of their own insensibility.[5] For they blame the author of all goods,[6] Christ, God and child of God.

Is not then this the God who is duly revered by the most percipient and intelligent nations and peoples,[7] exalted above all power and rising above all goodness?[8] It is a cause of greater praise, an outstanding marvel, that he has not availed himself of his great power to requite the insult, but has forgiven humans for their foolish thoughts, reckoning folly and error intrinsic to humanity, while himself abiding by his own decision[9] and abating not a jot of his natural love for humankind. Away with you, impious ones (for this command is laid on you on account of your incorrigible sin[10]) to the

1 Cf. 1 Tim. 2.3–5; the dedication of spoils to Christ resembles the Roman practice of consecrating the *spolia opima* to Jupiter. Elsner (1998), 187–88 contends that Constantine carried this practice further by spoiling the monuments of his pagan countrymen to adorn his arch.

2 Cf. Plato, *Republic* 466b, but Constantine is probably alluding to the notorious pederasty of Socrates.

3 The title used of the Father at John 17.3 and of the Son at 1 John 5.20.

4 Death, as at Rom. 6.23.

5 The idolater shares the properties of his idol, as at Isa. 44.18.

6 Cf. 1 Chron. 29.14, John 1.3, Col. 1.16. The accolade can be transferred to Christ because he is the one through whom all things were created.

7 Meaning above all the Jews, whose elevated monotheism was praised, e.g. by Lucan, *Civil Wars* 2.592–93 and Numenius, Fr. 57 Des Places. Cf. Justin Martyr, *1Apology* 5 for the contention that among the barbarians those who lived by reason were Christians.

8 In common with other Christians (e.g. Origen, *Against Celsus* 7.42), Constantine affirms that God's sublimity cannot be measured even by the loftiest terms in Plato; here he alludes to *Republic* 509b, where the Good is said to transcend even being in its dignity.

9 Perhaps the promise to Noah at Gen. 9.15–17, cited at Isa. 55.9; cf. Rom. 3.24–25 on God's forbearance in the days of sin.

10 Cf. Rom. 1.24, where the punishment of sinners is to be given up to sin. Drake (2000), 303 proposes that 'a secondary purpose of the *Oration to the Saints* was to argue in favour of a diversity of belief'. Surely it is evident that Constantine was a rigid partisan in the advocacy of his own religion, even if he did not believe that he had to be a persecutor to be an honest Christian.

slaughter of nations[1] and sacrifices, your revelry and feasting and carous-
ing,[2] as you profess to offer worship while you devise unbridled pleasures
and debaucheries, and pretend to make sacrifice while you are in thrall to your
own pleasures.[3] For you do not know any good, nor the first commandment
of the great God, who gave laws to the human race and committed the
government of their lives to his child so that those who lived rightly and with
discretion should, according to his child's judgment,[4] obtain a second life
that was good and happy.

I have rehearsed therefore the doctrine of God about the way of life for
humankind, not indeed ignorantly, like the many, nor from conjecture or
guessing. But perhaps someone might say, whence comes the appellation
'child', what sort of birth [was it], if there is only one God and this one is a
stranger to all intercourse?[5] In fact one ought to conceive the birth as
double,[6] first the familiar one by parturition, then the other from an eternal
cause, the rationale[7] of which was furnished by the prescience of God and is
also clear to any person who is dear to him. For anyone who is wise will
know the cause of the ordering of the whole. Since now nothing is without
cause, the cause of existent things will necessarily exist before them. Since
then there is a world and things within it, and a power that keeps them safe,
the Saviour will necessarily exist before them all. Hence Christ is the cause
of salvation, but the saving of existent things is what is caused, just as the
Father is the cause of the Son, but the Son is the one caused.[8]

1 This taunt is directed either to barbarians, or (if Constantine is not yet the sole ruler of the
Empire) to pagans who are still capable of waging war in the east.

2 On the immorality of pagan festivals cf. Tertullian, *Apology* 15.7, 17.5, 35.2.

3 A hopeless attempt at the grand style, which Eusebius, had he forged this speech, would
have bettered at least by hinting at a law against sacrifices, as at *Constantine* 2.45. The earliest
law to proscribe all sacrifices in the Theodosian Code was introduced by the son of Constantine,
Constantius (*Code* 16.10.2). Salzman (1993) is one of many who doubt that Constantine passed
such a law, which would surely have precluded the toleration implied at *Constantine* 2.56, as
well as the special measures described at *Constantine* 3.54–55 and *Tricennial* 8. Supporters of
Eusebius' testimony include Optatus, *Against the Donatists* 2.15; *Origin of Constantine* 34 in
Lieu and Montserrat (1996), 38; Barnes (1981), 220–21. If this speech is as early as I suggest,
this passage merely shows that Constantine had no choice but to tolerate pagan rituals in the
first years of his reign.

4 On Christ as Judge see John 5.21–27, Rom. 2.16 etc.

5 In contrast to the generated gods of pagan myth in Chapter 4.

6 A thoroughly orthodox position, anticipated by Ignatius, *Trallians* 7.2, Lactantius, *DI*
4.12–13 and the so-called 'Roman Creed' reconstructed by Kelly (1972), 102–03.

7 Playing on the term *logos*, which is sometimes the title 'Word'.

8 Again very far from heresy; cf. Basil, *Against Eunomius* 1.25.

His pre-existence has now, I think, been sufficiently established.[1] But how did he come down to humankind and the earth?[2] The motive for descent, as the prophets foretold, is care for the whole, for the maker will necessarily care for his works.[3] But, as he was going to approach a mundane body and tarry on earth, he contrived for himself a sort of spurious birth[4] as need required, for there was conception without marriage and childbearing by pure virginity, and God's mother[5] was a maid,[6] and there was a temporal origin of an eternal nature,[7] and perception of an intellectual being and matter for an incorporeal epiphany.[8] The rest too was consonant with the appearance: a radiant dove came flying from the ark of Noah and settled in the virgin's lap.[9] Consonant too was what followed these intangible nuptials, purer than all chastity and greater than lordship itself: the Wisdom of God from the cradle,[10] and the reverent reception of him by the Jordan which was the provider of ablutions.[11] Add to this the royal

1 According to Eusebius, as quoted by Athanasius, *On the Councils* 33.16, this teaching was repeated at the Council of Nicaea, where Constantine averred that Christ had been eternally present to the Father in potential, and only subsequently brought forth in act.

2 A question put by pagan controversialists: Origen, *Against Celsus* 4.15.

3 Cf. Hos. 11.1–4, Isa. 55.4–11 etc.

4 A bold phrase, perhaps alluding to Plato's depreciation of matter at *Timaeus* 52a.

5 Heikel, following Schultze (1894), brackets this phrase, which is not attested in any Greek author of the fourth century. Wright (1991) suggests that it is a calque upon some Latin title such as *dei genetrix*, and thus a clue to the original language of the speech.

6 Cf. Matt. 1.23, interpreting Isa. 7.14. The Greek term in the present passage is *korê* rather than *parthenos*, perhaps because the translator was usurping a pagan title, which belonged not only to the Greek Persephone when she was worshipped at the Eleusinian mysteries, but also, according to Epiphanius, *Panarion* 51, to the mother of the god Aion or eternity in Alexandria.

7 Not a Eusebian phrase, but fully consonant with the Nicene declaration of 325 that Christ is from the essence of the Father.

8 For similarly picturesque variations on the virgin birth see Tertullian, *Apology* 21; he doubts whether even God can be strictly incorporeal (*On the Flesh of Christ* 11.2), but Lactantius, *DI* 1.7 accepts this as an axiom, if only because God has no need to propagate his own species. Lactantius had been anticipated by Tatian, *Oration* 25.2. A more accurate writer than Constantine would, like Justin, *1Apology* 63.16, have contrasted the incorporeal apparitions to the patriarchs with the assumption of flesh in the reign of Augustus.

9 At Luke 1.35 a visitation of the Holy Spirit is foretold; for the equation of this with the dove at Gen. 8.9–12 cf. Hilary of Poitiers, *On the Mysteries* 14.

10 In contrast to the proverb that no-one is wise from birth; cf. Athanasius, *Against the Arians* 3.51.

11 Constantine may be thinking of the deference shown to Jesus by John the Baptist at Matt. 3.11–14 and parallels. The Jordan owes its reputation to this episode and to Elisha's cleansing of Naaman in 2 Kings 5.

anointing,[1] of a piece with his knowledge of all things,[2] his manner of educating and the power which accomplished miracles and healed the unhealable,[3] the speedy and unobstructed confirmation of his human prayers,[4] and generally his entire life which passed the human measure, his teaching which imparted not cleverness but wisdom, since those who frequented him learned not the so-called political virtues,[5] but the paths which lead to the intellectual world, as they labour for the vision of that order which never changes and are trained for the comprehension of the supreme Father.[6]

Nor was there any measure in his acts of benevolence. Instead of blindness there was sight, instead of paralysis health, instead of death resurrection to life.[7] For I leave aside the unstinting provision of necessities in the wilderness, and the fact that a little field repeatedly yielded every kind of abundance to large crowds.[8] This thanks I give you according to my ability, Christ our God and Saviour,[9] the supreme providence of the great God, because you save us from evils and teach us the most blessed teaching – yes, it is not as praise but as thanks that I say these things.[10] After all, who being human could hymn you as is due? For you are said to have brought forth things that are from what was not,[11] to have kindled light for

1 Presumably the descent of the Spirit at Christ's baptism (Matt. 3.17 and parallels), where the Father echoes his words to the king at Ps. 2.7. The psalm is quoted exactly at Acts 13.3 and Heb. 1.5. The name Christ means 'the anointed one', and is applied to priests, kings and prophets in the scriptures; Constantine's own royal status may not be far from his mind.

2 See especially John 2.24 and 18.4. By contrast, Mark 13.32 implies that the earthly Christ was ignorant of some things, and this text was adduced by 'Arians' as a proof that he lacked the omniscience of the true god: Basil, *Epistle* 236 etc.

3 On the difference between Christ's miracles, effected by his sovereign word, and the machinations of pagan sorcerers, see Arnobius, *Against the Nations* 1.48.

4 See e.g. John 12.28 and Mark 7.34–35.

5 On these, the ordinary virtues, see Plato, *Republic* 427e–434d; Plotinus, *Enneads* 1.2.1.16; Porphyry, *Sententiae* 32. Porphyry lists four categories: political, purificatory, intellectual, paradigmatic.

6 For contemplation as the end of the Christian life cf. 1 Cor. 13.12; 1 John 3.2; Origen, *First Principles* 1.4.1.

7 See e.g. John 9.1–7; Mark 2.1–10; John 11.1–46 etc.

8 See e.g. Matt. 14.14–21; Mark 8.19–20; John 6.1–14.

9 Cf. Titus 2.13 for the formula.

10 Cf. again Origen, *On Prayer* 15, rejecting prayers of adoration, but not prayers of thanksgiving, addressed to Christ. The reason offered by Origen, however, is the inferiority of the Son to the Father, not the inadequacy of human speech.

11 See Heb. 11.3, where faith informs us that God created the world. The Greek phrase *ex ouk ontôn* may mean either out of nothing or out of formless matter; in Latin *ex nihilo* can mean

them[1] and to have given order by regulation and measure to the irregular confusion of the elements. But the outstanding mark of your love for humankind is that you made those of good nature emulous of the divine and blessed life, and took thought that, becoming merchants of true goods,[2] they should give to more people a share of your wisdom and good fortune, procuring for themselves the eternal fruit of virtue;[3] that, freed from incontinence and partaking of love for humankind, with miseries before their eyes but the shield of faith before them,[4] they should embrace faith and every kind of virtue, which the former way of life had cast out of the human character. This life had been the cause, or rather necessity, for the descent of the Saviour who exercises providence over all. For there had been found no doctor[5] of the requisite skill for such great evils and the unrighteousness which prevailed over that life.

Now when that providence reached things here, it easily put in order whatever had been disordered by overweening and incontinence. And it did not do even this secretly, for it knew that, while some people were contemplating its power with intelligence and reason, others, as if resembling irrational creatures, were estimating nature rather by their senses. For this reason, so that no-one, whether virtuous or weak, should be in doubt, he brought his bountiful and marvellous healing into the open before their eyes, restoring life for a second time to those whose lives had ceased, and bidding those deprived of their senses to have them restored to health. And when he stilled the sea, ordained calm after storm,[6] then, after having completed his marvellous works and summoned human beings from faithlessness to sturdy faith, flew back up to heaven[7] – whose work was this but that of God and his pre-eminent power?[8]

---

only 'from absolutely nothing'. Cf. Tertullian, *Hermogenes* 18–20, where Christ rather than matter is said to be the origin of creation at Gen. 1.1; on the triumph of this doctrine in the Church of the late second century see May (1994), 148–78.

1 Cf. Matt. 4.16, John 9.5 etc.

2 Cf. Matt. 13.45–46, the parable of the merchant and the pearl.

3 Cf. Heb. 12.11 on the 'peaceable fruit of righteousness'.

4 Eph. 6.16 again.

5 See Matt. 9.12 etc.

6 See Matt. 8.26 and parallels.

7 On the ascension see Acts 1.9, John 20.17, Eph. 4.10. Here it is combined with the soul's recovery of its wings in Plato's *Phaedrus* 256b–d, to which Justin alludes at *Trypho* 2.5.

8 Christ himself is the power of God at 1 Cor. 1.24, but Constantine appears to make the distinction adumbrated in Origen's *Commentary on John* 14.28.

Not even was the time close to his suffering a stranger to these marvellous sights, when night, veiling the light of day, made the sun disappear.[1] For dread fell upon the peoples everywhere, that the consummation of all things had come, and that chaos was about to prevail like that before the regulation of the world.[2] And the cause of such a great evil was sought for, and whether human beings had committed some licentious act towards the divine until, in his gentle magnanimity, disdaining the insults of the impious, he restored[3] the heaven, adorning the whole of it with the ballet of the stars.[4] And no less indeed did the blear-eyed[5] aspect of the world return to its proper brilliance.

12. But one who is prone to blasphemy[6] will say that being God he was able to improve and mollify the natural impulses of humanity. What method then could be more effective, what attempt more likely to succeed in making the evil ones see wisdom, than his own appeal. Was not he himself present and visible to teach the well-ordered way of life? If then the proclamation of God when present had no success, what good could he have done when absent

---

1 Matt. 27.45 and parallels. The next sentence implies that the darkness covered the world, not merely 'the land', as most translators of the biblical text maintain. If Origen, *Against Celsus* 2.33 can be trusted, the Greek historian Phlegon described convulsions at this time exceeding those reported in any of the gospels.

2 As Mark 13.25 etc. would suggest. 'Chaos' is here borrowed from the poets (e.g. Ovid, *Metamorphoses* 1.7 after Hesiod, *Theogony* 116) a name for the state of formlessness (*tohu bohu*) described in Gen. 1.2 ; for *tohu bohu* come again cf. Jer. 4.23. Mic. 1.6 and Zech. 14.4 in the Septuagint use the term *chaos* of the state to which God threatens to reduce Israel after repeated disobedience, and the Roman (though Greek-speaking) author Hippolytus, *On the World* locates chaos in the underworld. Lactantius, *DI* 2.9 alludes to the Hesiodic usage, but insists that even chaos cannot antedate the beginning of creation; Chalcidius, *On the Timaeus* 122 identifies chaos with matter, which he believes to be a creation of God.

3 The restoration (*apokatastasis*) of all things, promised in Acts 3.21, is a frequent theme of Christian literature, e.g. Justin, *Trypho* 134.4; Origen, *Against Celsus* 3.1.15. But some (e.g. Nemesius, *On the Nature of Man* 35) were also familiar with the Stoic doctrine that successive worlds were engendered by a constant alternation of destruction and *apokatastasis*. Plato held (*Timaeus* 39d) that all the stars and planets return periodically to the same alignments; Chalcidius in his paraphrase of this theory seems to echo the diction of Virgil, *Eclogue* 4.5, cited below at Chapter 19.

4 At Job 38.7 the stars sing; at Plato, *Timaeus* 40c they dance – or rather both are implied by the Greek word *choros*, but only the motion is perceptible to mortals. See further p. 11 n. 1 above.

5 Possibly an allusion to Gen. 40.7, where Joseph (an acknowledged type of Christ) is restored to the brothers who thought that he was dead.

6 Perhaps thinking of the second-century heretic Marcion, who imputed the creation to a deity who was just but not good, inferior to the Father of Jesus Christ.

and unheard? What obstacle therefore arose against the most blessed teaching? The perversity of human beings.[1] For whenever we take offence at what is well and aptly proclaimed, then the sobriety of the intellect is debauched. What matter that they were inclined to neglect the decrees and to offer their ears reluctantly to the laws that had been laid down?[2] For if they had not ignored it, they would have had the due reward for their attention, both immediately and for the next life, which is life in the true sense. For indeed the reward of obeying God is incorruptible and eternal life,[3] which can be claimed as the due of those who know God and those who offer their own lives as an object of emulation, and as it were an eternal paradigm to those who have chosen the life of struggle.[4]

For this reason then the teaching was imparted to the wise, so that whatever these proclaim may be carefully maintained with inward purity by those who heed it, and the observance of God's command may be true and sure. For from this grows also fearlessness in the face of death through pure faith and absolute holiness with respect to God; and it withstands the tempests of the world with the irresistible <strength>[5] of divine virtue, fenced round for martyrdom.[6] And when it has overcome the greatest fears through magnanimity, it is deemed worthy of the crown[7] by the one for whom it bore an honourable martyrdom.[8] And it has no pride, for it knows

1 See e.g. Isa. 59.2, Rom. 1.18–20.

2 See e.g. Jer. 44.4; Ezek. 20.24; Rom. 3.7–20.

3 See Wis. 2.23, 1 Cor. 15.50 on incorruption; John 6.68 on eternal life.

4 Although Deut. 30.16–20 promises life to those who keep the Law, and Jesus (Matt. 5.20) makes righteousness a condition of entering heaven, eternal life is generally held by apostolic authors to be contingent on faith in Jesus (John 3.16 etc.). While the law is not abrogated (Rom. 3.31), and we are still required to imitate Christ's obedience (Phil. 2.5–9), faith makes us beneficiaries of his death, which at the same time atones for and diminishes our continuing propensity to sin (Rom. 6.1–8.4). Even the New Testament (James 2, Heb. 11) insists that faith is exhibited through works, and the apologists often represent Christianity itself as a law or *nomos* (cf. James 1.25, Rom. 8.2–4).

5 Supplementing the lacuna with Heikel.

6 Or 'for witness', as that is the original meaning of the Greek word *martus*. The two senses are conflated as early as Mark 13.9.

7 Cf. 2 Tim. 4.8, Rev. 4.4 etc.

8 Martyrs were highly regarded in the west, as is evident from the 25th and 60th canons of the council of Elvira, c. 305 AD, which restrict the application of the title and the honours which attend it. Constantine's respect for them is attested by his own words at Eusebius, *Constantine* 2.40.1, but his insistence that the martyrdom should be honourable suggests that he was already aware of the dubious claims advanced on behalf of some who had wilfully run upon their deaths or died for a sectarian form of Christianity. Opponents of the Donatists alleged that their defection had originally been prompted by the attempt of a catholic deacon, later the Bishop of

too, I think, that this too has been given by God[1] to help it stand and eagerly fulfil the divine decrees.[2] And to this way of life there succeeds enduring memory and eternal glory – and very reasonably, if indeed the life of the martyr shows discretion and mindfulness of the proclamations, and the death is found to be full of magnanimity and nobility.[3] Hymns follow this indeed, and psalms and blessings and praise to the overseer of all. And this is the sort of sacrifice of thanks that is performed by those who are pure from blood and pure from all violence; nor is the odour of incense desired nor burnt offerings,[4] but a pure light such as suffices for the illumination of those who pray,[5] and among many things the greatest discretion is shown in the feasts made for alms[6] and the recovery of the needy and the assistance of the fallen.[7] If anyone should deem these vulgar, he does not think according to the divine and blessed teaching.

Carthage, to correct the misplaced devotions of a wealthy noblewoman named Lucilla (Optatus, *Against the Donatists* 1.16).

1 Cf. Eph. 2.8.

2 These would include above all the commandment to love one another at the cost of life at John 15.12–13. As it was already the custom, at least in the eastern territories, to receive the pronouncements of emperors as 'divine scripts' (*theia grammata*), the audience at this point could be expected to draw the inference that only those who keep the laws of God have the right to administer those of men. See Edwards (1997), 171 n. 11; Mark the Deacon, *Life of Porphyry of Gaza* 50.

3 A layman's celebration of a practice which the leaders of the Church had long been striving to restrain. In the second century Montanists were accused of having propagated the worship of a false martyr; the survivors of the great massacre in Lyons in 177 found it necessary to state that they did not venerate the bodies of their brethren; eighty years later Cyprian of Carthage countermanded a widespread custom when he denied that it was possible for the dead to give absolution to the living (Letter 22). Yet Constantine was not afraid to dedicate his new capital to Lucian of Antioch even after the heretic Arius had used that martyr's name as a rallying-cry (Theodoret, *Church History* 1.5), and at *Life of Antony* 90, Athanasius reports that the shrines continued to be defiled by pagan rituals in the mid-fourth century.

4 Cf. Hos. 6.6 and Matt. 9.13.

5 Whereas pagans kindle lamps even in the daytime, according to Tertullian, *Apology* 35.4. Josephus, *Against Apion* 217–19 set the example of summoning martyrs to corroborate the truth of one's religion.

6 'Pity' (*eleos*) often means the giving of alms in Jewish and Christian literature; here there may be a reference to the 'feasts of charity' first mentioned at Jude 12. To judge by Athanasius, *Life of Antony* (cited above), these feasts were held at the martyr's tomb. In any case, these sober feasts are contrasted with the riotous celebrations of the pagans in Chapter 11.

7 The relief of the poor is enjoined throughout the New Testament, as in the Old (Rom. 15.26–27, 1 Cor. 8, Gal. 2.10). For the view that it is peculiar to Jews and Christians, see Veyne (1992), 30–33, who argues that the ostentatious benefits conferred by pagan donors were not generally extended to the neediest groups, non-citizens and slaves.

13. There are some indeed who also show their immaturity by finding fault with God.[1] 'What was his purpose in fashioning not one and the same nature for existent things, but enjoining the production of different things that are for the most part contrary to nature? This is the source of the differences in our characters and wishes. Perhaps it was better after all, for exact obedience to God's commands and for the exact apprehension of him and the confirmation of each person's faith, for everyone to be of the same habits. And of course this was possible, as it was God's affair.' Those who say this appear to find fault with the ordering of the whole, and not to expect the alternation of night, but to want the light of day to persist for ever, notwithstanding the necessity of rest; to be aggrieved by the bounds of Ocean and land, to find fault with the earth which furnishes so many things for the use of its inhabitants, and indeed to blame the sea, which provides a varied path for those who sail.[2] They demand that everything once for all should be of a single form, not thinking it right that woods and mountains should appear at all, and generally to abolish all the different products of nature along with their appellations. And are sentiments trite? Well, is it not utterly ridiculous to demand that all humans should be of the same habits, and not to reflect that the ordering of the world itself is not the same as that of the things within it, nor are physical and moral beings of the same nature, nor are the body's passions the same as those of soul? For God fashioned the whole world from different elements.[3]

For since the powers of bodies are different, there are necessarily many and different things supplied for the use of the world, seeing that the works of nature are many and innumerable, <many produced by earth>[4] and many by the sea and air. But the human he made a rational creature and endowed him with the knowledge of goods and evils,[5] so that he might flee evils and pursue goods. And having endowed him with a readiness for such wisdom, he left him with free will and permitted him to judge what character should

---

1 Possibly the Manichees, who urged that a world containing so many evils could not have been designed by an almighty and benevolent God. They were persecuted by Constantine's predecessor Diocletian: *Collation of Mosaic and Roman Statutes* 15.3.

2 This celebration of natural variety has a parallel in Constantine's tract against the persecutors at Eusebius, *Constantine* 2.58.

3 A point stressed also by Lactantius, *On the Wrath of God* 10.

4 Inserting a phrase, after Heikel.

5 Cf. Irenaeus, *Against Heresies* 4.39.1 for the argument that knowledge of good and evil (in both the moral and natural senses of those words) is intrinsic to the human, not merely the fallen condition.

be stamped on his own life, and this he did equally for all human beings.[1] Whence then comes the difference of habits? It comes, in my opinion, when we ignore the good with which providence has endowed us, and giving way to passion or appetite, we choose the worse instead of the better. For passion is highly belligerent, and appetite is violent, and they overthrow unthinking people whenever they get the better of reason. When reason prevails, however, the whole life is moderate and worthy of praise. It is applauded therefore when, like some good charioteer,[2] it pulls on the reins of its disorderly and demented team. Hence arise faith, piety toward God, righteousness, discretion and the happy enjoyment of every kind of virtue.

These and such as these are the amendments which lead souls[3] to the Holy Judge,[4] not to be condemned or incur exposure of their sins, but to receive the honours that he himself has promised to those whose lives have been the best.[5] But those who have sinned and taken their fill of bodily pleasures[6] retribution forcibly drives on, lamenting, to the appropriate punishment, in fulfilment of the righteous declaration of God. There an unquenchable and unceasing fire[7] awaits them, there awaits them too a precipitous and

---

1 Following the tradition of Irenaeus (*Against Heresies* 4.37) and Origen in assigning free will to all humans, even after Adam. In fact, only the Manichees and Gnostics were accused at the time of denying this liberty.

2 A clear allusion to Plato, *Phaedrus* 246a, where reason is the charioteer of the soul.

3 Notwithstanding the testimony of Paul (1 Cor. 15) and the admonitions of many previous writers (see for example [Athenagoras], *On the Resurrection of the Dead*), Constantine speaks as though the soul, and not the whole of the person, were the subject of reward and retribution. This Platonic doctrine had already begun to supersede the biblical one in Lactantius, *DI* 2.13, which defines death as the 'damnation of souls to eternal punishment'. At *DI* 3.12–13 Lactantius asserts the inherent immortality of the soul and seems to forget the resurrection of the body until 7.23. On the other hand, Constantine may have in mind such texts as Wis. 3.1 ('the souls of the righteous are in the hands of God'), where the word 'soul' may, as in biblical usage, denote the whole person; certainly the 'righteous souls' of Chapter 16 below are still embodied.

4 Cf. 2 Tim. 4.8.

5 Cf. 2 Tim. 4.8 on the judgment which the martyr awaits from God.

6 Early Christianity differs from Platonism, not in being less suspicious of pleasure, but in regarding vicious pleasure as a symptom of the fall that supervened upon the creation of the body. See Phil. 3.19 on those 'whose god is their belly', the precepts of sobriety in Titus 2 etc., and Rom. 7.8 on concupiscence as the origin of sin.

7 See Mark 9.43 and Justin, *Trypho* 120.5 for the unquenchable fire (*asbeston pur*). As can be seen from the first occurrence of the phrase at Homer, *Iliad* 16.123, such conflagrations sometimes run their natural course, although they cannot be curbed by any natural agency.

remote abyss.[1] Those who take offence at existent things are guilty of an impious reflection, desiring one and the same value in everything. It therefore seems unjust to the impious that the honourable should rank above the inferior, and that the immortal nature should surpass corruptible things and earthly creatures in blessedness, in the same degree as it is more solemn and divine. And the human race is not without a share in the divine goodness,[2] but this is neither simply universal nor fortuitous, but is only for those who have followed in the footsteps[3] of the divine nature and chosen the supreme pursuit of life, the knowledge of God.

14. To compare things that come to be with those that are eternal is in truth the most perfect madness. For the former have neither beginning nor end; the latter, inasmuch as they have grown and come into being and receive a temporal origin of their existence and life, are also subject to death as a necessary consequence.[4] Now how can things that come to be made equal to the one who ordered them to be given birth? For if the former are like the latter, the decree of birth could not properly be reckoned his. But even the things in heaven cannot be compared to the intellectual or images to paradigms.[5] How is this confusion of all things anything but ridiculous, when the dignity of the divine is concealed by comparison with humans and beasts? How can humans not be mad when they desire a lordship equivalent to God's, though they have rejected the life of discretion and virtue? For if we lay claim at all to the divine felicity, we ought to live our lives according to God's command. It is in this way that we shall pass our lives in immortal and unchanging abodes,[6] superior to all

1 The term abyss can be found at Deut. 32.22, cited by Justin, *1Apology* 32, and at Prov. 8.24. The precipice appears to come from Plato, *Phaedo* 112d–e, unless Constantine has in mind the deep valley of 1 Enoch 23, which finds partial confirmation in Zech. 14.4 and in Christ's sayings about Gehenna (e.g. Mark 9.47).

2 Cf. Gen. 2.7 on the gift of the Holy Spirit to Adam, and Rom. 2.14 on the conscience of the Gentiles. The doctrine that all human beings possess the image, if not the full likeness, of God was bequeathed to the Church by Irenaeus, *Against Heresies* 5.6.1, and Origen, *First Principles* 3.6.1.

3 For the image cf. Porphyry, *Sententiae* 54.17 etc. Constantine may also have in mind the myth that Justice, when departing from the world, left her footprints among the good: Virgil, *Georgics*, 2.473–74.

4 Again Plato, *Timaeus* 27d–28b overshadows 2 Cor. 4.18.

5 Cf. Exod. 25.40, where the archetype of the Temple is revealed to Moses on Sinai; 2 Cor. 4.18, where things seen are declared to be inferior to the invisible.

6 The plural is employed, no doubt, because John 14.2 avers that there are 'many mansions' in the house of God.

fate,[1] having lived according to the law ordained by God. For the only power in human beings equivalent to God's is the absolutely unfeigned veneration of God and the turning to him, the contemplation and learning of what pleases the higher power, and the fact of not having inclined towards the earth but, so far as lay in our power, of lifting our intellects toward what is upright and sublime.[2] For the victory that comes from this exercise, it is said, is superior to many goods. The difference between existent things, both in their value and in the comparison of their potencies, is explained on this principle, which those who think soundly and give condign thanks obey, while the fools who give no thanks receive the retribution that is worthy of their insolence.

15. And indeed the Son of God summons all to virtue, having made himself the expositor of his Father's decrees to people of intelligence.[3] That is indeed if we do not deceive ourselves by being culpably unaware that he went about on earth for our advantage, that is to confer beatitude on humankind, and having called to himself the best of that time, schooled them with a life-enhancing education, having taught them the remedy of a moderate life with faith and righteousness in a manner opposed to the jealousy of the contrary nature,[4] whose custom is to lure and deceive the inexpert. No indeed, he visited the sick, lightened the ills that beset the infirm,[5] comforted those who had reached extremes of poverty and distress, praised intelligent moderation that accompanies reason, bade it endure nobly and impeccably every kind of insult and every kind of disdain,[6] teaching that a thing of this kind was a sort

1 Cf. Plotinus, *Enneads* 4.40 and Zosimus, *Treatise on the Omega* 7 for the claim of the philosopher to be superior to fate. Christians such as Ignatius, *Ephesians* 19.3, asserted that Christ had broken the power of magic, which was often held to depend on cosmic sympathy (Plotinus, *Enneads* 4.40).

2 On the upright posture of human beings, which prepares for the knowledge of divine truths, cf. Lactantius, *DI* 2.1, citing Ovid, *Metamorphoses* 1.85–88.

3 This is perhaps what John intends by calling Christ the *logos* (John 10.24–26) and is certainly what Justin understands by the appellation at *Trypho* 109.2, citing Mic. 4.2 on the law and Logos coming forth from Zion. Cf. Origen, *Against Celsus* 4.15 on the continuing role of Christ as teacher.

4 On the jealousy of Satan cf. Wis. 2.28; Lactantius, *DI* 2.13; Prudentius, *Origin of Sin* 188. God is described by Plato, *Timaeus* 30e, as incapable of jealousy, though God gives a different account of himself at Exod. 20.5.

5 Cf. Matt. 8.17, applying Isa. 53.5 to the healing of the sick.

6 Constantine appears to have in mind the beatitudes (see Luke 6.20 on the blessedness of the poor; Matt. 5.5 on the meek and 5.10–12 on the persecuted). Matt. 5.44 bids the disciples pray for those who persecute them, while Matt. 10.16 enjoins a combination of dovelike meekness with serpentine intelligence.

of visitation from his Father, so that those who were magnanimous in enduring what befell them might be perpetually victorious.[1]

For as the transcendent and pre-eminent form of strength, he inculcated firmness of intellect with philosophy,[2] which is the knowledge of what is true and good, habituating those who are rich with righteousness to share what they have with poorer people by a philanthropic distribution.[3] He prevented lordship in every way,[4] showing that, just as he came to people of moderation, so in granting favour he would pass over those who neglected people of moderation, and that for humankind the prelude to life is need and nakedness, and likewise death brings an end in need and nakedness.[5] Only virtue, he said, is worthy of every care.[6] This then he proclaimed that we should honour, as the salvation of the soul which is seated in the rudder of perfect virtue,[7] and that we should practise the highest degree of piety, discretion and gentleness. For this was the method ordained against all the billows of our life.[8] And having instructed the souls of his disciples with these exhortations and many others like them, so that they might pursue the most salutary way of life not only with spoken proclamations but with their deeds, he went as their guide to lead them, as it were, through the long and uninhabited tract of a burnt and dehydrated desert.[9] He led them too through billows of a madding sea, enraged by winds, and sustained the waves as they bore like solid ground the footsteps of God and of the righteous as they

1 Cf. Rom. 5.3, James 1.3.

2 Cf. Pericles' boast that Athenians are 'lovers of wisdom without unmanliness' at Thucydides 2.40.

3 Cf. Luke 19.8–9, Acts 4.34, 2 Cor. 8.14. Clement of Alexandria, *On the Rich Man's Salvation*, explains how it is possible to retain one's wealth without incurring the condemnations pronounced at Mark 10, Luke 6.24 and James 5.1.

4 Cf. Matt. 23.8, Mark 10.42, James 4.1.

5 Cf. Job 1.21, Wis. 8.1, 1 Tim. 6.7.

6 Though the term 'virtue' is not unknown to apostolic authors (2 Pet. 1.5 etc.), the New Testament prefers to speak of righteousness in the sight of God. This formulation savours more of Plato and the Stoics.

7 For the metaphor cf. Methodius, *On Resurrection* 1.37; Numenius Fr. 18.3 Des Places.

8 As Constantine is now in parabolic mode, he may be alluding here to one of the episodes in which Jesus stills a storm, e.g. Matt. 14.24–33, Mark 4.35–41. Cf. Ps. 117.29.

9 The Stoic model would be Cato in Lucan, *Civil War* book 9. The more obvious prototype is of course the exodus from Egypt; on Christ as the leader of the Israelites in the wilderness see 1 Cor. 10.1–11. This and other features of Constantine's portrait of Christ appear to be parodied in Julian, *Oration* 7, 219c–d – perhaps an argument against Hanson (1973), who dates the *Oration* to the reign of Julian.

walked.[1] And having by such a great test proved the faith of the peoples who paid heed to him, he equipped them not only to disdain dreadful and fearful things, but also to be the most genuine disciples of the hope in him.[2] And when one of his companions was yielding too much to his passions he restrained him with words and set him right. This one was trying to ward off with a sword a swordsman who was advancing towards him, as though the Saviour's sovereign might were not present with him. Jesus bade him remain at rest and let go of the sword, reproaching him as one who had despaired of taking refuge in him, and openly laying down the rule that everyone who initiates unjust acts or undertakes to use the sword against the instigator of unrighteousness will perish by violence.[3]

This indeed is heavenly wisdom, to choose to be injured rather than to injure, and when it is necessary, to suffer evil rather than to do it. For since being unrighteous is the greatest evil, it is not the injured but the one who injures who is overtaken by the greatest retribution.[4] But it was open to one who pays heed to God neither to injure nor to be injured, taking courage in the protection of God, who is ever at hand and assisting, that none of those who pay heed to him will be harmed. How could he [otherwise] have given himself the best advice? Or could he have imagined, as it were declining the help of God, that he had to help himself? That would be a battle between two parties, and the victory would be dubious; but no-one of intelligence prefers what is dubious to what is fixed. And how could one who has been tried by such dangers, and has always been easily rescued from the terrors by God's mere nod,[5] be likely to doubt the presence and help of God, seeing that he has travelled through the sea which has been flattened by the Saviour's proclamation, and was furnishing a solid road for the peoples who traversed it?[6]

1 Cf. Ps. 116.9 on the crossing of the Red Sea. For walking on waves see Matt. 14.25–29, though here it is Christ who walks while Peter sinks.

2 The source of hope is the work of Christ, its destination glory: see Rom. 8.24, 1 Cor. 13.13, Eph. 1.18 etc.

3 See Matt. 26.51–52. The passage could be understood by the audience as a warning against insurrection or as a commendation of Christian forbearance under the recent persecutions.

4 A Platonic gloss on a biblical sentiment: see Plato, *Gorgias* 469b; Matt. 5.44; Rom. 12.21.

5 For this metaphor cf. *Iliad* 1.528, Constantine's letter to Aelafius at Optatus, *Against the Donatists*, Appendix 3, and Edwards (1997), 184n.

6 Cf. Exod. 15.19, Ps. 136.14. The allegory is transferred to Constantine by Eusebius, *Tricennial* 9. The exodus from Egypt was of cardinal significance in Christian typology, as the victory by which God proved himself the God of his people (Exod. 20.1) and the supreme act of

For this in my opinion is the evident support of faith and foundation of obedience, when we examine those marvellous and incredible things that have happened and been accomplished at the bidding of his providence.[1] Hence it comes about that we do not repent of faith even when one falls into the trial of evils, and keep undisturbed our hope in God.[2] For when this state comes about in the soul, God takes his seat in the intellect.[3] This person is invincible, and thus the soul that possesses this invincibility in its own intellect will not be overcome by the evils that surround it. And this we have learned by experience from the victory of God, who, exercising his providence over all things, suffered the besotted iniquity of the impious, yet reaped no harm from his affliction, but donned the greatest victory tokens and an eternal crown in defiance of wickedness,[4] bringing to fulfilment the choice made by his providence and affection for the righteous,[5] while he subdued the ferocity of the unjust and impious.

16. But his affliction was announced beforehand by the prophets; and announced beforehand also was his birth in a body.[6] Told beforehand too was the occasion of his embodiment, and the cause of his taking flesh was evident also, viz. that the brood which sprang from unrighteousness and incontinence, raging against righteous works and ways,[7] might be extirpated, and that the whole inhabited world might partake of intelligence and

---

deliverance commemorated in the Jewish Passover (Exod. 12), which was the forerunner of Easter (1 Cor. 5.7 etc). Yet most patristic commentary on the miracle at the Red Sea dwells on the typological meaning of the waters and neglects the pedestrian crossing. Exceptions are Arator, a Latin poet of the sixth century (*Apostolic History* 2.49–52) and Gelasius, the fifth-century compiler, whose *Church History* 1.5.4 contains the argument that Jews who believe in such events have no right to doubt the vision of Constantine. If (as is almost always the case) Gelasius had a source, it is therefore likely to have been Constantine himself, or one of the eulogists who were in the habit of likening him to Moses: Rapp (1998).

1 Cf. John 20.30–31, Acts 2.22 and Arnobius, *Nations* 1.48 for the argument from miracles, though Constantine, like most of the apologists, prefers to elaborate the proof from prophecy.

2 Cf. Rom. 5.3–5; James 1.2–4.

3 Rom. 7.23–8.5 has been conflated here with a pagan image, used e.g. by a previous emperor, Marcus Aurelius at *Meditations* 3.16.

4 Cf. Col. 2.15 and Heb. 2.9.

5 Cf. Rom. 8.28–31 and Eph. 1.5, though Constantine does not hint that the righteous were predestined, except in so far as God was sure to reward their works.

6 Cf. Matt. 1.23, citing Isa. 7.14, which in the Septuagint clearly prophesies birth from a virgin. Kamesar (1990) shows that the application of this text to the virgin birth was supported in antiquity by strong philological arguments, even by such proponents of the Hebrew text as Jerome.

7 Cf. Matt. 3.7, where the teachers of the Jews are called a 'generation of vipers'.

discretion, as the law dispensed by the Saviour prevailed in the souls of almost everyone,[1] reverence for God grew strong and superstition[2] was wiped out. This had given rise to the notion, not only of sacrificing irrational creatures,[3] but also of devoting human victims[4] and the unholy pollution of altars.[5] According to Egyptian[6] and Assyrian laws, people sacrificed righteous souls to idols of bronze and clay.[7] However, Memphis and Babylon[8] have received the fruit that was proper to such worship, having been laid waste and left uninhabited along with their ancestral gods. And this I say not from report, but I myself have been present to behold it, and have been an eye-witness of the miserable fortune of the cities.[9] Memphis is waste,[10] where Moses in accordance with the decree of God shattered the arrogance of

1 Whatever we believe about the spread of Christianity before Constantine, this is clearly an instance of the hyperbole which Lane Fox (1986), 269 discovers in many Christian apologists.

2 For this term see Chapter 1.

3 For the claim that sacrifice is a consequence of the fall, see Tertullian, *On Fasting* 4, where Noah's offering at Gen. 8.20 supplies the prototype. Eusebius, *Tricennial* 253.6 Heikel boasts of the bloodless sacrifices of Christians, alluding to Rom. 12.2. Pagan admirers of Porphyry's *On Abstinence* might be expected to look on such a cult with interest and goodwill.

4 The testimony of Eusebius, *Gospel Preparation* 4.15.6 and 4.17.4 that human sacrifices were offered in Africa up to the time of Hadrian, appears to be borne out by Tertullian, *Apology* 9.2, if this indeed states that the atrocities persisted up to the time of his father's military service. Plutarch, *On Superstition*, considers human sacrifice to be the most heinous case of false religion; he like other Greeks, imputes it only to barbarians. For this reason it was also a widespread calumny against Christians; Rives (1995) observes that, by throwing the obloquy back on the persecutors, Christians proved themselves the true custodians of an endangered humanism.

5 Cf. Dan. 8.13, Matt. 24.15 and parallels on the 'abomination of desolation'.

6 Herodotus, *Histories* 2.45 denied that the Egyptians ever practised human sacrifice, but Plutarch, *Isis and Osiris* 73 cites Manetho, a native priest, to the contrary. As Rives (1995), 68 observes, it was generally Busiris, a mythical tyrant slain by Heracles, who was accused of this atrocity. Constantine, however, is retorting upon the whole people the charges that Egyptians such as Apion had levelled against the Jews: see further Josephus, *Against Apion* 2.93–95 and Rives (1995), 71.

7 Eusebius, *Gospel Preparation* 4.17.3 relates that all the Syrians practised human sacrifice, and Tertullian, *Apology* 19.2 names Belus of Assyria (i.e. Baal) as the coeval of Saturn, King of the Titans, who was the most famous devourer of infants both in Greek myth and in Carthage.

8 Here apparently taken as the capital of Assyria; see below on Nebuchadnezzar.

9 Barnes (1976b), 184 cites Eusebius, *Constantine* 1.19 to show that Constantine may have accompanied Diocletian to these places in his march to Ctesiphon.

10 Strabo, *Geography* 17.32 agrees that Memphis in Egypt is largely desolate, though he attests its fame as a sanctuary of Apis; cf. Jerome, *Commentary on Ezekiel* 9.30.

Pharaoh,[1] the greatest potentate of the time, and destroyed his army, victor as it was over many of the greatest nations and fenced round with arms – not by shooting arrows or launching javelins, but just by holy prayer and meek adoration.[2]

17. And no people would ever or could ever have been more blessed than that one, had they not voluntarily cut off their souls from the Holy Spirit.[3] What could one say about Moses to match his worth? Leading a disorderly people into good order, having set their souls in order by persuasion and awe,[4] he procured freedom for them in place of captivity, and he made their faces bright instead of blear,[5] and caused their souls to advance so far that, through their excessive change to the contrary and the good fortune of their achievement, they became superhumanly boastful.[6] Moses excelled his predecessors in wisdom to such a degree that even those who were praised by the nations as wise men and philosophers came to emulate his wisdom.[7] For Pythagoras, by imitating his wisdom, obtained so great a reputation for temperance as to make his self-denial a model for the most temperate Plato.[8] And as for Daniel, who prophesied what was to come, performed the greatest works of magnanimity and excelled in the beauty of his character and his whole life, what grave and harsh offence he suffered from the then tyrant of Assyria whom he defeated![9] His name was Nebuchadnezzar, and

---

1 Though not mentioned in Exodus 14, Memphis is almost a synonym for Egypt at Hos. 9.6. It may already have been customary for Constantine's panegyrics to compare the immersion of Pharaoh in the Red Sea with the drowning of Maxentius and his army in the Tiber at the Milvian Bridge in 312: see Eusebius, *Constantine* 1.38; Rapp (1998), 686–88.

2 As in Chapter 11, an allusion to the passage of the Red Sea. Only a Christian audience would be expected to tolerate such an appeal to miracles; Josephus, *Against Apion* 2.154–63 accords an equally prominent place to Moses, but dwells on his wisdom and courage, omitting all the marvellous elements in the biblical narrative.

3 Combining Ps. 95.11 (cited at Heb. 3.18) with Ps. 51.11; the *Selections on the Psalms* ascribed to Origen assert that the latter text must have an allegorical meaning.

4 Cf. Philo, *On Virtues* 80 (Moses as lawgiver), and *The Heir of Divine Things* 81 (his disciples).

5 Cf. p. 27 and Gen. 40.7 on the restoration of Joseph to his guilty yet grieving brethren.

6 On the boastfulness of the Jews cf. Luke 18.11, Rom. 3.17, 2 Cor. 11.17 etc.

7 For Pythagoras' debt to the Jews see e.g. Porphyry, *Life of Pythagoras* 11; Iamblichus, *On the Pythagorean Life* 14.

8 Cf. Numenius, Fr. 1 Des Places on Pythagoras as the mentor of Plato.

9 Though Nebuchadnezzar was king of Babylon, he is styled king of Assyria at Jdt. 1.1. For Constantine the confusion is felicitous, as Virgil (see below) alludes to the Assyrian herb.

when his whole line was wiped out,[1] the awful and immense power of his passed to the Persians. For the wealth of the tyrant was celebrated,[2] and is so even now, as is his untimely concern for the wrong mode of worship, the abundant supply of metals for the construction of gods and ships of a heaven-scaling altitude,[3] and the terrible laws of worship that he laid down with savage intent.[4] But Daniel, spurning all these through his unsullied worship of the true God, foretold that the untimely zeal of the tyrant was going to be the cause of some great evil.[5] Yet he failed to persuade the tyrant, since unstinted riches stand in the way of sound intelligence.[6] At the end indeed the potentate revealed the wildness of his intellect when he ordered wild beasts to ravage the just one.[7]

Noble too was the unanimity of the brothers bearing witness.[8] Those who subsequently emulated them won immense glory for their faith in the Saviour. Not ravaged by fire and furnace and the terrible ones appointed to devour them, they drove back the encompassing fire in the furnace by the holy contact of their bodies. And Daniel, after the dissolution of the Assyrian state, when it was destroyed by the launching of thunderbolts,[9] went over to Cambyses, the king of the Persians,[10] by the providence of God. But there too was envy and with envy the pernicious attacks of the magi,[11] great and

1 See Daniel 31 on the fall of Nebuchadnezzar's son Belshazzar.

2 Not only in the Bible: see Lucretius, *On the Nature of Things* 4.

3 Cf. Ezek. 27.3–9. The conflation of scriptural prophecies is justified insofar as the prophets themselves often make use of generic images, rather than describing concrete phenomena.

4 See the command to worship the statue at Dan. 3.4–6.

5 Daniel interprets the evil omen of Nebuchadnezzar's dream at Dan. 4.22–27.

6 As Daniel hints to Belshazzar at Dan. 5.17: 'thy gifts be to thyself, O King'.

7 See Dan. 14.32–33 on the madness of Nebuchadnezzar who began to act like a beast. In the portion of the Greek version known as Bel and the Dragon, the unnamed king of Babylon has Daniel thrown to lions.

8 Shadrach, Meshach and Abednego were cast into the fiery furnace for refusing to worship Nebuchadnezzar's idol: Dan. 3.16–20. See also the 'Song of the Three Children', which forms part of the Greek text.

9 Assimilating the overthrow of this kingdom to that of Sodom and Gomorrah at Gen. 19.25.

10 The new king was Darius the Mede, according to Dan. 5.31. Even the translators of the Septuagint, who substituted the name Artaxerxes, knew that this Darius was fictitious. The name Cambyses has crept into the narrative here, either because this was the name of the father of Cyrus of Persia, the true conqueror of Babylon, or because a second Cambyses, the heir of Cyrus, was reckoned to be 'a second Nebuchadnezzar, spoken of in the book of Judith' (see Eusebius, *Chronicle* 104).

11 The traditional name for the Zoroastrian priesthood and hence for eastern magicians and astrologers. Although they paid homage to Christ at Matt. 2.1–10, the name was applied indiscriminately to the instigators of persecution, e.g. at Eusebius, *Church History* 7.10.4.

numerous dangers in succession, from all of which he was easily saved with the help of Christ's providence,[1] and easily excelled in the trial of every kind of virtue. For when the man prayed three times a day,[2] as he practised the great and eminent virtues that gave rise to his memorable works, the magi enviously slandered the very efficacy of his prayers, and slanderously telling the potentate that his great power was very dangerous, they persuaded him to sentence Daniel to be a sacrifice to savage lions, though he had been an instrument of such great public goods to the Persians. But Daniel's sentence and imprisonment led not to his doom but to his eternal renown. And set in the midst of beasts, he found the beasts milder than his jailers. For his prayer, assisting the virtue of rectitude and discretion, rendered docile those who were mad by nature. And when this was made known to Cambyses (for the achievements of such great and divine power could not be left in darkness[3]), he himself was staggered by the marvellous nature of what was reported, and regretted the easy credence that he had given to the slanders of the magi.[4] None the less, he dared to become an observer of this spectacle, and to see the man who was hymning Christ by the raising of both hands, the lions meanwhile submissive and as it were adoring the footprints of the man.[5] And forthwith he sentenced the magi who had persuaded him to the same penalty, and imprisoned the magi in the den of the lions. The beasts who a little before had been obsequious rushed on the magi and ravaged them in accordance with their own nature.[6]

18. But it rests with me also to commemorate foreign witnesses to the divinity of Christ. For these make it obvious that even those who blasphemed him knew in their minds that he was God and the child of God,

1 An inference from Dan. 3.25, where the three children are accompanied by an angel, whom Nebuchadnezzar calls a son of god. Moreover, Hippolytus, *Commentary on Daniel* 3.29 makes the prophet a type of Christ, chiefly because at 6.17 he is confined in a pit with a stone across its mouth.

2 Dan. 6.3–9. According to Eusebius, *Constantine* 3.49, Constantine set up an image of Daniel and the lions in Constantinople. Hippolytus, *Commentary on Daniel* 3.24 compares the outstretched hands of Daniel to those of Moses during the battle with the Amalekites (Exod. 17.11); this in turn could be read as a prefiguration of the Cross (Justin, *Trypho* 49.80).

3 Cf. Matt. 5.14–16.

4 Dan. 6.19–23, expanded in the Septuagintal version.

5 For this picturesque supplement to the biblical narrative cf. Hippolytus, *Commentary on Daniel* 3.27.

6 Dan. 6.24. Constantine omits the information that the wives and children of the malefactors perished with them.

if indeed they believe their own words. Now the Erythraean Sibyl,[1] saying that she was born in the sixth generation after the flood, was a priestess of Apollo, wearing a diadem on equal terms with the god whom she worshipped, in charge of the tripod round which the snake was coiled.[2] She made predictions for those who consulted her, her parents having foolishly presented her for this kind of service, from which come indecent passions[3] and nothing worthy of reverence, just as is reported of Daphne.[4] And once, having been led into the sanctuaries of untimely superstition and become full of truly divine[5] inspiration, she foretold in words what was to happen with respect to God, plainly revealing by the prefixing of the initial letters, which is called an acrostic,[6] the history of Jesus' descent:

1 On the Erythraean Sibyl see Lactantius, *DI* 1.6.10, though *DI* 7.19.9, which quotes a portion of this acrostic, implies that it was the work of a different sibyl. Sibylline eschatology is cited most frequently by Latin authors: cf. Athenagoras, *Embassy* 30, where the Sibyl is merely an authority on the nature of God.

2 Although the Delphic Sibyl was called the Pythia, and legend traced the name to Apollo's slaying of the serpent Python, the presence of a snake at Apollo's oracles is otherwise unattested. They did, however, serve as putative instruments of prophecy elsewhere: see e.g. Lucian's *Alexander* on the oracle of Glycon.

3 Cf. Prudentius, *Against Symmachus* 2.1064–113 on the unwholesome passions of the Vestal Virgins. Both he and Constantine imply a contrast between the impurity of pagan virgins and the chastity of their Christian rivals; prophecy is once again the privilege of virgins at Acts 21.9 (and one might add in Mary's Magnificat at Luke 1.46–55).

4 Readers of Ovid's *Metamorphoses* (1.452–563) would remember Apollo's attempted rape of Daphne as the first crime of the gods against humanity. Daphne was saved by being turned into a laurel, the leaves of which were said to produce a divine intoxication when they were chewed by the Delphic Sibyl. Had the speech been delivered at Antioch, a reference might be intended to the shrine of Apollo at neighbouring Daphne. Hanson (1973), citing Ammianus Marcellinus 22.12.8 and Gregory of Nazianzus, *Oration* 5.22, claims to detect an allusion to an episode in the reign of the Emperor Julian (*Passion of Artemius*, at Lieu and Montserrat (1996), 244–47). In that case the *Oration* would be a forgery; on the other hand, Constantine, who had once regarded Apollo as his patron, seems to have entertained a peculiar hostility to him after his conversion, which would suffice to explain this jibe. See Eusebius, *Constantine* 2.50 and 3.54. Lactantius, *Pers.* 11.7 corroborates this testimony to Apollo's hatred of the Christians; cf. the jibe at *DI* 4.13. Moraux (1954), II, 271 shows that Diocletian's devotion to Apollo is confirmed by epigraphy.

5 To judge by Acts 16.16–18, where Paul expels the spirit of false prophecy from a woman whom the author calls a *python,* Christians saw mantic inspiration as a form of demonic possession.

6 The acrostic spells the words *Iêsous Christos Theou Huios Sôter Stauros* (Jesus Christ, Son of God, Saviour, Cross). The first five words are a standard formula, often represented by a drawing of a fish because their initial letters make up the Greek word *Ichthus*. The full acrostic appears as ll. 217–50 in the extant text of the eighth *Sibylline Oracle*, but in Augustine's Latin version at *City of God* 18.23 the Stauros-lines are wanting. Lactantius, *DI* 7.16 and 7.19 cites

In sign of coming judgment earth shall sweat;
Eternal monarchy[1] shall come from heaven
Straightway to judge the flesh and all the world.[2]
Outcasts and the elect shall look on God,[3]
Uplifted at time's end with all the saints,[4]
Set on his throne to judge all flesh ensouled.[5]

Chaff now and earth shall all the world become;[6]
Riches and all their idols men shall break;[7]
Earth, sky and sea shall be consumed in flames;[8]
Invading fire shall breach the gates of hell.[9]
Sinner and saint shall rise to day's free light;[10]
Their flesh the fire shall test eternally.[11]
Of secret deeds none shall remain unknown,
Since God's torch shall unlock the heart's recess.[12]

Then shall all people wail and gnash their teeth;[13]
Eclipse shall hide the sun and dancing stars,[14]

---

only fragments of the same oracle in Greek with no acknowledgement of the acrostic. Since Augustine's version fails to reproduce the acrostic perfectly, it seems unlikely that Constantine was familiar with a more successful rendering. Had he quoted the lines in Greek to a Latin audience, few would have been capable of following the acrostic; but as this would be almost equally true for an audience of Greek speakers, the most probable conjecture is that the lines were added in a written version published after the delivery of the speech.

1 Heb. 1.8 applies Ps. 45.6 ('Thy throne, O God, is for ever and ever') to Christ. Other texts (Matt. 13.43, 1 Cor. 15.28) could be taken to assert that only the kingdom of the father is eternal. That Christ's kingdom shall have no end (Luke 1.33, Rev. 11.15) was already an article of the Roman creed according to Kinzig and Vinzent (1999).

2 That Christ would return for judgment was also an article of the Roman creed. It has the support of many texts, e.g. Matt. 16.27, John 5.22, Rom. 14.10

3 Cf. Isa. 40.5, Zech. 12.10, Mark 14.62, 1 John 3.2, Rev. 1.9.

4 See Dan. 7.27 on the everlasting kingdom of the saints; 1 Thess. 3.13 on the saints in the train of Christ.

5 Thus the poem insists on a corporeal resurrection, as 2 Cor. 5.10 insists that 'everyone shall receive for things done in his body'. For the throne see Matt. 25.41, Rev. 4.2 etc.

6 Cf. Matt. 3.12, Luke 3.17 on the winnowing-fan of Christ.

7 Cf. Mic. 1.7.

8 Cf. 2 Pet. 3.10–12

9 On the gates of hell cf. Matt. 16.18.

10 Cf. Dan. 12.2.

11 Cf. 1 Cor. 3.15, 1 Pet. 4.12

12 Cf. Matt. 10.26, Luke 12.2, 1 Cor. 4.5.

13 On the remorse of the damned cf. Matt. 14.42, 14.50.

14 Cf. Joel 2.10, Luke 23.44–45, Acts 2.20 etc.

Oblivion wrap the heavens and the moon's light,[1]
Uplifting hollows, casting down high peaks.[2]

Huge sorrow then shall fall on humankind.[3]
In peak and plain there shall be no distinction;
Ocean shall bear no ships, as thunderbolts
Strip the burnt land of springs and sounding rivers.[4]

Sounds of lament shall trumpet[5] forth from heaven,
Omen of squalor, grief and cosmic pain.
Then yawning earth shall open Tartarus;[6]
Emperors all shall come before God's throne;[7]
Rivers of holy flame shall pour from heaven.[8]

Signs manifest to all men there shall be:[9]
True men shall crave the branches of the Cross.[10]
As men grow pious Christ will shock the world,[11]
Unveiling the elect with his twelve springs.[12]
Rod shall be shepherd, ruling as with iron.[13]
Our God is this, set forth now in acrostics,
Saviour immortal, king who died for us.[14]

And by divine power these things were plainly appointed for the virgin to prophesy. And for my part I think her blessed, since the Saviour chose her as prophetess of his own forethought for us.

1 Cf. Isa. 34.4 and 51.6, Ezek. 32.7, Matt. 24.35, Mark 13.24–25 etc.
2 Cf. Isa. 40.4, Mic. 1.4.
3 As prophesied at Matt. 24.21 and parallels.
4 Cf. Rev. 21.2 on the disappearance of the sea.
5 Cf. Matt. 24.31, 1 Cor. 15.52, 1 Thess. 4.16, Rev. 8.16.
6 Cf. Rev. 20.13. For the name Tartarus see the Greek and Latin versions of the *Inventio* in this volume, and compare the use of Acheron, another mythological appellation for the underworld, by Constantine himself at Eusebius, *Constantine* 2.54.
7 Cf. Ps. 72.10–11.
8 Cf. Gen. 19.24 on the incineration of Sodom and Gomorrah. There may also be an allusion to the waters of the underworld in pagan myth, though Constantine slights these in Chapter 9.
9 Cf. Matt. 24.30–33 and parallels.
10 Literally 'horns of the Cross'; cf. Eusebius, *Constantine* 1.31. On the display of the cross in Rome see Eusebius, *Constantine* 1.40.
11 On Christ and his cross as a *skandalon* or 'stumbling-block' cf. Matt. 13.21, 1 Cor. 1.23.
12 Meaning the twelve apostles, as at Matt. 19.28.
13 Cf. Rev. 12.5, 19.15.
14 The Oracle, like Constantine and unlike Arius, does not hesitate to call Christ God. His cross bore an ironic proclamation of his kingship, as Matt. 27.37 and parallels attest.

19. The majority, however, do not believe, even though they agree that there was an Erythraean Sibyl who was a seer. Instead they suspect that someone of our own religion, not devoid of the poetic muse, composed these verses, and that they were spuriously called verses of the Sibyl, containing as they do life-enhancing maxims which curtail the strong authority of pleasures and conduce to discretion and well-ordered life.[1] But the truth is manifest, since the studies of our own men have calculated the times more accurately, so that no-one can hold the wild theory that the poem came into being after the descent and judgment of Christ and that a lie was put about that the words had been spoken long before by the Sibyl.[2] For it is agreed that Cicero, having encountered the poem, translated it into the Roman tongue and included it among his own compositions,[3] and that this man was destroyed during the ascendancy of Antony.[4] And then Augustus got the better of Antony and reigned for fifty-six years.[5] Tiberius succeeded him, and it was in his time that the presence of the Saviour shone forth,[6] and the mystery of the most holy religion prevailed.[7] Then a new race of people

---

1 Cf. Lactantius, *DI* 7.15.26.

2 See e.g. Lactantius, *DI* 1.6.7-15 on Varro.

3 That is, he cited it at *On Divination* 2.56, but arguing the contrary, viz. that lines penned with such labour cannot be divinely inspired. Hall (1998), 666–67 suggests that Constantine's claim to have conquered *instinctu divinitatis* ('by divine impulse') is based on knowledge of *On Divination,* but in my view the case for dependence ought to be qualified by an acknowledgement of the freedom with which Constantine used this and the other fruits of his education.

4 After the assassination of Julius Caesar in 44 BC Rome was briefly ruled by the triumvirate of Lepidus, Mark Antony and Octavian. Antony was Caesar's friend, Octavian his adopted son. Though Cicero attempted to make a protégé of Octavian, and reserved his most scurrilous rhetoric for Antony, the proscription which resulted in his death was the work of all three triumvirs. Edwards (1999a), 214 points out that Cicero receives honourable though not uncritical mention in Lactantius, who, like the Augustus of 27 BC, professed to think everything after the Republic decadent. Thus Constantine would naturally wish to remove the stigma of this crime from his predecessor, even before his panegyrists began to draw comparisons: see *Latin Panegyrics* 4(10).31, echoing famous lines from the *Aeneid.*

5 It was only in 31 BC that Octavian finally vanquished Antony, and only in 27 BC when proclaiming a disingenuous 'restoration of the republic' that he assumed the title Augustus and initiated that epoch of Roman history which we call the Principate or the early Empire. As Augustus died in 14 AD, Constantine is dating his reign from 41 BC, when victory at Perusia put his hegemony in Rome beyond dispute. The *Chronicle* of Eusebius takes the same view.

6 For the metaphor cf. 1 Tim. 3.16.

7 Luke 3.1 dates the inception of Jesus' ministry to the fifteenth year of Tiberius, i.e. 29/30 AD.

was established, of which I think the most eminent of the Italian poets[1] spoke:

> Whence then appeared a novel race of men[2]

And again, in another passage of the *Bucolics*:

> Sicilian Muses, let our theme be great[3]

What could be plainer than this? For he adds:

> The oracle of Cumae is fulfilled[4]

Obviously the expression 'of Cumae' refers enigmatically to the Sibyl. And he was not content with this but advanced further, as though the matter required his own testimony. What did he say?

> For us[5] the roll of ages starts anew.[6]
> The Maid returns with our beloved King.

---

1 To a Greek assembly, this circumlocutory reference to Virgil would be a cryptogram; to a Roman one it would be both perspicuous and endearing. The Fourth Eclogue, the most majestic of Virgil's early poems, purports to have been composed in 40 BC. It prophesies the birth of a marvellous infant, who has been identified as: (a) the child of Asinius Pollio, addressed as consul in the poem; (b) the child of Antony and Queen Cleopatra of Egypt; (c) the child of Antony and his bride Octavia, sister of Octavian; (d) the child of Octavian and his bride Scribonia; (e) the prophesied Messiah of Jewish scripture; (f) the child of the east whose reign is foretold in the *Third Sibylline Oracle*; (g) a purely symbolic figure, for whom the poet himself may not have had a name. The classic study of parallels between the Eclogue and messianic literature, including the Sibylline Oracles, is Norden (1924). Nisbet (1978) remains a useful survey and appraisal of rival critical approaches. The edition consulted in my annotations is that of Coleman (1977).

2 Virgil spoke of a 'new scion' (*nova progenies*); the plural may have been put into the mind of the translator by *Sibylline Oracles* 3.282, or by the ancestor of this at Hesiod, *Works and Days* 90–92.

3 In Virgil, 'somewhat greater'.

4 Eclogue 4.4, where the Latin speaks of a 'final age'. Constantine no doubt deleted this because the end had not yet come. Cumae in Campania was the abode of the sibyl visited by the hero in Book 6 of the *Aeneid*.

5 Edwards (1999b), 259 surmises that the speaker has confused Eclogue 4.5 (*magnus ab integro saeclorum nascitur ordo*, 'the great order of ages is born from the beginning') with *Aeneid* 7.44 (*maior rerum mihi nascitur ordo*, 'a new order of things is born for me') to precipitate a new line: *magnus ab integro rerum mihi nascitur ordo*. In Latin the confusion is facilitated by metrical and verbal similarities which are unlikely to have been preserved in Greek, even if both lines had already been translated.

6 The translator has omitted the words *Saturnia regna* ('kingdom of Saturn'), perhaps because Greek readers, who knew Saturn only as the Latin equivalent of the child-devouring

Who therefore would this returning maiden be?[1] Would it not be she who became full and pregnant by the divine Spirit? And what was to prevent the maid who was impregnated by the divine Spirit from being and always remaining[2] a virgin? And she will come a second time when God also for a second time relieves the inhabited world by his advent. And the poet adds:

> Worship the newborn child, light-bearing moon,
> Who gives the age of gold for that of iron;[3]
> For when he rules all human wounds are healed
> And all the groans of sin are put to death.[4]

Now we understand that these things have been said through allegories, at the same time manifestly and obscurely, the divinity of Christ leading to vision those who examine the force of the words more deeply.[5] In order that

---

Cronos, would not be aware that this was a Latin name for the Golden Age. His substitution of the term 'of ages' for *ab integro* 'from the beginning' is probably designed to acquit the emperor of holding a doctrine of the eternal recurrence such as Christians reprimanded in the Stoics. Cf. Justin, *2Apology* 7.3

1 Most scholars would answer, Justice, who is said to have been driven from the world by the immorality of the human race: Aratus, *Phenomena* 133; cf. Virgil, *Georgics* 2.473–74 and *Sibylline Oracles* 3.9. As she was represented by the constellation Virgo – see Nisbet (1978), 71 – the poet may be announcing the completion of some astronomical cycle.

2 Notwithstanding the references to Jesus' brothers and sisters at Mark 6.3 and parallels, the perpetual virginity of Mary was already assumed by Origen, *Homilies on Leviticus* 8.2, and by the fourth century had become a dogma for orthodox writers. This new status not only enabled Mary to displace the maiden goddesses of Greece (Athene, Hecate, Persephone and Artemis), but invested her with the typological properties of Israel, whose chastity in the Old Testament, though not inviolable, is perennially renewed.

3 *Eclogue* 4.8–10a. The Lucina of the original has been replaced by the moon in this translation – a Christianizing touch, as the moon is bidden to worship God at Ps. 148.3. The age of gold is the first state of the world in ancient theories deriving from Hesiod, *Works and Days* 111. Where other Latin apologists denounced the *Saturnia regna* as a fable of the poets (Tertullian, *Apology* 10; Lactantius, *DI* 1.11), Constantine is happy throughout this speech to equate the biblical paradise with the fanciful topographies of philosophers and poets. A political undertone may be suspected, as Virgil had attributed spontaneous fertility to the Italy of Augustus in his *Georgics*, while the satellites of Maximian and Diocletian claimed to have witnessed a doubling in the crop throughout the Empire: *Latin Panegyrics* 11(3).15.

4 *Eclogue* 4.13–14. In the original line 13, the Latin was *te duce*, 'thou as leader', alluding to the consulship of Pollio, and line 14 suggested release from fear rather than sin. The translator has been able to improve on the original; Constantine's commentary simply ignores what is alien to his purpose.

5 Cf. Origen, *Philokalia* 5.4 and *Against Celsus* 4.15 on Christ as the teacher who is concealed within the written word of scripture. Augustine later took up this theme in his treatise *On the Master*.

none of those who held power in the royal city shall have grounds to reproach the poet as one who writes in defiance of paternal laws and repudiates the customary practices of his ancestors with regard to the gods, it conceals the truth.[1] For he knew, as I believe, the blessed and laudable end of the Saviour, but in order to avert the rage of savagery, he directed the mind of his audience towards their own tradition, and says that it is necessary to establish altars, build temples and perform sacrifices to the newborn one. And for intelligent readers the rest of his composition is in keeping with this, for he says:

20.   He shall receive God's deathless life[2] and see
            Heroes his massed companions –

Obviously the righteous –

                    He himself
            To home and yearning blest ones shall appear,[3]
            Steering the world with his paternal virtues.
            For thee then, child, earth's earliest gifts do grow,
            Barley and oats, acanthus mixed with bean.[4]

A marvellous man, with all the ornaments of learning, who, accurately perceiving the savagery of the present times, says:

            For thee rich goats, their udders overflowing,
            Shall of themselves produce sweet springs of milk;
            Nor shall fierce lions terrify the herds.[5]

He speaks truly; for faith will not fear the potentates in their royal halls.

            Thy swaddling-clothes[6] shall bring forth fragrant grass;
            The venomed snake shall perish, perish too
            Plague; and in vales the Assyrian herb shall thrive.[7]

---

1 Constantine is more generous to Virgil than Lactantius (*DI* 7.22), who imputes the poet's obscurity to his ignorance of the truth.

2 The Latin of *Eclogue* 4.15 has *deum vitam*, a poetic contraction of *deorum vitam*, 'the life of the gods'. The Greek translator may have mistaken *deum* for the accusative singular.

3 *Eclogue* 4.17, though the translation is reminiscent of *Odyssey* 21.209 etc.

4 A loose rendering of *Eclogue* 4.19–20, with analogues at *Sibylline Oracles* 3.744–49.

5 *Eclogue* 4.21–22, with analogues at *Sibylline Oracles* 3.788–95.

6 The Latin is *cunabula* ('cradle'). To judge by the following commentary, Constantine seems to take this word to mean something like 'the occasion of thy birth'. See Kurfess (1936), 99.

7 *Eclogue* 4.23–25, though there is no mention of plague in the Latin.

No-one could say anything truer than this, or more germane to the virtue of the Saviour; for his very swaddling-clothes, the power of the Holy Spirit,[1] engender as it were a fragrant flower in freshness. And the snake perishes, and the venom of that snake, who deceived the first creation,[2] leading their minds away from the <discretion>[3] planted in them to the enjoyment of pleasures,[4] so that they might know the destruction appointed for them. For before the descent of the Saviour, he used to break the souls of humans, who, not knowing the immortality of the righteous,[5] were supported by no good hope. But when the Saviour suffered, and at the due time the body which enclosed him was separated[6] the possibility of the resurrection was revealed to humankind through the Holy Spirit;[7] and if some dirt of human unrighteousness was left, all of this was washed away by holy ablutions.[8] Then indeed he bids those who heed him to take courage, and from his own awesome and splendid resurrection, he bade them hope that a like fate would be theirs.[9]

Justly therefore the whole breed of venomous creatures has perished, and death too has perished[10] and the resurrection has been sealed.[11] The race of the Assyrians has perished too, which was a contributor to faith in God; but in saying that the herb grows abundantly and everywhere, he describes the multitude of those who worship. For it springs up like a multitude of

1 Cf. Luke 1.35, where the Holy Spirit overshadows Mary.

2 The subtle beast of Gen. 3.1, identified as Satan in Rev. 12.9.

3 Supplying a word with Heikel.

4 Before Augustine identified pride as the root of Adam's sin, the transgression of Adam and Eve was generally traced to carnal appetite, as by Origen, *Homily on Genesis 1*. Constantine is probably imagining an incremental history of corruption, rather than a single decisive instance, and he appears to have the Old Testament on his side.

5 Dan. 12.2 is the only passage in the Hebrew Bible which undoubtedly predicts the resurrection of the righteous. Mark 9.10 says that the disciples were still ignorant of the 'rising from the dead', though this was now a tenet of the Pharisees (Acts 23.6).

6 On the severance of body and spirit in Christ see Luke 23.46 and John 20.30. For Constantine, however, the separated element is not spirit but body, the latter being a temporary adjunct to the essential nature of Christ.

7 Cf. Rom. 1.3.

8 On baptism cf. Matt. 28.19, 1 Cor. 6.11, Tit. 3.5, Heb. 10.22. etc. If Constantine was indeed baptized on his deathbed, as a credible but not uncontested report affirms, he must none the less have regarded himself at this stage as a catechumen preparing for the rite.

9 Cf. Rom. 8.11.

10 Cf. Isa. 25.8, 1 Cor. 15.54, Rev. 20.14.

11 Cf. 2 Cor. 1.22, Eph. 1.13.

branches from a single root,[1] thriving with fragrant flowers and watered evenly by dew.[2] And learned too, O Maro[3] wisest of poets, and consistent is all that follows:

> Heroic virtues thou shalt learn, the feats
> Of thy great sire, with fortitude adorned.[4]

– signifying by heroic virtues the deeds of the righteous, and meaning by the virtues of his sire the organization of the world and the realization of eternal stability. Equally he means the laws that the devout Church observes when it practises the life of righteousness and discretion. Marvellous too is the progress toward consummation of the life between goods and evils, which declines the suddenness of an instant change:

> First came the acres of the golden flowers,[5]

(that is, the fruit[6] of the divine law came at need)

> And on red brambles sprang the clustered grape[7]

(which did not happen in the unrighteous life)

> Down the pine's hard flanks runs a stream of honey

He is sketching the stupidity of humans at that time and their hardened characters. Equally he is teaching that those who labour in God's toil will receive some sweet fruit of their own endurance:

---

1 This simile for the kingdom of Nebuchadnezzar (Dan. 4.12) is transferred to the kingdom of God at Mark 4.32.

2 Cf. Isa. 35.1, Ps. 72.6.

3 The rhetorical device of addressing an absent person is called 'apostrophe'; Virgil's full name was Publius Virgilius Maro. The *cognomen* Maro is frequently employed in Latin, especially when, as at Lactantius, *DI* 1.13.12, the author wishes to express a sense of kinship; it is unlikely that this usage would mean anything to a Greek audience at this date.

4 *Eclogue* 4.26–27.

5 *Eclogue* 4.28. The word *paulatim* ('gradually') is omitted in the translation but presupposed in the comment that introduces the verse. Thus Constantine clearly has the Latin in mind; he may be concerned to justify the slowness of his own reforms.

6 On Christ as the fruit of Mary's womb cf. Luke 1.42; on the fruits of the kingdom see e.g. Matt. 21.43.

7 *Eclogue* 4.29. The Greek has transposed the Latin words *rubeus* ('red') and *incultis* ('uncultivated').

> Yet traces of that old infatuation[1]
> Remain: the sea traversed, the cities walled,
> The ploughman's glebe churned up by dragging oxen.
> Tiphys shall come again, and, glad[2] with heroes,
> A new Thessalian Argo. Greece and Troy,
> Tried by a new Achilles, fight again.[3]

Well said, O wisest of poets![4] For you wielded the authority of poetry to its fitting limits. Of course it was not for you to give oracles, since you were not a prophet,[5] and you were prevented, I think, by a certain danger attaching to those who censure ancestral customs. But you set forth the truth in a secure and guarded manner, so far as was possible, for those with the power of understanding, making towers and wars the agents, which even now are to be found in human life. He warred indeed directly against the opposing evil power,[6] sent forth by his own providence at the bidding of his great Father.[7] What then does the poet say after this?

> But when the hour and fruit of manhood come[8]

---

1 Meaning either the murder by Romulus of his brother Remus on the day of Rome's foundation, or else the folly of the Trojan king Laomedon, whose refusal to pay the divine masons of his city led eventually to its downfall and the flight of Aeneas from Troy to Italy. Even Christians who did not believe that Adam's sin was the cause of every other were familiar with biblical phrases tracing the source of evil to the beginning (John 8.44, Rom. 5.17–18, 1 Cor. 15.22).

2 The translator has mistaken the word *delectos* ('chosen') for *dilectos* ('beloved, desired').

3 *Eclogue* 4.31–36. The Argo, built by Tiphys, was commonly reputed to have been the first ship, and was used for the capture of the Golden Fleece. The Trojan war, in which Achilles figured as the best warrior of the Greeks, marked the end of the age of heroes, and was often used as a touchstone in chronology.

4 What Greek, even if forging an oration on behalf of a Latin speaker, would have given such an accolade to Virgil?

5 Justin, *1Apology* 44–45 and Clement of Alexandria, *Stromateis* 6.42–43 both allow that certain pagan seers were directly inspired by God, but in Greek texts it would have been surprising to find Virgil numbered among them. Latin hearers of Constantine would have been aware that poets of the Augustan era often described themselves as seers or *vates*, but the claim is always more flattering to the bard himself than to the anonymous source of his inspiration.

6 Cf. Rev. 17.14. There is no evil power in the Eclogue, but Lactantius found the devil, under the guise of Jupiter, at *Georgics* 1.126 (*DI* 5.5).

7 Cf. John 10.17–18. Constantine is here close to affirming the equality of the Father and the Son.

8 *Eclogue* 4.37 in fact means 'when the strength of ages has made thee a man'.

(that is, when having come to manhood, he eradicates the troubles that beset human life and brings a peaceful order[1] to the whole world),

> No sinful crews shall then profane the sea,
> The fruitful earth shall yield abundant growth,
> Herself unsown, unploughed; nor shall the vine
> Desire the sharp edge of the pruning-knife.
> Nor shall men dye the fleece, but of itself
> The ram shall blaze with unction brought from Tyre
> And change drab wool for Sardic indigo.
> Come, take the glorious rod of kingly power
> From the right hand of thy loud-thundering Sire!
> Behold the mighty world, its strong foundations,
> The joy of earth, of heaven and of sea,
> Glee and the stout heart of unending time!
> Would that the boon of strength might give me years
> To sing thy deeds, so far as in me lay!
> The godlike bard of Thrace[2] would not affright me,
> Nor Linus, nor Arcadian Pan himself.
> No, Pan himself would not bear off the crown.[3]

Behold, he says, the joy of the mighty world and all the elements.

21. One of those who lack intelligence might think that this is said of a human generation. But when a human child is born, in what sense is the earth unsown and unploughed and the vine not desirous of the edge of the pruning-knife or any other tendance?[4] How could this conceivably have been said of a human generation? For nature is the minister of the divine

---

1 Does Constantine have in mind here the injunction to 'impose the custom of peace' (or 'impose custom on peace') that is given to Rome at *Aeneid* 6.852?

2 That is, Orpheus, putative author of many religious and mythological verses. Linus in the next line is another famous Thracian singer; Pan, a goat-legged god who appears to shepherds, is also a great singer, as in Theocritus, *Idyll* 1; Virgil, *Eclogue* 10 etc.

3 *Eclogue* 4.38–59. At 4.38 the notion of profanation has been added by the translator. At 4.39 a vague phrase has replaced the name of Jove (i.e. Jupiter). Where Virgil spoke of the *mundus* or heavens at 4.50, the translator echoes Job 38.4, Prov. 8.23 and Isa. 40.21 on the foundations of the earth. The expression 'stout heart' at 4.52 derives from Homer (*Iliad* 2.851 etc.), the application perhaps being prompted by Empedocles, Fr. 29 DK. 4.58–59 has been mistranslated, but as the divinity of the nymph Arcadia is left intact, I doubt the suggestion of Lane Fox (1986), 649 that the translator means to reduce Pan to the status of a mortal.

4 Tarn (1932) none the less contends that the poem was written in honour of the forthcoming child of Antony and Octavia; when the child proved to be a girl, Antony perhaps applied the prophecy to his illegitimate son by Cleopatra, Alexander Helios. Nisbet (1978), 69 n. 122 is

decree,[1] not the performer of a human bidding. But also the joy of the elements indicates the descent of a god,[2] not any human parturition. And the poet's prayer that his term of life might be extended is a sign that God is being invoked; for it is from God that we are accustomed to ask for life and preservation, not from a human being. Indeed the Erythraean woman says to God, 'Why, O Lord, do you impose on me the necessity of prophecy and not rather, having raised me on high from the earth, sustain me until the most blessed day of your coming?'[3] As for Maro, he appends these words also to what has been said:

> Seeing thy mother's gentle smile,[4] begin
> To know her, for she bore thee many months.
> Thy parents never smiled on thee by day,
> Nor hast thou touched the bed or nuptial feast.[5]

For how could his parents have smiled upon this one, who was their God, unqualified power without a shape,[6] circumscribing other things but not

---

able to show that similar portents attended the birth of Alexander the Great in the romantic account of his life attributed to Callisthenes.

1 Cf. Constantine on the sovereign laws of nature in his letter to the oriental provinces at Eusebius, *Constantine* 1.48.1.

2 Cf. Ps. 98.8, Isa. 55.12. From pagan sources, Nisbet (1978) can cite Nonnus, *Dionysiaca* 7.344; but the evidence of Nonnus is always suspect, both because of his fifth-century date and because of his metrical paraphrase of the Fourth Gospel.

3 On the Sibyl's reluctance to prophesy cf. Virgil, *Aeneid* 6.77–78; *Sibylline Oracles* 3.5–6. Yet Constantine was later to report (*Constantine* 2.50) that he had heard of a different reason for the silence of the oracles, namely that the 'righteous on earth' had stopped the mouth of Apollo.

4 The closing lines of *Eclogue* 4 (60–63) have been subject to emendation in both ancient and modern times. Constantine may have read 4.60 as *risentem agnoscere matrem*, 'recognise your smiling mother', where Coleman has *risu cognoscere matrem*.

5 Most editors now read: *incipe, parve puer; cui non risere parentes/ nec deus hunc mensa, nec dea dignata cubile est* ('begin, little child; the one on whom his parents have not smiled, the god does not deem him worthy of the table, nor the goddess of the bed'). Edwards (1999b), 259 suggests that Constantine read: *incipe, parve puer, cui non risere parentes, nec deus hunc mensa, nec dea dignata cubile est*. This is to assume that *hunc* ('this one') in the second line refers to the boy who is being addressed with the vocative in the previous one; but Quintilian, a better rhetorician than Constantine, was willing to tolerate something equally harsh, viz. *qui non risere parenti* ('those who have not smiled on their parent', which entails a change from plural to singular in the following line). See Coleman (1977), 149.

6 For the word *askhêmatistos* cf. Clement, *Stromateis* 5.83. The application of privative terms to God was very common, and a full bouquet of epithets can be found at Arnobius, *Against the Nations* 1.31.

THE ORATION TO THE SAINTS

possessing a human body?[1] And who is unaware that the Holy Spirit has no experience of the bed?[2] What desire or appetite could there be in the constitution of the Good to which all aspire?[3] What is there in common at all between wisdom and pleasure? But let such statements be left to those who pursue some human and vulgar education and are unschooled in the divine education.[4] For the latter parade themselves for the sake of display and glory, whereas the former prepare to purify their souls from every evil deed and word.

And you yourself I summon as an ally in what I say, O godly piety![5] – you who are a sort of holy law, the much prayed-for hope of all goods, teacher of holiness, indefeasible promise of immortality. You I beseech, piety and love of humankind, and it is to your cures that we who are healed owe eternal thanks. But the mob, which through its implanted hatred of you has no experience of your protection, rejects God as well, nor does it have any notion of the cause of life and being,[6] that what is proper to the higher power sustains it[7] and the other impious ones. For all the world is his possession and whatever is in the world.

22. For my part, I ascribe to your goodwill all my good fortune and that of those who are mine. And the evidence is that everything has turned out according to my prayers – acts of courage, victories, trophies[8] over my enemies. Even the great city is conscious of it and gives praise with reverence, while the people of the most dear city[9] approve, even if it was deceived by unsafe

1 Cf. Arnobius, *Against the Nations* 1.31; Origen, *On Prayer* 23. Constantine means, of course, that God, qua God, does not have a body; he is not denying the Incarnation, which is styled a *perigraphê* or circumscription at Clement of Alexandria, *Excerpts from Theodotus* 19.

2 Cf. e.g. Origen, *Homilies on Leviticus* 8.3 on the conception of Christ without carnal intercourse.

3 Cf. Plato, *Republic* 509b–c and the God of Aristotle, *Metaphysics* 1074b–1075a.

4 A distinction between divine and secular wisdom which originates with Philo, e.g. *On Coming Together* 74. The utility of a 'common education' (*enkuklia mathêmata*) is defended by Clement of Alexandria, *Stromateis* 1.25–30.

5 Later a title, here (as it would seem) a mere abstraction. Cf. Constantine's letter to the provincials of the east at Eusebius, *Constantine* 2.52.

6 Cf. Acts 17.28.

7 That is, the mob. For the argument that even evil is sustained by good, cf. Augustine, *On the Nature of the Good*.

8 The trappings of all panegyric, as we see from *Latin Panegyrics* 10(2).2; 11(3).19 etc.

9 See introduction for the argument that the most dear city, the venue of the *Oration*, is Rome. It is not clear whether the great city and the dear one are the same, but the syntax seems to me to imply a distinction, and I shall argue in Chapter 25 that the former is Nicomedia.

hopes into choosing a protector unworthy of it, who was suddenly overtaken in a fitting manner worthy of his atrocities,[1] one that it is not right to recall, least of all for me as I speak with you and strive with all solicitude to address you with holy and auspicious speech. And I shall perhaps say something neither unseemly nor improper. Be that as it may, there was a time when a war of surpassing madness and savagery, a war without a treaty,[2] was proclaimed against you by tyrants,[3] O godly piety, and against all your most holy churches;[4] and there were not wanting some in Rome[5] who delighted in the magnitude of these public evils, and a field was prepared for battle.[6] But you, coming forward, gave yourselves up, relying on your faith in God.[7] And the savagery of impious mortals, incessantly encroaching like fire, attached

---

Having assumed the unusual position of an encomiast, the emperor was bound to turn for precedents to his own courtiers, and Rome appears as the lodestar of his ambitions at *Latin Panegyrics* 4(10).13–14; 12(9).18–19 etc. The city had of course been accustomed to flattery at all periods, and we cannot doubt that eulogists of Maxentius will have honoured it with the same incidental tributes that survive in the panegyrics to his father: *Latin Panegyrics* 10(2).13; 11(3).12 etc.

1 Barnes (1976a), 422, proposing Serdica as the venue, surmises that the allusion is to the death of Galerius there in 311, which would still be remembered when Constantine retired to this 'second Rome' in 316. The identification is, of course, less probable if the speech was delivered as late as 321, as Barnes (1981) now holds. Even in 316 the deaths of Maximinus and Maxentius might have effaced Galerius from popular recollection.

2 Although the locution *polemos aspondos* is used by Eusebius only of the war declared against Constantine by Licinius in 321 (*Constantine* 1.50), it is conventional enough to be applied to any conflict which the speaker wishes to paint in stronger colours.

3 The word here bears its usual Greek meaning of usurper or unconstitutional ruler. It is used by Constantine of his pagan predecessors in edicts of repeal, e.g. *Theodosian Code* 15.14.4, which Corcoran (1996), 157 regards as the epitome of an oration to the Senate.

4 It is not clear whether piety is here used as a title of the Roman Church or of the whole Church catholic. In either case, we see that, just as Constantine has attributed to Christ the magnanimity and philanthropy that would grace an earthly ruler, so he credits the Church here with the virtue that would commonly be ascribed to the subject of a royal panegyric: cf. *Latin Panegyrics* 11(3).11 etc.

5 Lane Fox (1986), 778 n. 16 contends that if Rome is openly named here it cannot be the 'most dear city' of the preceding paragraph. In reply Edwards (1999b), 266 quotes *Latin Panegyrics* 10(2)1.1 and 2.1, where an honorific sobriquet for the capital is followed by the name.

6 On my reading, this is the battle of the Milvian Bridge in 312, on the eve of which Constantine beheld the Cross in a dream as a pledge of victory.

7 No popular demonstration of this kind is recorded for Serdica in 316/7 or 321 (Barnes), Antioch in 324 (De Decker, Lane Fox), Thessalonica in 324 (Piganiol) or Byzantium in 325 (Mazzarino); but on the reception of Constantine in Rome in 312 cf. Eusebius, *Constantine* 1.39 and *Latin Panegyrics* 4(10)11.2.

to you a marvellous glory,[1] worthy of everlasting song. For awe took hold of those who beheld, on the one hand the executioners and tormentors of the bodies of the pious growing faint and struggling in the face of terrors,[2] and on the other the chains loosed, the very tortures relaxed, the burnings diminishing as they were applied, the hardiness in toil of God's indomitable servants who compromised their freedom of speech[3] not even for a moment. What profit was there for you in this atrocity, O monster of impiety?[4] And what was it that made you lose your wits?[5] You will say that it was honour towards the gods.[6] What gods are these? Or what sort of conception have you that is worthy of the divine nature? If they were as you thought, you ought to have treated their rulings with amazement, rather than obeying the shameless decrees of those who unrighteously demanded the sacrifices of the righteous.[7] Or perhaps you will say, because of ancestral custom and

1 Cf. 2 Cor. 4.17, which promises a 'more exceeding and eternal weight of glory' after light and momentary affliction.

2 An earthly premonition of the divine reversal promised by Tertullian, *On the Shows* 30.

3 As Van Unnik (1962) explains, *parrhêsia* is a term of some importance in the New Testament, denoting first the outspokenness of Christ (Mark 8.32), then the dauntless proclamation of the gospel by the apostles (2 Cor. 3.12), and finally the enfranchisement of Christians in the kingdom of the next world. It retained its significance also in the instruction of catechumens, as is clear from Van Unnik (1962).

4 The chapter heading at p. 183.2 Heikel identifies this tyrant as Maximinus, who died in 313 as the opponent of both Constantine and Licinius. Barnes (1976a) emends to Maximian, another name for Galerius, but Lane Fox (1986), 633–35 argues that Eusebius (or his editor) is correct. Drake (1985) also accepts the authority of the manuscript reading, and advances the theory that Constantine, addressing a Roman audience, is alluding to the letters of Maximian to Maxentius, which were discovered after Constantine entered Rome, and exposed his rival as a supporter of persecution.

5 Assimilating the tyrant to Nebuchadnezzar (Dan. 4.30–34) and Herod Agrippa (Acts 12.21–23). Galerius appeared to have suffered the most condign affliction, dying in the manner of Herod Agrippa and Antiochus Epiphanes (Eusebius, *Church History* 8.16.2), but Maximinus, overthrown by Licinius in the name of God and dying slowly of his own poison, gave more open testimony when he implored the mercy of Christ (Eusebius, *Church History* 9.10.13 and *Constantine* 1.58–59; Lactantius, *Pers.* 49).

6 As Maximinus did in the edicts summarized by Corcoran (1996), 149–50; see Eusebius, *Church History* 9.7.3–14 and 9.9.1. Lactantius, *Pers.* 10.6 reports that Diocletian's advisers regarded Christians as enemies of the gods

7 The tyrant is assumed to be relying on the same response from Apollo which provoked persecution under Diocletian at Eusebius, *Constantine* 2.50–51. See note on Daphne at Chapter 18.

the verdict of humanity.[1] I agree. For the customs are very close to these proceedings, and come from the very same insanity. You thought perhaps that there was some eminent power in human forms carved by carpenters and craftsmen.[2] No doubt you spoke to them,[3] taking great solicitude lest they be soiled – great and eminent gods who needed human solicitude![4]

23. Examine our mode of worship against your own.[5] Is there not here true unanimity and enduring love of humankind, with reproach of lapses bringing not destruction but correction,[6] a regimen not of savagery but of salvation and strict faith first toward God, then toward the natural community of humankind, and pity for those embattled with misfortune, a simple life which does not cloak its wickedness in any variegated cunning, and knowledge of the true God and his monarchy?[7] This is true godly piety, this is strict worship, utterly unblemished, this is a prudent life, whose followers advance toward eternal life as by some sacred highway.[8] For no-one wholly dies if he keeps on with such a life and purifies his soul from his body; he does not so much die as fulfil the ministry decreed for him by God. For the one who confesses God does not become an instrument of insult or of passion, but, nobly enduring necessity,[9] has the trial of his fortitude as a passport to goodwill from God. For there is no doubt that the

---

1 A point stressed in the edict of Galerius at Lactantius, *Pers.* 34 and Eusebius, *Church History* 8.17.4. Moraux (1954), II, cites *Collation of Roman and Mosaic Laws* 6.4.1, 6.4.3 and 15.3.2 to illustrate the appeal to antiquity, together with the ironic comments of Lactantius at *DI* 5.19.3.

2 Cf. Isa. 45.6.

3 He may be thinking of Diocletian's embassy to the oracle of Apollo, which returned the answer that he was prevented from speaking the truth by 'the righteous on the earth' (Eusebius, *Constantine* 2.50). The speechlessness of idols was a biblical commonplace: 1 Kgs 18.26–27, Isa. 45.7.

4 Both Minucius Felix (*Octavius* 24) and Tertullian (*Apology* 29.1–2) had sneered at the inability of the gods to protect their images and shrines.

5 A common challenge in apologetic, beginning with Josephus, *Against Apion* 2.150.

6 Cf. Gal. 6.1 on the restoration of a brother 'taken in a fault'.

7 As we learn from Tertullian, *Against Praxeas* 3, the monarchy or sole rule of God was a premiss of all theology in the Latin west. It could also be the foundation of an analogy between the divine economy and the power of a single ruler on earth, be he spiritual or secular. See Fowden (1993) on imperial government, Brent (1995) on the papacy.

8 Perhaps a reminiscence of the old trope of the two ways, on which see now Aldridge (1999). But Constantine may also have in mind the dry-shod crossing of the Red Sea (see Chapter 16). For a parallel with Eusebius, *Tricennial* 216.3 see Edwards (1999b), 275 n. 83.

9 Meaning no doubt the will of God revealed in suffering; cf. Luke 22.22, Acts 22.23.

divine[1] welcomes human virtue. It would indeed be one of the greatest absurdities if human beings, when they happen to receive benefits either from their superiors or their inferiors in authority should be grateful for whatever relief their benefactors happen to have given them, and give benefits in return, while the one who is over all and ruler of all and the Good itself[2] should neglect the recompense. This is the one who accompanies the whole of our lives, and is present to us at whatever time we do any good, who immediately gives benefits when one receives courage and uprightness, but postpones the full measure of his recompense until the full measure of our lives. For the whole verdict on a life is determined at that time when the body is forsaken by the soul, and the soul itself, in unblemished purity, approaches the pure and unblemished divinity.[3] This then is divine righteousness, and this the test of the righteous, when the faith and continence of a whole life are brought to trial. And when it is well with these, the reward of eternal life follows, but the fitting retribution pursues the wicked.[4]

24. I put the question to you now, Decius,[5] you who trampled upon the toils of the just in hatred of the church and appointed retribution for those who lived a holy life: how do you fare now after your life? What kind of state are you in, what miseries surround you? The time between life and death showed your good fortune, when, falling with all your army on the Scythian fields,[6] you led the renowned power of Rome to contempt against the

1 Cf. Constantine's usage of the term *theion* (more usual in pagan than in Christian allusions to the Deity) at Eusebius, *Constantine* 2.28. The term is often applied to the gods as arbiters of mundane affairs: e.g. Herodotus, *Histories* 1.32, Plotinus, *Enneads* 2.3.9. The Latin equivalent is perhaps *divinitas* or *numen*: see L.J. Hall (1998) on the ambiguity of the terms in which the faith of Constantine was proclaimed to the west.

2 After a reminiscence of Eph. 4.6, the Father is once again equated with the Platonic Good of *Republic* 509 etc.

3 Again, as in Chapter 13, ignoring the resurrection of the body. The precept that we should not call anyone happy before his death was made proverbial by Herodotus, *Histories* 1.33.

4 Cf. the bombastic assertion of this unconvincing platitude in Constantine's letter to Palestine at Eusebius, *Constantine* 2.27.

5 Cf. Lactantius, *Pers.* 4. Roman emperor from 249–51 AD, Decius is generally credited with the first general persecution of the Christians. As Rives (1999) is the latest to observe, the terms of his edict or edicts remain unclear and the Church may have been a casualty, rather than the intended target, of a decree ordaining universal sacrifice.

6 In fact, as we see from Aurelius Victor, *Caesars* 29, Decius fell in battle while pursuing the Goths who had crossed the river Danube from the north. See Bird's commentary on Aurelius Victor (1994), 128–31 for the ancient authorities on this poorly documented reign.

Getae.[1] But you Valerian, who showed the same murder-lust toward those who heeded God, you made the holy judgment manifest when you were caught and led as a prisoner in bonds with your very purple and all your royal pomp, and finally, flayed and pickled at the behest of Sapor the King of the Persians, you were set up as an eternal trophy[2] of your own misfortune![3] And you too Aurelian, beacon of all injustices, how conspicuously, when you were traversing Thrace in your madness, you were cut down midway and filled the furrows of the road with impious blood![4]

25. And Diocletian after the murder-lust of his persecution, having voted himself down, unwittingly renounced himself as one unworthy of power, and confessed the harmfulness of his folly in the confines of one contemptible dwelling![5] What good did it bring to this man to have kindled

1 The Goths of northern Europe and the Getae of Thrace were frequently confused because of the likeness of names; here the Thracian seat of war facilitates the error. The Scythians of the Russian steppes are superimposed on the Getae in the lordly manner of Ovid, *From Pontus* 1.106–08. Greek authors tend to be more fastidious, since the Thracians were their neighbours and the Scythians sometimes resident in their cities.

2 To be contrasted with the trophies secured by Constantine in Chapter 22.

3 Lactantius, *Pers.* 5 describes the same episode with uncharitable relish; the *Augustan History, Valerian* 7, can only attribute the fall of so good a man to a 'certain necessity'. Although he temporarily rescinded the edict of Decius and restored the property taken from the Church, Valerian (253–60) returned to persecution in 257, allegedly at the instance of his adviser Macrianus (Eusebius, *Church History* 7.10.4). Constantine ignores the role of the satellite, just as he ignores the widespread belief that Diocletian's persecution was instigated by Galerius. This silence might appear to confirm the scepticism of Davies (1989), who argues that Galerius has been cast in the role of Macrianus by our Christian witnesses; it is possible, however, that as an emperor reciting the acts of his predecessors, Constantine thought that the dignity of his office would be best preserved by adhering to the official record rather than to a secret history.

4 Both Lactantius (*Pers.* 6) and Eusebius (*Church History* 7.30.20–21) report that Aurelian (270–275) was mediating a persecution of Christians at the time of his death. The claim is not absurd, as Aurelian might have seen the cult of Christ as a rival to that of the unconquered Sun, which he himself was promulgating. It is, however, possible that Christians, in the manner of the Old Testament Book of Chronicles, invented a reason known to God for the fall of an otherwise estimable ruler. The *Augustan History, Aurelian* 41 and 43 hesitates whether to include Aurelian among the best or merely among the mediocre emperors.

5 On 1 May 305, after a reign of twenty years, Diocletian reached the apogee of statesmanship by laying aside his power, and forcing his reluctant colleague Maximian to do likewise. He was succeeded by Galerius, his own crown prince or Caesar, in the east, while the authority of Maximian passed in the same way to Constantius, father of Constantine. Constantine exaggerates the pains of abdication, which he treats as a divine punishment rather than as an act of statesmanship. It was painful to Christian authors to observe that, while

war against our God?[1] I suppose that of passing the rest of his life in fear of the thunderbolt. Nicomedia tells it, and the witnesses are not silent, of whom I happen to be one.[2] For I saw him cry out, when he was mentally enfeebled and in fear of every sight and sound, that the cause of the evils surrounding him had been his own folly when he invoked against himself God's protection of the just.[3] Nevertheless the palace and his house were destroyed, after the dispensation of the thunderbolt and the fire from heaven.[4] The outcome of these actions had indeed been foretold by people of intelligence. And they did not keep silent or hide their misery over the undeserved events, but evidently and publicly they spoke with freedom[5] to one another:

'What great madness is this? What arrogance it was in the sovereign power that human beings should dare to make war on God, should wish to rage drunkenly against the most holy and righteous form of worship and to contrive the destruction of righteous people in such great numbers when there was no antecedent wrongdoing.[6] And this when times were

---

Diocletian suffered obloquy, he failed to die in a manner that passed judgment on his sins. On his return to humble status see Lactantius, *Pers.* 19.5; on his chagrin at being alive to witness the destruction of his statues see *Pers.* 42.

1 Cf. Constantine's denunciation of the persecutors in his letter to Palestine at Eusebius, *Constantine* 2.25.

2 Lactantius, *Pers.* 18.10 attests the presence of Constantine in Nicomedia in 305, though not in 303. Barnes (1976b) argues that if Constantine had accompanied Diocletian on his earlier campaign he would have remained in Nicomedia on his return. Be that as it may, the speech that follows would be patently fictitious, even without the biblical allusions and the implied justification of Constantine.

3 Perhaps a variant on the report of the oracle which Constantine relates at *Constantine* 2.50; Lactantius, *Pers.* 10.7 implies that it was already common knowledge. It is possible that the *Augustan History*, *Valerian* 42, is mocking such claims to private information when the putative author alleges that his father had overheard and taken note of Diocletian's political maxims even before he seized the throne (and therefore even before his name was Diocletian).

4 Lactantius, *Pers.* 14.2 holds Galerius accountable for the fire, which he blamed on the Christians. Constantine's description, recalling his account of the destruction of Assyria, is perhaps symbolic: cf. Gen. 19.24, 1 Kgs 1.10, Luke 9.54. He thus exonerates the Christians from the charge of arson by making God himself the incendiary. Cf. the comparison of Maxentius to Pharaoh in Eusebius, *Constantine* 1.38, entailing an obscurely metaphorical account of his overthrow.

5 See note at Chapter 22 on *parrhêsia*, which signifies here a defiant frankness in the neighbourhood of an evil ruler.

6 Cf. the (possibly spurious) rescript of Hadrian quoted at the end of Justin, *1Apology*, which advises that no prosecutions should be brought against the Christians unless they had committed other wrongs. On the hollow pretexts of the persecutors, cf. Constantine's letter to Palestine at Eusebius, *Constantine* 2.26.2.

prosperous,[1] both privately and publicly, when all things were proceeding well and unanimity prevailed among the sovereigns.[2] There will be a requital for this, there will be judgment for the blood unjustly poured,[3] and perhaps indeed the same misfortune will overtake both the blameworthy and the blameless. For the divine[4] is justly indignant with the wicked.'

And when they said this, their conjectures were not improbable. For they beheld a great and excessive savagery, since when everything that savagery is disposed to conceive was exhausted, impiety went after obscene punishments. For the aforesaid king[5] judged that holy virgins and respectable women should suffer the outrage of insolence, summoning the young men to pleasure with shameful ordinances.[6] In this case the self-restraint of the commoners was superior to the incontinence[7] of the tyrant. For no-one gave himself up to unholy passion, and the sentence of the king was unable to overthrow the discretion of the people. O what an excellent custodian of the law, what a teacher of discretion to all his subjects, O what concern the army showed for its own citizens! Those who had never seen the backs of their enemies in the battle-line pierced the breasts of their compatriots![8] For all that, at last the providence[9] of God came to judge the unholy deeds, not indeed without harm to the people: there was slaughter on a scale that, had it

1 For the claim that Diocletian's persecution destroyed the prosperity of his reign cf. Eusebius, *Church History* 8.13.9; Lactantius, *Pers.* 9.11–12; Constantine at Eusebius, *Constantine* 2.54.

2 Constantine wishes to intimate that the discord which arose after his usurpation in 306 could be traced to the godless policy of his predecessors rather than to his personal ambition.

3 Cf. Gen. 4.10 on the blood of Abel crying from the ground.

4 A more natural expression in the mouth of a pagan than in that of a Christian: see Chapter 23.

5 In Latin the use of *rex* ('king') was generally pejorative, as it commemorated the rule of the Etruscans which was ended in 509 by the expulsion of the last Tarquin and the establishment of republican institutions. The rape of a married woman was the fatal crime which felled the Etruscan dynasty.

6 Standard allegations, though not elsewhere brought against Diocletian. Cf. Eusebius, *Church History* 8.14.2 on Maximinus, *Constantine* 1.33–34 on Maxentius and *Constantine* 1.55.2 on Licinius; Lactantius, *Pers.* 38.1 on Maximinus. Christians such as Minucius Felix (*Octavius* 25) pointed out that Rome was founded and populated with the help of similar atrocities.

7 The characteristic vice of a tyrant in ancient literature, as at Plato, *Republic* 578a.

8 A similar jibe is attributed by Lactantius, *Pers.* 13.2 to the Christian Euetius, who tore down the first decree against the Christians.

9 The term now implies an interest in the course of history, not merely in the cosmic regularities which were the subject of *pronoia* when discussed by Greek philosophers.

occurred among barbarians, would have sufficed to bring about eternal peace. For the whole army of the aforesaid king, subject to the authority of some good-for-nothing who had seized the Roman Empire by force,[1] was exterminated by many wars of all kinds.[2]

But what more clear and obvious token of divine judgment could be advanced? The world itself cries out, and the pageant of the stars shines brighter and more conspicuous, rejoicing (as I believe) in the fitting judgment of unholy deeds. The very times that succeed the wild and inhumane life are reckoned to rejoice because of their own good lot, and show the goodwill of God toward humankind. While as for the invocations of God by those who were being oppressed and longed for their natural liberty,[3] and their praises of thanksgiving to God after the release from evils, when liberty and their contract with justice had been restored to them, how do these fail to delineate in every way the providence of God and his affection for humankind?

26. But when they praise my service,[4] which commenced with the inspiration of God, do they not confirm that God is the cause of my feats? Absolutely. For it is God's prerogative to decree the best things, and that of human beings to obey God. Now in my view a ministry is most lovely and excellent when someone, before the attempt, ensures that what is done will be secure.[5] And all human beings know that the most holy devotion of these hands is owed to God with pure faith of the strictest kind, and that all that has been accomplished with advantage is achieved by joining the hands in prayers and litanies, with as much private and public assistance as everyone

---

1 Barnes (1976a), 422 identifies this person as Licinius, later arguing at (1981), 323 that the speech must therefore follow the rupture in 321. Lane Fox (1986), 632 endorses this deduction as confirmation of his own dating of the speech to 324. Nothing, however, prevents us from supposing that this prodigal is once again Maximinus; he cannot have been Maxentius, since, as Drake (1985) observes, he never took charge of Diocletian's troops.

2 On wars as a ruinous consequence of impiety cf. Constantine at Eusebius, *Constantine* 2.27.1.

3 That is, citizens. On the abridgement of their rights to litigation under Diocletian's edicts see Corcoran (1996), 180.

4 For the term *hupêresia* cf. Eusebius, *Constantine* 2.28. Constantine also styles himself God's servant or instrument at *Constantine* 2.64, Gelasius of Cyzicus, *Church History* 2.7.35 and Optatus, *Against the Donatists*, Appendix 5. Elliott (1992) deduces from the Greek passages that Constantine professed to have been acting in the cause of God before his march on Rome in 312.

5 Cf. Luke 14.28 on the cost of war and fortification.

might pray for on his own behalf and that of those dearest to him. They indeed have witnessed the battles and observed the war in which God's providence awarded victory to the people, and have seen God co-operating with our prayers. For righteous prayer is an invincible thing,[1] and no-one who pays holy adoration is disappointed of his aim. For no place is left for disappointment, except where faith's part fails, since God is always present with goodwill to welcome human goodness. Thus it is human to lapse sometimes, but God is not to be blamed for human lapses.[2] Those who pursue piety should, however, confess their gratitude to the Saviour of all for our own salvation and the good state of public affairs, and petition Christ for one another with holy prayers and litanies,[3] that he may continue his benefits to us. For he is an unconquerable ally and defender of the righteous, he himself is the best judge, the guide to immortality, the bestower of eternal life.

The fifth book of Eusebius Pamphilus[4] on the life of Constantine the king.[5]

---

1 Cf. James 5.16.

2 Cf. Plato, *Republic* 617e: 'the blame is with the one who chooses; God is not to blame'.

3 As for Origen, *On Prayer* 14.4–15.1, Christ remains primarily the recipient of petitions.

4 Eusebius took the name Pamphilus in memory of his teacher, a fellow-lover of Origen who also became a martyr.

5 Here the word 'king', being written by a Greek-speaking annotator, carries no pejorative sense.

HERE BEGINS THE COMING[1] OF THE HOLY CROSS

In the year 233,[2] when God's servant[3] the great man Constantine was reigning, in the sixth year of this reign,[4] a great host of barbarians[5] gathered

1 The Latin is *adventus* rather than *inventio*, though the latter would be a more accurate translation of the word *heuresis* which appears in the title of the Greek work. Perhaps the noun is intended as an allusion not only to the vision of Constantine, but to his subsequent exaltation of the Cross when he entered Rome in 312: see Dufraigne (1997), 73–83. Borgehammar (1991), 151 and 241–42 surmises that there was once a separate narrative of the *Vision*. See note on closing rubric also.

2 Borgehammar (1991), 181–82 is no doubt correct to argue that this means the 233rd year since the accession of Trajan on 28 January, 98. The edition of A.D. Holder (1889), 15 credits Eberhard Nestle with this conjecture; see further Nestle (1889), 41–42 on the burial of the Cross under Trajan. Drijvers and Drijvers (1997), 55 remark that one of the Syriac versions, which says that the Cross was recovered for a second time by Helena, is alluding to the legend that Protonike, the wife of the Emperor Claudius, was the first to unearth the trophy, which was then consigned to earth again under Trajan. By the reckoning explained below, the second year of this emperor began with the month of Easter in 98, and the Easter of 329 marks the inception of his 233rd year.

3 Constantine styles himself a servant of God in a letter at Eusebius, *Constantine* 2.55 and is followed in this by Eusebius, *Constantine* 1.2. Cameron and Hall (1999), 186 and 188 observe that the term is in keeping with Eusebius' assimilation of Constantine to Moses, and, since Moses was the first to win a battle with the sign of the Cross (Exod. 17.11–12), this parallel would not be out of place in the present work.

4 In the Syriac version it is the seventh year and in the month of Kanun. This is the second in the Palmyrene calendar, according to Samuel (1972), 179. Constantine became undisputed master of the Empire on 8 November in 324, and since the present text appears to date the year from Nisan, the month of Easter, his sixth year will have commenced in the second quarter of 329. Nisan is the seventh month in the Palmyrene reckoning, and if it began as late as 24 May (cf. Samuel (1972), 176 on Heliopolis), the first Kanun of the emperor's reign would commence in late December 324. In that case, by the Palmyrene computation, it would fall in the second year of Constantine, which would already have begun in late November. Kanun of the seventh year in Palmyra would span late December and early January of 329/30, though for the Latin text translated here the seventh year would not begin until Easter 330. A mediaeval Latin version of the legend confirms that the miracle took place in 'January of the seventh year': Borgehammar (1991), 282. It may not be an accident that Constantine's conversion has been assigned to the Christmas season.

5 The barbarians are not named in the Latin text. See Zosimus 2.21 (perhaps also Eusebius, *Constantine* 4.6, though the date is vague) for the battle against the Sarmatians which appears

and came over the Danube in preparation for war against the Roman state.[1] Now this was announced to king Constantine Augustus,[2] and he also gathered a multitude of troops, and set out to join issue with them, and he found those who had crossed into Roman territory and were over the Danube.

Now when Constantine Augustus saw that the multitude [of barbarians] was beyond counting, he was deeply distressed and sorely afraid. But that very night, there came to him a man in great splendour,[3] who roused him and said to him, 'Constantine, do not be afraid,[4] but look up again into heaven and behold!' And gazing up into heaven, he beheld the sign of the Cross of Christ, formed out of brilliant light, and above was inscribed this rubric in letters: *In this sign*.[5] Thereupon Constantine Augustus made a likeness of the Cross that he had seen in the sky, then took the sign and had

---

to be commemorated here. An earlier victory (305/6) over this tribe is alleged in the little work *On the Origin of Constantine* 4, but this event could not be said to have fallen in the sixth or seventh year of Constantine on any chronology of his reign. The same is true of the success in 307 deduced by Barnes (1976c), 149 from the place of the title Sarmaticus in an inscription. The Sarmatians, a tribe on the north-eastern frontier of the Empire, acquired an excessive prominence in Christian hagiography of Constantine and his family, perhaps, as Lieu suggests, because they were confounded with the Persians: Lieu and Montserrat (1996), 142 nn. 2 and 3.

1 A Byzantine life of Constantine, dating from the ninth century according to Lieu and Montserrat (1996), 102, records at chapter 25 (p. 128 Lieu and Montserrat) that Constantine saw a third vision of the Cross when he bridged the Danube in defiance of the 'Scythians'. The second vision occurred before the capture of Byzantium, and these three divine signals therefore marked the three great victories of his career (see ch. 3, p. 139 Lieu and Montserrat).

2 The title 'king' is biblical, *rex* being a term distasteful to all writers of classical Latin because it was reminiscent of the Etruscan rulers who had been expelled from the city in 509 BC. Augustus had been the standard title of emperors since 27 BC, and was first assumed by Constantine, without legal forms, on the death of his father Constantius in 306 AD (see Lactantius, *Pers.* 24).

3 The angel does not figure in other accounts, but would typically be required in the Old Testament at a moment of vocation: see e.g. Josh. 5.14, 1 Sam. 13.6.

4 A typical salutation; see e.g. Luke 2.10.

5 Eusebius, *Constantine* 1.28 reports, on the emperor's sworn word, that in the course of the campaign which led to the capture of Rome, he saw in the early afternoon a Cross above the sun, 'formed out of light', which bore the rubric, *Conquer by this*. What is described, however, is not so much the Cross as a *labarum*, a combination of the Greek characters X and P, which Eusebius construes as the first two letters of Christ's name, although pagans might have recognized here an icon of the sun. For Lactantius, *Pers.* 44 it is again a form of the *labarum* that his hero sees at the Milvian bridge on the eve of his battle for Rome; Prudentius, *Against Symmachus* 1.487 confirms both the location and the nature of the sign.

it put in the van,[1] and making an onset with his troops against the barbarians, he fell upon them the following dawn; and the barbarians were afraid and took to flight through the mists of the Danube. And no small number perished, and God in that day gave victory to King Constantine through the power of the Holy Cross.

Now when King Constantine came to his own city,[2] he summoned all the priests of all the gods or idols, and inquired of them what god this sign was or to what god it belonged; and they could not tell him.[3] There remained, however, one of them, who said to him, 'This is the sign of the God of heaven'. A few Christians who were present at that time[4] came to King Constantine and preached to him the mystery of the Trinity and the advent of the Son of God, how he was born and crucified and on the third day rose from the dead.[5]

1 The Latin has *in fronte*, which is inelegant and ambiguous; but Borgehammar (1991), 220 cites an alternative version which states that the Cross 'went before' the army, and that is also the meaning of the Syriac. Lactantius, *Pers.* 44 reports that, by divine admonition, Constantine had the 'sign of Christ' inscribed on his soldiers' shields; Eusebius, *Constantine* 1.37 says that the Cross was carried at the head of Constantine's troops in his engagement with Maxentius.

2 To judge by the sequel this means Rome and not Byzantium. But Constantine entered Rome in 312.

3 Compare Dan. 4.18–19 and 5.14–17, where the Babylonian kings apply in vain to their own advisers, and discover that only Daniel the Jew can expound their visions. Such literary somersaults, reversing the position of the Gentiles with regard to the Jews, are common in the literature of the early Church, prefigured as they were by Paul himself at Gal. 4.24.

4 At Drijvers and Drijvers (1997), 54 the Syriac says that Christians in the army were known as Nazarenes. This is usually the word for a Palestinian sect originating with converts from Judaism; perhaps the author means to anticipate the story of Judas. The service of Christians under pagan generals is attested with reluctance in Tertullian's *On the Soldier's Crown* (third century), happily if not honestly by Eusebius in his tale of the 'Thundering Legion' (*Church History* 5.5) and more credibly in Lactantius' account of Diocletian's purge in 297 (*Pers.* 10). The Roman legionary was by occupation a citizen of the world, and so perhaps by inclination a monotheist; thus Maximinus Daia and Licinius fought each other in the name of different universal gods: Lactantius, *Mort.* 46–47.

5 All these had been essentials of the Christian faith since apostolic times: see Rom. 1.3 and 1 Cor. 15.3. The author will of course have been familiar with the epitome of Christian belief called the Apostles' creed, which seems to have originated in Rome in or before the mid-fourth century, as well as with the formularies issued at the Councils of Nicaea in 325, Constantinople in 381 and Chalcedon in 451. Even the simplest creed would have informed the king that Christ was the son of God, that he came down for our salvation, that he ascended and will come again in judgment, and that the Church also confesses the Holy Spirit, the remission of sins by baptism and the resurrection to everlasting life. If the 'Nicene Symbol' of 325 or its successor, the more familiar 'Nicene Creed', had been employed in his instruction he would also have learned that the Son was consubstantial with the Father, true God from God, begotten and not made. These were not stated doctrines of the Church before the Council of Nicaea in 325.

Then King Constantine sent to Eusebius the bishop of Rome,[1] and caused him to come to him, and [Eusebius] instructed him in the whole of the Christian faith, and taught him the mysteries of all things[2] in the name of Our Lord Jesus Christ;[3] and, when assured of his faith, he enjoined him to build churches of Christ everywhere,[4] but bade him destroy the temples of the idols.[5]

[6]Now the blessed Constantine was perfect in the faith and served in the Holy Spirit, and became versed in the holy gospels of Jesus Christ. When he had learnt where the Cross of the Lord is,[7] he sent his mother Helena[8] to seek

1 A Eusebius was bishop of Rome in 308–9, but on no chronology can he be the man intended, and Constantine did not become a Christian at that time. Drijvers and Drijvers (1997), 23 suggest that the name Rome is a misinterpretation of the Syriac word Rum, which designates the Roman Empire. If, as is generally held, it was Eusebius of Nicomedia who baptized the dying Constantine (Jerome, *Chronicle, ad* 337), it is no surprise that an author who aimed at orthodoxy should (consciously or unconsciously) have substituted his namesake, for Eusebius of Nicomedia had signed the creed of 325 reluctantly, and was exiled for his refusal to endorse the anathemas appended to it. Fowden (1994b), 161 traces the name Eusebius of Rome as early as 460 in the (lost) work of the historian Agathangelos.

2 It is not clear what the king had still to hear if he had already imbibed the mysteries of the Trinity, as the text above declares. After 451 the Chalcedonian definition of the person of Christ as fully God and fully man, though not contained in any creed, was thought by the dominant party in Byzantium, and by everyone in the Latin west, to be binding on the whole Church.

3 The author no doubt means that he was baptized in the triple name of Father, Son and Holy Spirit, as at Matt. 28.19. The older form, represented in Acts 2.38, was generally superseded by the time of Constantine, though, to judge by Hippolytus, *Apostolic Tradition* 21.19, anointing in the single name survived in Rome until the third century. It is possible that Eusebius of Nicomedia, unwilling as he was to admit that the Father and Son were both God, would have eschewed the Trinitarian formula; historical verisimilitude is not, however, a point of great concern with the present author.

4 Constantine was extolled as a founder of sacred buildings even before his conversion to Christianity at *Latin Panegyrics* 6(7).22. His labours as a Christian are rehearsed by Eusebius, *Constantine* 3.47–51.

5 Paulinus, Letter 31 asserts that this destruction was carried out under Helena's auspices. Eusebius, *Constantine* 3.54–58 implies that most of the demolitions took place after her death.

6 At this point a group of manuscripts includes an account of the burial of the Cross and the erection of a temple of Aphrodite above it, which seems to depend on Eusebius's *Onomasticon* or else the *Church History* of Rufinus and is later presupposed in the present narrative. See Borgehammar (1991), 302 and Taylor (1998), 190–91.

7 This means, presumably, in Jerusalem, since all the rest remained to be discovered.

8 In the following sentence, as in the Greek, it is clear that Helena undertakes the mission of her own accord. Thus we seem to see here a clumsy attempt to join two narratives originally discrete. The Latin version implies, more clearly than the Greek, that Helena was converted at the instance of her son; cf. Eusebius, *Constantine* 3.47, as well as Constantine's allusions to his pagan upbringing in *Oration* 11.

the holy wood of the Cross of Our Lord, and to build in the same place a church of the Lord.[1] Now the grace of the Holy Spirit reposed in the blessed Helena, mother of the emperor Constantine. She versed herself in every mansion[2] of the scriptures of the Lord, and possessed an intense love of our Lord Jesus Christ. Later indeed she also sought out the saving wood of the Holy Cross. Now when she had read intently about the advent of salvation[3] in our Saviour Jesus Christ and the erection of his Cross and resurrection of the dead, she could not live with herself until she had also found the victorious wood of Christ's Cross, on which the body of the Lord had been fixed.

Now this is the way she found it.[4] On the twenty-eighth day of the second month[5] she entered the holy city of Jerusalem and then convened the vile[6] mob of Jews, not only from[7] Jerusalem but from the neighbouring cities, castles and estates, so that the total of Jews was found to be three thousand.[8] To these the blessed Eternal[9] one said, 'I have learned from the holy prophets that you were beloved of God, but because[10] all of you, spurning wisdom,[11] poured curses on the one who wished to redeem you from the curse, you abused him who cleansed your eyes from unclean spirits with his

1   The construction of this building is reported by Rufinus, *Church History* 10.8.

2   John 14.2.

3   Or 'the advent of humanity', reading the apparatus in Holder, p. 17. Borgehammar (1991), 238 suggests that this is a clumsy rendering of the greek *enanthrôpêsis* ('becoming man'), which, unlike the alternative *ensarkôsis* ('incarnation'), cannot be rendered by a single Latin word.

4   Paulinus of Nola, Letter 31 appears to be the earliest witness to Helena's convocation of the 'most learned among the Jews'. Though he does not name Judas, the hero of the present narrative, he also shows no acquaintance with the rival account in which it is Bishop Macarius of Jerusalem who counsels Helena.

5   In the Syriac at Drijvers and Drijvers (1997), 56 the month is Iyas, eighth in the Palmyrene calendar and the first after Nisan, in which the Easter celebration falls. The Latin therefore appears to be dating the months from Eastertide, just as the Jews began the year with Nisan.

6   The epithet *impiissima* is not found in the Greek.

7   This construction also is unparalleled in the Greek; in general the diction of the Latin tends to the hyperbolic.

8   A small number, as the Syriac observes: Drijvers and Drijvers (1997), 56–57 cite testimony that Hadrian was held to have been responsible for the desertion of the territory. Nevertheless, Stemberger (2000), 17 accepts an estimate of 700,000 Jews in the whole territory of Palestine in 140 AD; even if the majority lived in Galilee, there would be far more than 3,000 in Judaea.

9   Aeterna being no doubt a scribal error for Aelena, one form of the empress's name.

10   Introducing a more complex sentence than we find in the Greek.

11   Paul avers at 1 Cor. 17–30 that God confuted the wisdom of the world by the folly of preaching, and above all by the crucifixion, whereby Christ became the wisdom of God for us. Reminiscences of Jewish 'wisdom literature' (Prov. 8.22, Wis. 7.25–26) reinforced the Christian tendency to use 'Wisdom' as an appellation of Christ (cf. also Luke 11.49).

spittle,[1] and you handed over to death the one who raised your dead,[2] you have once and for all exchanged light for shadows and truth for falsehood.[3] Upon you has fallen the curse that is written in your scriptures.[4] Now, however, choose from among yourselves men who have diligently learned your law, so that they may answer me about the matters on which I shall interrogate them.'

Having withdrawn in fear, and held a long debate among themselves, they found those men who claimed to have learned the law well to be a thousand in number. And they brought them to the blessed Helena, producing on their behalf the testimonials that they had a deep knowledge of the law. To these the blessed Helena said 'Hear my words and take note of my words with your ears. For you do not understand in the words of the prophets how they prophesied about the coming of Christ.[5] The reason that I am interrogating you today, is that *A boy shall be born to you and his mother shall not know a man.*[6] And the writer[7] David also knows the Lord, saying *I saw the Lord always before my face, because he is at my right hand lest I be moved.*[8] And Isaiah says of you, *I have begotten sons, but they have reviled me. The ox knows his master and the ass his crib, but Israel does not know me and my people have not understood me.*[9] And the whole of scripture has spoken of this man; therefore you who used to know the law are in error. Now, however, choose some who have diligently learned the

1 See Mark 7.33 and 15.19.

2 For the verb 'hand over' see Matt. 27.2, Rom. 4.25, 1 Pet. 2.23 etc. For resurrections by Jesus see Matt. 9.25 par, Luke 7.14, John 11.43.

3 Cf. John 3.19, Col. 2.7, Heb. 10.1.

4 See Deut. 18.15, Ps. 95.11 etc.

5 A pervasive theme of early Christian literature, from Matt. 1.22 on. See further Skarsaune (1987).

6 A variant of Isa. 7.14, stressing the virginity of Mary. Although the word *almah* in the Hebrew text is now customarily rendered as 'young woman' rather than 'virgin', Kamesar (1990) shows that the arguments advanced by ancient exegetes in favour of the latter are not entirely nugatory.

7 That is, scriptural author.

8 Ps. 16.8 in the Vulgate (generally 17.8 in English renderings of the Hebrew), cited at Acts 2.25 by Peter. Whatever he understood it to mean, Athanasius (298–373) argued at *Against the Arians* 1.61 that 'the Lord' is God and Christ himself the speaker, notwithstanding such famous texts as Mark 14.62, Acts 7.56 and Rom. 8.34 where it is Christ who sits at the right hand of the Father.

9 Isa. 1.2–3, cited against the Jews as early as the mid-second century: Justin Martyr, *1Apology* 63. The logic appears to be that as Israel clearly knows the Father, the God whom they do not know is Christ.

knowledge of the law, so that they may give an answer to my interrogations.' And she commanded that they be kept in custody with the greatest care. And taking counsel among themselves, they chose fifty men who were the greatest experts in the law.[1] And coming to the queen they stood before her face. She said 'What are these?', and they said, 'These are the ones most learned in the law'. And again the blessed Helena began to instruct them: 'You who are truly foolish sons of Israel, who in accordance with the scriptures have followed the blindness of your fathers, who say that Jesus is not the Son of God, who read the law[2] and understand not the prophets'.[3]

But they said, 'We do indeed read and understand. But for what reason do you say such things to us? Tell us, so that we may know and answer what is being said.' And she said to them again, 'Come here and choose better people'. And when they came, they said to one another, 'For what reason do you think the queen is imposing this labour upon us?' And one of them, Judas by name,[4] said, 'I know that she wants to put a question about the wood on which our fathers hanged Jesus.[5] Take care, therefore, that no-one confesses to her; for then indeed our paternal traditions will be destroyed and the law will be reduced to nothing. Zaccheus[6] declared this to my father,

---

1 'peritissimi' is the word used by Paulinus of Nola, Letter 31.

2 A play on words (*legitis legem*), not paralleled here in the Greek; but a few words later the Greek has an untranslatable play on *anagignôskein* (read) and *gignôskein* (know). The Latin translator should be given credit for his success in reproducing the bad taste of the original.

3 Cf. Matt. 15.14, John 10.36 and 5.46, Luke 16.49, 2 Cor. 3.13–18.

4 For the earliest intimation of his presence in the legend, see Sozomen, *Church History* 2.1, which denies that God could have chosen one of the impious race, as some believe, as his means of revelation. Sozomen attests the other elements of the legend – the inscription, the resurrection and the adornment of the reins – without, however, implying that all were included in the legend of the Jew. The significance of the name Judas is clear enough, as it belonged not only to the traitor Iscariot, but also to the eponymous ancestor of all Judaeans, if not strictly of all Jews. Cf. Severus of Minorca at Bradbury (1996), 95, where the name of Reuben, the 'first-born son of Jacob', is given to the first Jew in Minorca to undergo spiritual rebirth.

5 Jesus is often said to have been hanged because Paul associates the Cross with the biblical curse on 'him that hangeth on a tree' (Gal. 3.10; see also Acts 5.30). Justin, *Trypho* 86 contrasts the tree of life with the wood of the Cross. The term 'wood' (as well as 'Cross') is used repeatedly by Egeria, *Pilgrimage* 37 in her account of the public veneration of the relic.

6 The name of the redeemed tax collector at Luke 19.2, but Johanan ben Zakkhai ('son of Zacchaeus') is also among the most famous rabbis of the first century. Although he is said to have lived into the reign of Trajan, he is also reported to have fled Jerusalem after foreseeing the destruction of the temple in 70 AD ; he resembled Christians also in attributing this calamity to the unbelief of Israel, in teaching that the world would be reconciled through charity rather than substitutionary offerings and in representing life as a choice between the paths to paradise and Gehenna. See further *Encyclopaedia Judaica* X, 248–54.

and my father as he was dying communicated it to me, saying "Take care, my son, when a question is put about the wood on which those who were before us condemned the Messiah, reveal it before you suffer crucifixion. Now the race of Hebrews has ceased to reign,[1] and the kingdom belongs to those who adore the crucified one. As for him, his reign is unto ages of ages,[2] for he is Christ, the Son of the living God."[3]

'Then I said, "Father, if then your fathers knew that this is the Christ, why did they lay hands[4] upon him?" And he said, "My son, you know his ineffable name[5] because I was never in their counsels and never joined with them, but from time to time I spoke against them. [The fact is] that the elders argued against me, and the priests therefore condemned him to be crucified, imagining that they could put to death the immortal one who was buried when they took him down from the Cross. He, however, rose from his burial after three days, and revealed himself to his disciples. Hence also your brother Stephen[6] believed and began to teach in his name. And, after taking counsel, the Pharisees and Sadducees condemned him, and getting together a crowd, stoned him to death.[7] None the less, that blessed one, as he gave up his soul, spread his hands and prayed to heaven, saying, *Lord, do not requite*

1 The 'supersessionist' doctrine, according to which the Church has unseated Israel in the plan of God, was prevalent in the early Church, and foreshadowed by Matt. 8.12, Mark 12.9–10 and Heb. 3.11, 18 (citing Ps. 95.11).

2 Cf. Luke 1.33.

3 Matt. 16.16.

4 Mark 9.31.

5 Christ has the 'name above all names' at Phil. 2.9 and Eph. 1.21. Jews held that the name of God was too holy to be uttered (Mark 14.61–62 etc.), while the predicate 'ineffable' was commonplace in Christian thought by the end of the second century (e.g. Clement, *Stromateis* 5.81).

6 It is not clear whether the meaning is that Stephen was a relative of Judas, or even that he was a fellow Jew; neither assertion would be true to Acts 6.5, which makes it clear that Stephen was a 'Hellenist' or Gentile Christian. It was, of course, impossible for the grandfather of Judas to have been a contemporary of the events that he describes, so the legend of Judas must have been contaminated at some stage with that of Protonike, wife of Claudius (41–54 AD). See also my note on the Greek which introduces a distant familial relationship. It may be significant that Stephen appears in the story of Judas Kyriakos; see also following note.

7 Acts 8.1. No relics of Stephen were known to the Church until 415, when a certain Lucian claimed to have discovered them by revelation. For a summary of his account and of the removal of the bones to Minorca see Bradbury (1996), 16–25. Van Esbroek (1984) suggests that the *Passion* and *Revelation of Stephen* in which this miracle is recounted were composed at the instance of Bishop John of Jerusalem, who is one of the principal figures in the narrative and also promoted the veneration of the Cross.

them for this sin. Listen to me, therefore, my son, and I shall teach you about the holy Christ and his righteousness. [The fact is] that Saul, who sat before the temple exercising the art of a tent-maker,[1] was a persecutor of those who believed in Christ.[2] It was he who roused the people against our brother Stephen,[3] but in his righteousness the Lord made him one of his own holy disciples. This is the reason why I and my fathers have believed that he is truly the Son of God.[4] And now, my son, do not blaspheme him, nor those who believe in him, and in this you shall possess eternal life." This is the witness of my father Simon. There, you have heard all; what do you wish to do if she interrogates us about the wood of the Cross?'

The others said, however, 'We have never heard such things as we have heard today from you. If a question is put about this, take care that you do not tell; after all, it is obvious from your saying this that you also know the place.' As they were saying this, soldiers came to them, saying, 'Come, the queen summons you'. Now when they had come before her they were put to the test by her. And they did not wish to say anything true. Then the blessed Helena ordered them all to be cast into the fire.[5] In their fear, they handed Judas over to her,[6] saying, 'This man is the son of one who was upright and a prophet, and he has the best and most exact[7] learning in the law. This man, mistress, will tell you faithfully all that your heart desires.'[8] And as they all

---

1 Holder's text reads *scaenografiam*, which ought to signify 'scene-painting', but Paul's profession is known from Acts 18.3, and the variants collected by Borgehammar (1991), 238 imply that the original term was intended to represent the Greek *skênoraphos*. This is one of a number of passages which Borgehammar cites as proof that the Latin is indebted to the Greek and not the Syriac, but he also admits that *skênoraphos* is only one of three variants in the Greek manuscripts. The Greek of Acts 18.3 is *skênopoios*, which received the calque *scenofactorius* in the Vulgate.

2 Gal. 1.23, 1 Tim. 1.13.

3 A cruel inference from Acts 7.58, 8.1 and 9.1.

4 Perhaps alluding to Matt. 27.54, and also to Paul's confession of Christ as Son of God at Gal. 1.16.

5 The Jews of the Christian era do not display the fortitude of their countrymen, the 'three children', who were cast into the furnace by Nebuchadnezzar for their refusal to worship his statue in Daniel 3. In chapter 1 of this text the children were also proof against hunger, whereas Judas is soon to yield after seven days of enforced starvation

6 As the Jews had handed over Jesus to a pagan suzerain: Matt. 27.2, Rom. 4.25 etc.

7 If with Holder's apparatus on p. 21 we read here *cum acribia*, we must agree with Borgehammar (1991), 238 that it is a borrowing from the Greek original, where *akribôs* ('exactly, accurately') is the term used.

8 See my note to the Greek text on this echo of Ps. 37.4.

gave the same testimony,[1] she dismissed them and detained Judas alone. Thereupon the queen called him to her and said to him, 'Life and death are set before you; choose for yourself which you prefer, life or death'.[2] Judas said, 'And who, placed in the wilderness with bread close by, will eat stones?'[3] The blessed Helena said, 'If you wish to live in heaven and on earth,[4] tell me where the precious wood[5] of the Cross is hidden'.

Judas said, 'As to the truth about matters that were two hundred years more or less[6] before our time, how can we, latecomers as we are, know this?' The blessed Helena said, 'In the same way as we know that before the present generation a war took place in Ilium[7] and the Troad,[8] and all now remember the dead, and there is a written tradition about the monuments and places'. And Judas said, 'Of course, mistress, seeing that they have been written down'.[9] The blessed Helena said, 'And a certain man has confessed a short while ago the things that you have done'. And Judas said, 'I have the blessed witness of the gospels to the place of his crucifixion'. {The blessed Helena said} 'Just show me the place that is called Calvary,[10] and I shall

1 The syntax is confused, but if the original was *omnium simul testimonium perhibentium* (cf. Holder's edition p. 21), then we have here a genitive absolute, which, as Borgehammar (1991), 238 contends, betokens a Greek original.

2 As Joshua set them before the Jews at Deut. 31.15. On the persistent theme of the 'two ways' in Christian literature see Aldridge (1999).

3 This utterance, apparently proverbial, may already have been known to the author of Matt. 4.3–4, where Christ is incited to turn stones into bread. Cf. also Luke 11.11.

4 She appears to insinuate that he will otherwise be guilty of the sin against the Holy Spirit, which cannot be forgiven in this world or the one to come: Matt. 12.32.

5 These words do not occur in the Greek, and indeed the Latin generally uses *lignum*, as the Greek employs *xulon*, as a synonym for the Cross.

6 Three centuries having now elapsed since the passion, this phrase ought to be taken as a reference to the burial of the Cross in the time of Trajan.

7 Another name for Troy, but the Syriac appears to speak instead of the tomb of Ilus, founder of Troy, whose tomb is mentioned at *Iliad* 11.371–72 etc. See Drijvers and Drijvers (1997), 62n.

8 The Trojan war, described in Homer's *Iliad*, was a touchstone of antiquity in Greece, although the Jews (and Christian readers of the Old Testament) were fond of pointing out that the works of Moses were more ancient. Both Strabo (13.1.34) and Pliny the Elder (*Natural History* 16.238) professed to know the site of Troy, though modern archaeology has not entirely vindicated either: see Cook (1973), 94–113, esp. 111.

9 The author may be reminding us that the Jews retained no memorials of their prophets, except perhaps those of some that they had killed (Deut. 34.6; cf. Matt. 23.39).

10 Luke 23.33. This Latin name, derived from the word for 'bald', translates the Hebrew Golgotha, 'place of the skull' (Matt. 27.33). According to Drijvers and Drijvers (1997), 64n, the Syriac reads simply 'skull', and therefore it is derived not from the Latin but from the Syriac version of the New Testament.

cause the place to be cleansed in case by any chance I may find my desire'. Judas said, 'I do not know the place as I have never been there'. The blessed Helena said, 'Nevertheless, by the Crucified One,[1] I shall have you put to if you do not tell me the truth'. And she ordered him to be thrust into a dry well[2] and remain there without food for seven days.

But when seven days had passed, Judas cried out from the well, saying, 'I beseech you, pull me out and I shall show you the Cross of Christ. When, however, he had come up from the pit and did not know for certain the place where the Cross lay, he lifted his voice to the Lord in Hebrew:[3]

> Aisaarabrimilas/filomabon.achuiroiloemlemetdochzod/
> failemfaudiubariccataadonaheluielecanro/
> abraxioetadalbarucadtamdextrambuzima/
> tuccatadavidauiatherahelbememonsegen/
> geminiihm.[4]

The meaning of this is:

> God, God, who madest heaven and earth,[5] who in thy palm hast laid out the heaven and with thy fist hast measured the earth,[6] who sittest above the chariot of the Cherubim,[7] and these fly in the courses of the air, in the

---

1 I take this to be the sense of *per crucifixum*, though the Greek does not contain an oath, and threatens starvation.

2 The Latin is *lacus,* which ought to mean 'lake', but is best construed as an equivalent for the word *lakkos* ('pit' or 'ditch') in the Greek original. Cf. the Latin translation of Jer. 2.13.

3 As Rendel Harris (1894) and Staubinger (1912), 59–60 point out, this prayer (which is not represented in the Syriac narratives, though a version of it occurs in the Kyriakos legend) is gibberish of a kind well known from the Nag Hammadi Codices and the magical papyri. Unlike the latter, however, it never invokes the names of Iao and Adonai, and Borgehammar (1991), 171 suggests that its structure is based on those in 2 Kgs 19.15–19, Isa. 37.16–20 and Esth. 13.9–17. The last may be of particular importance if I am right to associate the conclusion with the end of the book of Esther and the aetiology of the feast of Purim. In the *Revelation of Stephen* the position of the martyr's bones is revealed by an inscription which purportedly contains four Hebrew names: see Bradbury (1996), 19.

4 Variants are recorded by Borgehammar (1991), 272–78 and Holder, p. 23 with some pertinent observations on the use of specious Hebrew in magical practice. See Preisendanz, *PMG* 13.63 for a prayer to the creator, which attributes to him the regulation of the sun and moon. To judge by Philo, *On the Cherubim* 21–25, cherubs could be taken as personifications of the great cosmic cycles.

5 A commonplace since Gen. 1.1, but also the foundation of Christian confidence at Acts 4.24.

6 Isa. 40.12.

7 2 Chron. 3.10, Ps. 80.1.

immeasurable light[1] to which human measure cannot extend, for it is thou who hast made these six creatures with their sixfold wings for thy service; and four[2] of these who fly and serve thee, singing with unceasing voice, *Holy, holy, holy* are called the Cherubim,[3] while thou hast placed two of them in paradise to guard the tree of life, and these are called[4] Seraphim.[5] Thou, however, dost hold dominion over them, thou who didst consign the unbelieving angels to the depths of Tartarus,[6] and now they are beneath the bottom of the abyss,[7] to be tortured by the breath of serpents,[8] and they cannot speak against thee. And now God, if it is thy will that the son of Mary should reign – and had he not been from thee he could not have done such works of power, and had he not indeed been thy Son thou wouldst not have raised him again from the dead – give us therefore, God, a miracle, such as when thou didst hear thy servant Moses and didst show to him the bones of our father Joseph.[9] And so, Lord, if it be thy pleasure to show us the secret

1 1 Tim. 6.16.

2 As at Ezek. 1.6, where, however, they have four wings. Their song, already known to Ephraem, *Epiphany Hymn* 2.5, is recorded at length in *Zohar* 231a–b, cited by Lachower and Tishby (1989), 636–37. Knowledge of the nomenclature of angels is a precondition of efficacious magic in both Jewish and Gnostic literature: Schürer (1986), 347–49; Robinson (1988), 2.5.105.

3 The chant 'holy, holy, holy' (the Trisagion) is in fact ascribed to a retinue of Seraphs at Isa. 6.2–3, but the author perhaps confounds them with the Cherubim because elsewhere the latter are the only angelic beings who support the throne of God. Isaiah's Seraphs have six wings, as do the beasts who intone the Trisagion at Rev. 4.6–8, but the faces of the latter resemble those of the Cherubim in Ezek. 1.4–14. One aim of this prayer may therefore be to vindicate the superiority of the Christian prophet. See further my note on the Greek.

4 A singular verb in Latin, though following the word *duo* ('two'), the word *animalia* being understood. Borgehammar (1991), 238 notes that the neuter plural takes a singular verb in Greek, though not in Latin, and infers that the solecism here is occasioned by adherence to the Greek original.

5 At Gen. 3.24 they are Cherubim. Since, however, Seraphim were serpentine in form, they might be thought better suited than the Cherubim to the task of excluding human beings from paradise – all the more so if Satan himself is taken to have been a Seraph, as cabbalists have asserted, notwithstanding Ezek. 28.14: see Horowitz (1996), 222. Ephraem, *Paradise Hymn* 3.15 places Seraphs in Eden, and at 14.16 it is they, not the Cherubs, who inhabit heaven.

6 See my notes on the Greek text for parallels to this name.

7 Cf. Preisendanz (1973–74), 4.1249 for a prayer to Christ consigning a demon to the abyss of chaos. Elsewhere in the same papyrus, other deities are evoked from Tartarus, where they seem to govern rather than suffer: 4.1370, 104, 1451, 2337, 2537.

8 Reading *cruciandi* with Holder's apparatus, p. 24. The Greek has a different reading, but this one seems to combine a reminiscence of the 'worm that dieth not' (Isa. 66.24, Mark 9.44) with a reminiscence of the desolation of Jerusalem (Isa. 35.7, Jer. 9.11).

9 Ginzberg (1920), 181–83 records a legend that the bones of Joseph were sealed in a leaden coffin and submerged in the river Nile. Having located the coffin with the help of Serah,

treasury, cause to ascend from that same place the smoke of the aromatic
odour of sweetness,[1] that I may believe in the crucified Christ, that he is the
king of Israel now and unto ages of ages.[2]

As soon as Judas had intoned this prayer the place trembled and a mass
of aromatic smoke, the odour of sweetness, ascended from the place, so that
Judas in wonder clapped both his hands, and said, 'In truth thou, Christ, art
saviour of the world. I give thee thanks, Lord, because, unworthy as I am,
thou hast not deprived[3] me of thy grace. {I} Pray then, Lord, that thou
mayest be mindful[4] of my sins, and mayest number me with my brother
Stephen, who is enrolled among thy twelve apostles.'[5] And, having said this,
he girded himself and, taking a spade, began to dig. And when he had dug
twenty fathoms,[6] he found three crosses hidden. And the blessed Helena
demanded of him which was the Cross of Christ, 'for we know that there are

---

daughter of Asher, Moses divided Joseph's cup into quarters and cast these one by one into the
river. The pieces bearing images of a lion, an ox and an eagle were ineffective, but the one that
bore the likeness of a man brought up the coffin to the surface, and it was then carried in the
wilderness as a shrine by the Israelites. See the Greek for a reading that commemorates the
immersion of the body.

1 Conventional imagery of sacrifice, with a probable reminiscence of Eph. 5.2, where Christ
himself is said to be a sweet savour. A similar fragrance is said to have accompanied the
exhumation of Stephen: Bradbury (1996), 19. It may not be out of place to note that the Cross
is said to exhale an odour in Gregory of Elvira, *Song of Songs* 3.1 (fourth century), and that
signing with the Cross accompanied chrism, the pouring of the oil, in the rite of baptism as
prescribed e.g. by Hippolytus, *Apostolic Tradition* 22.

2 Luke 1.32–33.

3 This word in the Latin is followed by a genitive, not the usual ablative – another vestige for
Borgehammar (1991), 238 of a Greek original. In fact, however, there are cases in Latin of the
fifth century when the genitive displaces the ablative without Greek precedent. See e.g.
Augustine, *On the Work of Monks* 9.10, where the *vetus latina* (pre-Vulgate) rendering of 1 Cor.
9.15 contains the phrase as *nullius usus sum* ('I used none'). This is not a slavish rendering of
the Greek, which has the regular dative, and the Vulgate employed the ablative demanded by
classical usage.

4 No doubt the better reading is 'unmindful', which is suggested by the Greek and occurs in
Holder's apparatus, p. 24.

5 Meaning perhaps that he was ranked with them, as Constantine is emblematically at
Eusebius, *Constantine* 4.60.3. The author may have forgotten that Stephen was not a Jew, but
surely he must have been aware that he had not been one of the first apostles. The Greek at this
point styles Stephen the Protomartyr and affirms that he and the speaker are of the same *genos*
(race or family).

6 This being the depth at which the Cross had been buried in Trajan's time: Drijvers and
Drijvers (1997), 66.

two others, robbers, who were crucified with him'.[1] And they carried it into the midst of the city, waiting for Christ to show his glory. And about the ninth hour[2] a certain young man was brought dead on a bed. But Judas, full of joy, said, 'Now you will know, mistress, which is the much-desired wood, and its truth'.[3] And taking hold of the bed, Judas caused the dead man to be put down, and put upon him particular crosses, and the dead man did not rise. But when he placed the third Cross, that of the Lord, upon the dead man, straightway the youth who had been dead got up; and all who were present glorified the Lord.

But the devil, always jealous of all things good, flew through the air[4] with furious cries, saying, 'Who is it this time who does not permit me to take their souls, Jesus of Nazareth?[5] Have you not drawn all to you and revealed your Cross against my people? Judas, why have you done this? Was it not through a Judas that I first produced betrayal,[6] and see, now it is through a Judas that I am expelled. For my part, I have discovered what to do against you; I shall raise up another king who will forsake the Crucified and follow my counsels, adding wrongful torments, and now you will deny the Crucified.'[7] But Judas, brimming with the Holy Spirit,[8] said, 'And Christ

---

1 See Matt. 27.38 par. Ambrose, *Death of Theodosius* 46 asserts that, though three crosses were discovered, that of Christ was instantly recognized by its inscription, 'Jesus of Nazareth, King of the Jews', in Latin, Greek and Hebrew. In Rufinus, *Church History* 10.7, Socrates, *Church History* 1.7 and Sozomen, *Church History* 2.1, the wood that bears the rubric has become detached, and in Paulinus, Letter 31, no trace of it remains. Although the present author says nothing of it, the rubric was preserved in the time of Egeria: *Pilgrimage* 36.

2 This being the hour at which Christ himself expired: Matt. 27.46.

3 Rufinus, *Church History* 10.7 gives a longer speech to Helena's mentor (in this case Bishop Macarius), and has him work the miracle on a moribund female rather than a dead youth. Borgehammar (1991), 54 believes that this was also the test related by Gelasius, while Drijvers and Drijvers (1997), 66n observes that in the Protonike legend, the power of the Cross is exhibited in the resurrection of the empress's daughter. Paulinus of Nola, Letter 31 relates that the corpse of a man was brought to Helena at her own behest as a means of ascertaining the identity of the True Cross.

4 On the devil as prince of the air cf. Eph. 6.12, and on his persecution of the elect see 1 Pet. 5.8. To this cry we may compare that of Apollo leaving Delphi at Prudentius, *Apotheosis* 412, or that of God himself in the (fourth-century) *Handing Over of Pilate* at Elliott (1993), 210–11.

5 Cf. the exclamation of the demon at Mark 1.24.

6 John 13.27. The Greek adds the word 'traitor' to the name of Judas.

7 A reference to Julian, 'the Apostate', whose repeal of Christian privileges was represented as a persecution, and gave rise to many accounts of martyrdom, most of which, including that of Cyriacus, are likely to be fictitious. See Luigi (1904) and (1906).

8 As is said of his 'brother' Stephen in the hour of martyrdom: Acts 7.55.

who has raised the dead[1] condemns you to the abyss of eternal fire'.[2] The blessed Helena heard this, and wondered at his faith. With great zeal she encased the precious Cross in gold and precious stones. She had a silver chest made[3] and in it she encased the Cross of Christ, and she erected a church in the actual place of Calvary.[4]

Judas received the baptism of incorruption[5] in Christ Jesus. As they prayed a faithful flame was shown to them. She commended him to the bishop who was then in place, and he baptized him in Christ Jesus.[6] But while the blessed Helena was still preaching in Jerusalem, it came to pass that the blessed bishop received the sleep in the Spirit.[7] The blessed Helena summoned to her presence Eusebius, bishop of Rome, and he ordained Judas bishop over the church of Christ in Jerusalem.[8] He changed his name, however, and he was called Cyriacus.[9] Now the blessed Helena was full of faith in God, and understood in scripture both the Old Testament and the New; filled with the teaching of the Holy Spirit, she began once more to look earnestly for the nails that had been fixed in the Cross, whereby the unrighteous Jews had crucified the Saviour. And calling to her Judas, who

1 The construction *qui mortuos suscitavit Christus* is sufficiently unusual to warrant the verdict of Borgehammar (1991), 238 that it bespeaks a Greek original.

2 Cf. Matt. 25.41and Rev. 21.8. The Greek speaks more precisely of the 'lowest abyss'.

3 In imitation perhaps of the ark of God in which the scrolls of the Law were housed at Exod. 25.10–16 etc. Egeria, *Pilgrimage* 36–37 records that the contents of this were taken out and exhibited on Good Friday in Jerusalem. After it had received the adoration of the people, the Cross was carried along the way of sorrows at the head of the congregation.

4 Both events are briefly recorded by Rufinus, *Church History* 10.8 and Socrates, *Church History* 1.17. Paulinus, Letter 31 furnishes the most opulent description of the church: 'Brilliant with gilded webs and rich with golden altars, it preserves the Cross stored in a sacred chest.' He adds that the bishop of the city exhibited the Cross every year 'while the passover of the Lord was being celebrated', but not on any other day except at the request of ardent pilgrims. On the archaeology of the church in Jerusalem and related monuments much has been written, most recently by Cameron and Hall (1999), 273–94.

5 This phrase, which couples Acts 13.34 with 1 Cor. 15.53, is first attested in the *Acts of Thomas*, a writing often supposed to be of Syrian provenance. The Greek has 'baptism of regeneration', echoing Tit. 3.5.

6 See above on the baptism of Constantine. It is possible to argue that Matt. 28.19 is enjoining baptism in the Trinity for the nations, whereas Acts 2.38 implies that Jews, who know God already but not Jesus, need only to confess the single name.

7 Cf. the phrase 'sleep in Jesus' at 1 Thess. 4.14; also John 11.11 on Lazarus.

8 The Syriac version states that the original bishop, Macarius, had died, but that good man is entirely absent from the present narrative.

9 Derived from *kurios*, 'Lord'. Rev. 2.17, which says that every saint possesses a new name, may have given rise to the custom of adopting a new name on baptism.

was also called Cyriacus,[1] she said to him, 'Although the desire that I had with regard to the wood of the Cross has been fulfilled, yet sadness hangs over me on account of the fastenings that were fixed in it. No indeed, I shall have no peace in this matter until the Lord has fulfilled my desire. Come here now, and pray to the Lord about this.'[2]

The holy bishop Cyriacus, coming to the place of Calvary along with many brothers who had believed in Jesus Christ on account of the finding of the Sacred Cross and because of the sign that was worked in the dead man,[3] lifted his eyes to heaven and at the same time beating his breast with his hands, cried out from the fulness of his heart to the Lord, confessing the ignorance of former times and blessing all those who had believed in Christ and those who were still going to believe. Now when he had prayed for a long time that a sign would be revealed to him concerning the fastenings in the same way as with regard to the Cross, at the end of the prayer where the *Amen* belongs, such a sign occurred that all of us who were present saw it. A brilliant light shone forth from the place where the Holy Cross was found, brighter than the radiance of the sun, and all at once those nails which had been fixed in the Lord's body[4] appeared like gold glowing in the earth, so that all, believing with no doubts, said 'We know now in whom we have believed'.[5] Receiving two with great awe, he presented them to the blessed Helena, who, falling on her knees and bowing her head, did reverence to them.

Filled as she was with wisdom and knowledge, she wondered long and hard what she ought to do about them.[6] When she had bound herself to search out every avenue of truth, the grace of the Holy Spirit came into her senses,[7] to tell her to make from them at that place a memorial for the

1 Cf. Acts 13.9 on Saul 'who is also called Paul'. Having persecuted the Christians as his predecessor persecuted David, the second Saul had also assumed a less ill-omened name.

2 It is Helena, under the guidance of the Spirit, who discovers the nails in Ambrose, *Death of Theodosius*, 46–47.

3 Miraculous signs evoked belief, according to John 7.31, although the demand for signs is mocked at 4.48.

4 Borgehammar (1991), 238 suggests that the Latin construction, *qui in cruce confixi fuerant*, is a calque upon the Greek of the original.

5 Cf. 2 Tim. 1.12, where Paul speaks of his own belief.

6 Ambrose, *Death of Theodosius* 46 writes 'she knew not what to do' before the discovery of the nails.

7 See Ambrose, *Death of Theodosius* 46 and Paulinus, Letter 31 for prototypes of this eulogy, though only the former goes on to record this anecdote. Socrates, *Church History* 1.17 is the first to use the term 'memorial'.

generation whose coming the prophets had prophesied many generations before. And calling to her a man of great faith and learning, to whom many gave testimonials, she said to him, 'Obey the King's command and perform a royal duty. Take the nails and make from them bits in the rein of a horse that belongs to the King.[1] They will be an invincible weapon against all his adversaries. There will be victory for the King and peace from war.' This was so that what was said by the prophet might be fulfilled: *And it will be in that day that what is in the rein of a horse will be called holy to the Lord.*[2]

As for the blessed Helena, who had confirmed her faith in Jerusalem and completed the whole task, she launched a persecution[3] against the Jews who had not believed, and drove them with threats from Judaea.[4] And such was the grace that attended the holy Bishop Cyriacus that demons were put to flight by his prayer[5] and he healed the infirmities of everyone.[6] And the blessed Helena, bequeathing many funds to the holy Bishop Cyriacus for the relief of the poor, she slept in peace sixteen days before the Kalends of May,[7]

1 Ambrose, *Death of Theodosius* 48 and Rufinus, *Church History* 10.8 report this appropriation of the nails, but do not cite Zechariah or imply that they had any other than a cosmetic function. Borgehammar (1991), 55 reckons both the action and the prophecy among the details likely to been contained already in the narrative of Gelasius.

2 Zech. 14.20. The first narrative of the miracle to cite this verse is Sozomen, *Church History* 2.1; Cyril of Alexandria, however, had alluded to the legend in his *Commentary on Zechariah* 94, while Jerome, in his comment on the same verse, mocks the simplicity of those who would apply it to this event. On the transmission and significance of this prophecy in accounts of the discovery, see Drijvers (1992), 109–13.

3 The Jews suffer from Christians what the latter suffered from both Jews and Gentiles; but the Jews succumb where the Christians survived.

4 Thus repeating the work of Hadrian after Bar-Kokhba's rebellion in 135, and perhaps also imitating the Jews' revenge upon their persecutors in Esther 9, an event commemorated by a festival on the 14th of the month Adar. According to Socrates, *Church History* 7.16, the Jews were wont to re-enact the execution of Hamann at this festival (Esth. 9.25) in open mockery of the Crucifixion. Drijvers and Drijvers (1997), 71n observes that the Protonike narrative ends with the expulsion of the Jews from Rome by Claudius.

5 Exorcism, or the expulsion of demons from a human body, is regarded by almost all our ancient witnesses as a practice confined to Christians and Palestinian Jews: see Acts 16.20 and 19.13–16; Josephus, *Antiquities* 8.2.4; Lucian, *Lover of Lies* 12; Minucius Felix, *Octavius* 27; Preisendanz (1973–74), 4.1227; Origen, *Against Celsus* 5.45; Athanasius, *On the Incarnation* 30.6. Too many scholars have cited Philostratus, *Life of Apollonius* 3.38 and 4.20 as though these singular passages were proof of a widespread custom in the Hellenistic world.

6 Such miracles were attributed to the apostles by their admirers (Acts 3.1 etc.), and even perhaps by Paul to himself (Rom. 15.19).

7 That is on 16 April by inclusive counting. Cf. Bradbury (1996), 121 and 130 on the equally illusory precision of Severus of Minorca.

requesting all men who love Christ, along with their wives, to keep a festival in remembrance of the day on which the Holy Cross was found, the fifth day after the Nones of May.[1] And may all those who keep the Cross in remembrance receive a portion with holy Mary the mother of the Lord.[2] HERE ENDS THE FINDING[3] OF THE HOLY CROSS.

1 That is, by inclusive counting, on 11 May, though it may be that *post* here is a mistake for *ante*, since the usual date for the celebration of the discovery in the west was 3 May (i.e. five days by inclusive counting before the seventh). Neither date falls within Eastertide, which never fell later than 21 April in the Roman world. Paulinus, Letter 31 appears to say, by contrast, that Easter was the only season at which the Cross was commonly on display. Egeria, *Pilgrimage* 37 confirms that the occasion was Good Friday. Nevertheless, the feast of the elevation of the Cross was 14 September, according to the Greek and to Borgehammar (1991), 96–104. The Syriac does not specify a date.

2 The title 'Mother of God' is already bestowed by Constantine on Mary at *Oration* 11, and may translate the formula *dei genetrix* which occurs in the present passage. Wright (1991) observes that a variety of Latin titles continued to be current in Latin authors after Constantine.

3 The title of the original rather than the composite narrative; see n. 1 above.

STORY OF THE DISCOVERY OF THE HONOURABLE AND LIFE-GIVING[1] CROSS

The three hundred and third year since Our Lord's Passion[2] was being accomplished, when the seeking and discovery of the life-giving Cross took place. The ruler at that time was Constantine, that man most beloved of God,[3] whose mother was Helena, the right worshipful lover of Christ.[4] Having made a diligent study of the incarnation[5] of Our Lord Jesus Christ and his elevation on the Cross[6] and his resurrection from the dead, and possessed as she was of great intellect, she strove with zeal and faith to seek out the august and precious Cross of Christ and to show this to the world. And she journeyed to Jerusalem on the twenty-eighth day of the second month[7] with a host of soldiers. And having convened an assembly,[8] she called together the Jews who were in Jerusalem and those who were in the neighbouring cities and villages. And the total number of Jews who were gathered was found to be two thousand,[9] and when she had summoned them,

1 Both these epithets are explained in the text below.

2 Reckoning from the fifteenth year of Tiberius in 29/30 (Luke 3.1), this brings us to 331/2.

3 The adjective *theophilos* (of which the superlative *theophilestatos* occurs here) can mean 'loving God' (Clement of Alexandria, *Rich Man's Salvation* 34), but when accompanied by explicit reference to a person's secular or sacred office, almost always means 'loved by God' (see e.g. Athanasius, *Apology to Constantius* 1). Cameron and Hall (1999), 138–39 believe that Eusebius applies it to both Helena and Constantine in the former sense at *Constantine* 3.43.4, and in the latter at *Constantine* 3.47.1.

4 The Greek word is *philochristos*. When applied by Eusebius to Constantine's father in the titular inscriptions to *Constantine*, p.3.25 Winkelmann, the epithet *philochristos* indicates a sympathetic disposition to Christianity, rather than formal adherence. *Christophilos* may bear the same sense in chapter 7 of the Byzantine life of Constantine at Lieu and Montserrat (1996), 113. Both compounds seem to be most frequently epithets of the laity (cf. Mark the Deacon, *Life of Porphyry* 69, 70, 76, 84, 93. 103).

5 *Enanthropêsis* (literally, becoming man, rather than becoming flesh as John 1.14 and the Latin *incarnatio* suggest) was a technical term in Greek since the early third century: Hippolytus, *Commentary on Daniel* 4.49.1. See note to the Latin text on the rendering of it.

6 Cf. John 3.19 and 12.31.

7 That is 28 February, so the year is 302.

8 Using the term *ekklêsia* in its classical and secular meaning, rather than in the sense of 'Church', which was now more usual.

9 Three thousand in the Latin, on which see my note.

the blessed Helena spoke as follows: 'I have learned from the divine and holy scriptures that you were a righteous seed beloved of God,[1] yet you did not understand, but, deeming light to be darkness and truth to be a lie, poured curses on the God who wished to redeem you from the ancient curse, you chose to reckon among the dead the one who raised the dead and the one who brought you light with his spittle you spat on with unclean spitting.[2] Now, however, I say to you, choose for yourselves those whom you consider precisely learned in the Law, so that perhaps you may answer me about the matter on which I am about to interrogate you.'

Now they came in great fear, and after examining themselves, they found that those who reckoned themselves learned in the law were a thousand men;[3] in a body they came before the blessed Helena, testifying about the thousand men, that 'these are the ones who are well and precisely learned in the law'. For her part, she repeated what she had said and after much study[4] said, 'Hear what I say and pay heed to the words of my mouth.[5] You have not heard the holy scriptures, how the prophets made predictions about Our Saviour Jesus Christ, because the Holy Spirit was speaking through the prophets. *A boy has been born to us and his mother shall not know a man.*[6] And again the hymn-writer David [says] *I saw the Lord always before my face, because he is at my right hand lest I stumble.*[7] And Isaiah declared of you, *I have begotten sons, but they have set me at nought.* And again he says *The ox knows his master and the ass his crib, but Israel does not know me and my people have not understood me.*[8] See then, you who con the law, you do not know it, and hence I command that you be detained by the soldiers, and that after discussion you choose for yourselves those who reckon to be precisely learned in the law.'

---

1 This phrase could be constructed from Wis. 10.16, Ecclus. 47.22, Isa. 44.2 and 61.9 in the Septuagint, though the closest parallel is perhaps at *Testament of Levi* 2.

2 See Latin version for biblical references. Such antitheses would have been familiar to the author and his readers from paschal liturgies: cf. Melito of Sardis, *On the Pasch* p. 12.10–14.

3 A surprisingly high proportion (50%) of the total of 2000. The Latin text estimated the total at 3000, which yields a slightly more plausible fraction.

4 A longer clause than in the Latin version.

5 The first part of the sentence is commonplace, the second alludes to Ps. 53.2 in the Septuagint.

6 Isa. 9.6, but with an added reference to the virgin birth which is not found in the Septuagint or in any other witness known to me.

7 See note to this citation of Ps. 16.8 in the Latin.

8 Isa. 1.2–3.

Soon they went away again and holding a council among themselves,[1] they chose fifty men who were precisely learned in the law. And when they came to the queen she said 'Who are these?', and they said, 'These are the ones who are precisely acquainted with the law'. And beginning again the blessed Helena taught them the lore of truth, saying 'How long have you, foolish Israel, not been content with your ancient error and the blindness of your fathers, saying that Jesus is not the Son of God while you have the prophets in your possession and con them yet have no knowledge of the law?'[2] But they said, 'We do indeed con[3] and know, and we understand the law well. But tell us, mistress, the purpose of your interrogation, so that knowing it we may give an answer to the things you say.' And she replied to them, 'Go away on your own again, and choose for yourselves with great precision those who are credited with learning in the law, and consider the more precise inquiries I shall put to you.'

And when they came, they said to one another, 'For what reason do you think the queen is visiting these labours and interrogations on us?' And one of them, Judas by name,[4] answered them, 'I know that she wants to make an inquiry about the wood[5] on which our fathers[6] hanged the Messiah. Take care, therefore, that no-one confesses to her; for then indeed our paternal traditions will be absolutely destroyed. For Zaccheus my grandfather as he was dying enjoined this on my father, and my father as he was dying enjoined it on me, saying "Know, my son, that an inquiry is to take place about the wood on which the Messiah was hanged. When, therefore, the

1 When used of Jewish gatherings, the word *sumboulion* has the connotation of conspiracy, e.g. at Mark 15.1.

2 See the Latin for the biblical allusions here.

3 Playing on *anagignôskein* (to read) and *gignôskein* (to know), perhaps with an unconscious reminiscence of the contrast between reading and understanding drawn by Paul at 2 Cor. 3.14–15.

4 See my note to the Latin for the obvious significance of the name. Borgehammar (1991), 174–75 proposes that the author may have been acquainted with the traditions now preserved in the Aramaic targums or paraphrases of the Hebrew. Targum Onkelos construes Gen. 49.8 as though it had glossed the name of Judas as 'you will confess and not be ashamed'; Targum Neofiti states that 'all Jews shall be named after him'; Targum Pseudo-Jonathan combines these interpretations.

5 The word *xulon* (wood) often functions in biblical Greek as a synonym for tree, e.g. in the curse on the hanged malefactor at Deut. 21.22–23. Our author observes the apostolic practice of styling the Cross a *xulon* in its patibulary function (Acts 13.29; cf. Gal. 3.13), and a *stauros* when considered as an instrument of faith (1 Cor. 1.18).

6 The speaker may be attempting to reduce the culpability of the murderers by applying to them a phrase more properly used of the patriarchs, e.g. at John 6.31 and 1 Cor. 10.1.

quest for the Cross is about to commence, reveal it quickly before you suffer painful retribution. For no longer does the race of Hebrews reign,[1] but the kingdom and the glory will be of those who adore the crucified one, for he will reign for ages of ages."

'And I said to him, "Father, if you knew that this Jesus was the Christ, why did our fathers lay hands upon him?" And he said to me, "Listen, son. His stainless name[2] is aware that I never sat in counsel with those who reviled him, but even spoke against those who disbelieved in him. For that matter, neither did our fathers[3] join the conspiracy, nor did they concur[4] with those who crucified Jesus, but when he denounced the elders and the chief priests,[5] they condemned him, imagining that it was in their power to put him to death, while in fact they put him to death in his manhood, but he himself, being true God, remained impassible and immortal. And when they took him down from the Cross, they placed him in a tomb, setting over him also soldiers as guards, and rising within three days he revealed himself to his disciples. Hence also Stephen, the brother of my grandfather's father,[6] believed and began to teach the people the facts about Jesus. And, after convening a council,[7] the Sadducees with the Pharisees condemned him, and brought the whole of the multitude together, and they stoned him to death. None the less, that blessed one, as on the point of giving up his soul, spreading his hands to heaven, said, *Lord, do not lay this sin to their charge.* Listen, therefore, my son, so that I may teach you about the holy Christ and his goodness. [I tell you] that Saul too, who sat by the temple and was also a

1 The Jews have lost their character as a royal priesthood (Exod. 19.6) and will not be the beneficiaries of the promises at Dan. 2.44 and 7.27.

2 A hyperbolic instance of the notorious reluctance of the Jews to allude to God directly: cf. Deut. 12.21. The word *akhrantos* ('stainless') is used at Exod. 17.6 and Lam. 4.7 in non-Septuagintal versions, but not applied to the name of God in these passages or in other texts known to me. On the exalted name of Jesus see Phil. 2.9–10.

3 In the Latin only the first person is used, and the confusion of the Greek MSS at this point suggests to Borgehammar (1991), 252 that the Latin has preserved the original sense. In view of what is later said about Stephen, a redactor may be attempting to purge the impossible suggestion that the grandfather of Judas was a contemporary of Stephen, but his previous words 'I never sat in counsel' reveal that this was indeed his original claim.

4 The word used of Paul when he consents to Stephen's death at Acts 7.60.

5 These are the ones who try Jesus at Matt. 27.1 and Luke 22.36.

6 Stephen is now alleged to have lived two generations earlier than the grandfather of Judas; the interval is still impossibly short. See my introduction on the chronology, where I assume, with Borgehammar, that the Latin is truer to the primitive version.

7 Cf. Acts 6.12 for the term *sunedrion,* which may denote the sanhedrin (ruling body of the Jews in major cities) or a more informal gathering.

tentrope-maker,[1] was himself a persecutor of those who did not put their faith in the law. And he it was who roused the people against our father Stephen,[2] and was consenting to his death; but taking compassion on him, the Lord made him also one of his own illustrious disciples. This is the reason why I and my fathers have believed that he is truly the Son of God.[3] And you therefore, son, do not blaspheme against him, nor those who hope in him, and you shall possess eternal life."

'This, friends, is what my father Simon[4] enjoined on me when he was about to die. There, you have heard all; what do you wish to do about this? If the queen interrogates us about the Cross, what shall we say to her?' And in answer they said, 'We have never heard such things as we have heard today from you. But if an inquiry takes place about this, no-one is to confess.' As they were saying this, soldiers came to them, saying, 'Come, the queen summons you'. Now when they had come before her they gave her many answers, but did not speak the truth. Finally the queen, moved by the Holy Spirit, ordered them all to be cast into the fire. In great fear they handed Judas over to her, saying, 'This man is the son of one who was upright and a prophet, and is precisely learned in the law beyond all of us. Detain this man alone, and he will impart to you the desires of your heart.'[5] And as they all gave testimony as one, she dismissed them apart from Judas, and calling him to her, said, 'Life and death are set before you; choose which you prefer'. Judas said, 'And who, placed in the wilderness with bread close by, eats stones?'[6] And she said to him, 'If then you wish to live, both on earth and in heaven, tell me where is the Cross of Christ hidden?' Judas said, 'As is contained in the records,[7] it is three hundred and three years, and how can we, latecomers as we are, learn the facts about the Cross and where it is

1 Cf. Acts 18.3. The Greek is *himantomos* in the version here translated, on which see Borgehammar (1991), 238 and the Latin text on the word *skêno(g)rafia*.

2 Either he means simply a blood-relative of an earlier generation, or else he is already speaking as a Christian, as though the apostles were his patriarchs.

3 Cf. Mark 15.39 and Matt. 27.54.

4 The name has been deferred, as is common in both Greek and biblical narratives: Luke 7.40 etc.

5 Reminiscent of Ps. 37.4, this phrase, on the lips of mandarins in the fourth century, connotes a pious wish that is not to be satisfied without recourse to some uncommon measure: Mark the Deacon, *Life of Porphyry* 36.

6 See the Latin text for the biblical references in these sentences.

7 It was only to be expected that the Jews would have their own records (*hypomnêmata*) of the Passion, to match those disseminated by the pagans under the title *Acts of Pilate*: Eusebius, *Church History* 1.9.3.

hidden?' The blessed Helena said to him, 'How is it that so many generations ago a war broke out in Ilium and those who died there are held in remembrance, along with their sites and tombs?'[1] And Judas said, 'Begging your pardon, mistress, from written accounts, but we have not even one in written form'. The blessed Helena said, 'A short while ago you confessed to me that there are records'. Judas said, 'Pardon me, I was guessing when I spoke'. And the blessed Helena said, 'I have the certain and inspired voice of the holy gospel as to the place where Christ was crucified, just show me the so-called Place of the Skull, and I on my own authority shall give orders to everyone and have the earth of that place dug up, and the Lord God will fulfil my desire'. Judas said, 'Mistress, do as you will with me, for I am not acquainted with the place, nor have I found anything written about it'. Then the queen said to him, 'I want you to understand that if you do not confess to me I shall starve you to death'.[2] And having said this, she ordered him to be thrust into a dry well, in which there was no water, and ordained that he should remain there without food for seven days.

But after the seven days he cried out from the well of the pit,[3] saying, 'Pull me out and I shall show you the place Christ was crucified'. Then Judas was pulled up from the well, and went to the place in which Christ had been crucified. Not knowing, however, precisely where it was situated, he lifted his voice, praying in the Hebrew language and speaking thus:

> God, who madest heaven and earth, who with thy span hast measured the heaven and hast the earth in thy hand, who sittest upon the chariot of the Cherubim, and these swim in their courses in the immeasurable light to which human nature cannot attain, for it is thou who hast made them for thy service; and they minister unto thee saying with ceaseless voice, *Holy, holy, holy*, some of whom are also called the Cherubim, while some thou hast placed in paradise to guard the tree of life, and these are called Seraphim.[4] Thou, however, dost hold sovereignty over them, thou who didst consign the

1 See note to the Latin text.

2 The Latin contains only a threat to kill.

3 The word *lakkos* is used by the Septuagint at Genesis 37 of the pit in which Joseph was imprisoned on the advice of his brother Judah. The author may also be glancing ironically at Jer. 2.13 where the faithlessness of Israel is likened to a dry well.

4 I have suggested in a note on the Latin that an authentic Jewish tradition may be commemorated here. However, we should also take note of the theory of Borgehammar (1991), 176, that the author has misread 2 Enoch 21.1.

disobedient angels to the depths of Tartarus,[1] and now they are beneath the barricaded doors[2] of the abyss, undergoing punishment until the end, and they cannot speak against thy commandment. And now, sovereign Lord God, if it is thy will that the son of Mary the beautiful dove,[3] the one you sent, should reign – for had he not been from thee he would not have done such works of power, and had he not indeed been thy Son thou wouldst not have raised him again from the dead – perform for us therefore this miracle. As thou didst hear thy servant[4] Moses and didst show to him the bones of our brother Joseph[5] when they were hidden, so too now, Lord, reveal to us thy hidden treasure and where the Cross of Christ lies, cause to ascend from that same place the smoke of the fragrance of sweetness, so that I also, sinner as I am, shall believe in the crucified Christ, that he is the king of Israel and saviour of the world and of Jerusalem,[6] unto the ages.

As soon as Judas had intoned this prayer the place was shaken, and a mass of smoke, as it were the fragrance of aromas,[7] ascended from that place, so that Judas in wonder clapped both his hands, and said, 'In truth thou, Christ, art saviour of the world, thou art the Son of the Living God. I give thee thanks, Lord, because, unworthy as I am, thou hast not deemed me unworthy to be a partaker[8] of thy grace. Wherefore I pray, Lord, that thou mayest not be mindful of my sins, and mayest number me with thy first martyr[9]

1 Cf. Job 40.15 for this use of the Homeric name Tartarus to denote the infernal regions, together with *Testament of Solomon* 6 and 1 Enoch 10 on the imprisonment of the fallen angels. At 1 Enoch 20–21 the name of Tartarus and a word which seems to mean 'chaotic' are juxtaposed.

2 This seems to be the meaning of this unusual pair of words – perhaps a fortified variant of the 'gates of hell' at Matt. 16.18; cf. Rev. 1.18.

3 This may be the earliest application of Song of Songs 1.15 to Mary.

4 Borrowing the word *therapôn* from Exod. 4.10 etc.

5 Some MSS add 'in the river'. Borgehammar (1991), 176–77 notes that, whereas Gen. 50.25 does not say in what manner the bones of Joseph the patriarch were recovered, the story that his bones were found in the Nile may be the subject of an allusion in Philo, *On Dreams* 2.109. The typology is dense here, for not only was Joseph imprisoned in a well (Gen. 37), but the burial of his bones was interpreted by some Christians as an allegory of the sealing of the tablets of the Law within the ark: see Ephraem, *Nisibene Hymn* 43.1. Borgehammar goes on to point out that an analogy may be implied between the ark of the law and the casket of the Cross.

6 The reference to Jerusalem is peculiar to the Greek, which no doubt has in mind such prophecies as Gen. 49.10, Isa. 28.16 and Rev. 21.2.

7 See the Latin on the significance of Eph. 5.2 and other references.

8 Cf. 2 Pet. 1.4, where Christians are said to be partakers (*metokhoi*) of the divine nature.

9 The title protomartyr was perhaps first applied to Stephen in Jerusalem and in the fourth century.

Stephen, seeing that I too am of his stock.'[1] And, having said this, Judas, taking a spade, began to dig with the rest of the great multitude, and when they had dug as far as twenty ells, they found three crosses buried. Judas took these and brought them up to the city. Now those in Jerusalem were waiting for the glory of God,[2] and behold it was close to the ninth hour, and Judas brought the three crosses to the queen. And she, receiving the crosses with great joy, and clasping them said to him, 'And how shall I know now Judas, which is the cross of Christ? For we know that along with Jesus were crucified two good-for-nothing robbers, as the evangelists write, and that the three are equal.' Then he placed them in the midst of the city, and behold after a short time, a dead youth was brought in lying on a bed. And Judas, full of joy and filled with spiritual understanding, took hold of the bed and caused it to be put down on the ground, saying to the queen, 'Now you see, mistress, which is the desired Cross, and the power of it'. And as he placed the two crosses, one by one, upon the dead man, no sign occurred with them. But when he came to the third Cross and placed it upon the corpse, forthwith the gates of death were opened, and the dead youth arose, and to all was revealed the glory of God. Thereupon many of the Jews, seeing the immediate resurrection of the corpse, believed in our Lord Jesus Christ. Upon the occurrence of this great wonder, there came a voice from the air; it was that of the devil, saying in fury, 'Who is this who does not permit me to receive human souls? Jesus of Nazareth, you have drawn them all to you and has your Cross once more been revealed against me? Judas, why have you done this? For it was through Judas the traitor that I first caused the people of Israel to go astray; and now through a Judas I am driven hence. I too shall devise a Judas plan, and carry it out against you, for using my authority and power I shall contrive to raise another king, who will forsake the crucified one and readily follow my counsels and my will.[3] You I shall give over to terrible and manifold torments, so that after long retribution you will deny the crucified one.' Judas heard this, and enraged against the unclean spirit, he said, 'Wicked demon, may Christ who has raised the dead drag you down to

---

1 The Greek word is *genos*; but notwithstanding the genealogy constructed for him in the present text, Acts 6.5 implies that Stephen was a Gentile.

2 Cf. Matt. 15.43 ('waiting for the kingdom'). The crowd appears to be engaged in commemoration of the Passion, hence the significance of the ninth hour, which marks the time at which Jesus expired (Mark 15.34 etc.).

3 See notes to the Latin text on Cyriacus' martyrdom under Julian.

the lowest abyss of fire[1] for your own destruction'. And on hearing this the devil forthwith became invisible.

The blessed Helena glorified the power of God and wondered at the faith of Judas. Then the blessed Helena shielded the precious Cross of Christ very securely in gold and precious stones, and, having constructed a silver casket, she used it to shield for the Cross in a dignified and honourable manner. And having ordained the building of a church on the Place of the Skull, she deposited the Cross in the church to be guarded; as for Judas, once he had received the washing[2] of faith in Christ, she presented him to the bishop of that time. But while the blessed Helena was still dwelling in Jerusalem, it came to pass that the most holy bishop rested[3] in the Lord. The blessed Helena therefore summoned the bishop of Rome, Eusebius by name,[4] and he installed Judas as bishop to govern the church of Christ, having changed his name to Cyriacus. Now the thrice-blessed Helena, schooled as she was in the power of the law of God, had also learned with precision the teachings of the new instruction of Christ; recalling the statements of the holy scriptures, she next resolved to search for the nails that had been fixed in the Cross of Christ. So a second search began, and the blessed Helena said to Judas, who was also called Cyriacus, 'Although the desire that I had with regard to the wood of the Cross has been fulfilled, yet great sadness rests upon me on account of the nails that were fixed in it. Therefore I shall have no peace until the Lord has fulfilled my desire in this matter too.' Then the holy bishop Cyriacus, coming to the Place of the Skull along with many brothers who had believed in our Lord Jesus Christ on account of the finding of the Sacred Cross and the resurrection of the corpse, lifted his eyes to heaven and beat his breast with his hands, praying strenuously to the Lord. He made a long prayer in the Hebrew tongue[5] that

1 For the geography of Hell cf. 1 Enoch 21.

2 That is, baptism, which is described as a washing at 1 Cor. 6.11 and Tit. 3.5. The wording (a partial echo of Gal. 3.26–27) implies that faith ought to accompany the rite, though this need not exclude a practice of infant baptism, which was common throughout the Church in this author's day. Here it is not said that Judas was baptized in the name of the Trinity, as Constantine was; baptism in the name of Jesus alone is the usual rite in Acts, and Cyprian, Letter 63 explains that it was reserved for Jews, who already knew the Creator as their Father.

3 'Sleeping in Christ' is a Pauline synonym for death: 1 Thess. 4.14. Not so common in prose as in verse among pagan Greeks, the usage may have gained currency among Christians because it was attributed to Christ at Matt. 9.24 and John 11.11.

4 Here introduced for the first time, though in the Latin and Syriac he is already the minister of baptism to Constantine; see notes to the Latin at this point.

5 The words 'in the Hebrew tongue' are not in the Latin.

the nails fixed in the Cross would also be revealed to him; the prayer went on for a long time, and he had pronounced the Amen, when a sign occurred which was also witnessed by the bystanders, for a glow like a flash of lightning shone forth from that place. The nails of the Cross shone too in that place, flashing like gold more than the rays of the sun, so that all, without doubting, said 'We know now in whom we have believed'.[1] Receiving them with great awe, the bishop presented them to Helena, God's favourite, who on beholding them fell to her knees and bowed her head, and with great awe she thanked the Lord, the giver of good things.

As she was pondering deeply what she was to do with the glorious nails, the wisdom of God put it into her mind to be the cause of great salvation to forthcoming generations. And calling to her a man of great faith and wisdom, she said to him, 'Honour the King's command and the mystery.[2] Take the nails and make from them a bit in the rein of a horse on which the King sits, and they will be an invincible weapon against all his adversaries – victory for the King and peace from war.' And he took them and did what was commanded. This was so that what was said by the prophet might be fulfilled: *And it shall be in those days that what is in the rein of the King's horse will be called holy to the Lord.*[3] The blessed Helena had confirmed her faith in Jerusalem and completed everything in a holy, righteous and pious manner; having bequeathed many funds to the most holy bishop Cyriacus for his ministry to the poor, she also launched a persecution against the Jews, and those who had not believed in Christ the Saviour were driven from Judaea and scattered throughout the earth.[4] And such was the grace that was given the holy Bishop Cyriacus that he even drove out demons by his word

1 Cf. 2 Tim. 1.12.

2 Matt. 13.11 and Eph. 5.22 appear to authorize the use of the term *mustêrion* as a synonym for 'parable' (cf. Justin, *Trypho* 68.4). But Helena, in applying the term to a relic of the Cross, may have in mind the Pauline use of it to denote God's hidden purpose as revealed in Christ, and especially the disclosure of the true intent of scripture in opposition of the Jews (Rom. 11.25). When Christians began to describe their feats in the vocabulary of the pagan rites, it was naturally the eucharist or *pascha* that was reckoned to be the mystery *par excellence*, as already in Melito's paschal homily of the second century (p. 2.7), and the Passion itself is spoken of as 'the mystery' by authors such as Cyril of Alexandria, *To Nestorius* 3.6.

3 Zech. 14.20 in the Septuagint (the Hebrew says nothing of a king). See note on the Latin text.

4 Whereas the Latin speaks of a persecution, the Greek word *diasparêsas* recalls the dispersal (*diaspora*) of the Jews by Hadrian in 135, which is commemorated with pleasure by Eusebius, *Church History*. If, as I have suggested in the introduction, this narrative was originally set in the reign of Domitian, the penalty will have been inflicted by Hadrian himself.

and breath.[1] Now [Helena] took the precious and holy wood of the most venerable and life-giving[2] Cross, along with the holy and august nails by which Christ our God[3] allowed himself to be transfixed for our sake, and set them up in Jerusalem and Byzantium. Perfect in faith, piously revering the holy and consubstantial[4] Trinity, and having spread the faith of Christians in every place where she had tarried, she fell asleep,[5] enjoining all who believed in Christ to celebrate in remembrance of the day on which the Holy Cross was found, the fourteenth of the month of September,[6] so that all those who keep the Cross in remembrance may receive the portion of the Mother of God and all the saints, through our Lord Jesus Christ, to whom be glory and majesty, now and always and unto ages of ages.[7] Amen.

1 The fourth-century Bishop Cyril of Jerusalem, *Catechetical Homilies* 16.19 and 20.3 is the first witness to the role of breath (*emphusêma*) in the exorcism of demons, though the breath of Christ had already infused the Holy Spirit into his apostles at John 20.22.

2 The term *zôopoios* (applied to Christ at 1 Cor. 15.45) is used of a pictorial representation of the Cross, though not of the relic itself, by Eusebius, *Tricennalian Oration* 9 (p. 219.8 Heikel).

3 Christ is styled our God as early as Tit. 2.13; the corollary that God died on the Cross, though freely stated in a *Paschal Homily* by the second-century Melito of Sardis, was seldom drawn so explicitly as in the present passage by ecclesiastical writers of the fifth century (see e.g. Cyril of Alexandria, *Third Letter to Nestorius*, anathema 12, which states only that God the Word tasted death for us).

4 The term introduced at the Council of Nicaea in 325 as a test of clerical orthodoxy. It means that the Second Person of the Trinity shares the nature of the Father, and by the late fourth century was taken to imply that that there is no gradation in dignity between them. No conciliar formula declares (although the Nicene Fathers certainly believed) that the Holy Spirit is consubstantial with the Father, and the epithet would not have found its way into Helena's orisons to the Trinity, or indeed into any such prayer before the late fourth century.

5 Cf. John 11.11, 1 Thess. 4.13.

6 According to Borgehammar (1991), 100, this was the Encaenia of the Church of the Holy Sepulchre. See the Latin for a different date.

7 The familiar termination of the Lord's Prayer, found neither in Luke nor in Matthew, but first at *Didache* 9.2 or at 1 Clement 38.

THE EDICT OF CONSTANTINE TO POPE SILVESTER

1. In the name of the holy and indivisible[1] Trinity, namely the Father, the Son and the Holy Spirit,[2] the Emperor Caesar Flavius Constantine, in Christ Jesus, one of that same Holy Trinity, our Saviour[3] the Lord God, [Constantine] the faithful, benign[4] and beneficent, the pious, fortunate and triumphant victor over the Alemanni,[5] Goths,[6] Sarmatians,[7] Germans,[8]

1 The assertion that the Father, Son and Spirit are indivisible, and therefore one, is an axiom of all Trinitarian arguments after the Council of Nicaea in 325. It may have found its way into a confession when the would-be-orthodox heretic Marcellus of Ancyra appealed to the bishop of Rome in 341. For his creed see Epiphanius, *Panarion* 72.2–3, with Kinzig and Vincent (1999), 550–52.

2 Not an entirely gratuitous amplification, as the first Christian who is known to have used the Greek word *trias,* Theophilus of Antioch (*To Autolycus* 2.15), named the three as Father, Logos and Sophia. Although the Greek word *trias* has a wider sense than our word 'Trinity', the essentials of Trinitarian theology after 325 were always that: (a) God is Father, Son and Spirit; (b) the Son and Spirit both depend for their existence on the Father; (c) each of the three has its distinct or hypostatic existence; (d) none the less, there is one God, indivisible and unchanged.

3 Meaning Christ, if this is an echo of Tit. 2.13, and the verse is so interpreted as to make 'God' and 'Saviour' titles of the same party. Huyghebaert (1976), 61 observes that the title Saviour is employed in the *Donation* even where it did not appear in the *Acts of Silvester*, and draws the tenuous inference (cf. Huyghebaert (1979), 181–82) that the author was a cleric, not a monk.

4 Mirbt and Aland (1967), 251 and Fuhrmann (1968) add the epithet Maximus, 'supreme'.

5 A variant of this title, Alamannicus, is attested in an inscription cited by Barnes (1976c), 150; for numismatic and epigraphic evidence of the occasion see Barnes (1981), 66 and n. 31. Cf. *Latin Panegyrics* 4(10).18, although the title Alamannicus is not attested here or in any literary account of Constantine. Consequently, unless he possessed an accurate written source that we have lost, there is good reason for suspecting that author has transferred to him a title of Theodosius (*Panegyrics* 2(12).5), or else that he wishes Constantine to anticipate the victory of Clovis, the founder of the Frankish kingdom, over this people. Gregory of Tours, *History of the Franks* 1.30 clearly has the Milvian Bridge in mind when he asserts that this was the battle in which Clovis turned to Christ and that his baptism was an almost immediate sequel.

6 Following Eutropius, *Breviary* 10.7.1, Barnes (1976c), 153 opines that it was only after 324 that Constantine acquired the title Gothicus in his own right, though he may have shared an earlier accolade with Galerius (Eusebius, *Church History* 8.17.3). A late victory over this Germanic people is also recorded by Eusebius, *Constantine* 4.5.1; Aurelius Victor, *Caesars* 41 names only the Goths and Sarmatians as Constantine's adversaries, while *Epitome on the Caesars* 41 thinks only the Goths worthy of record.

Britons[1] and Huns,[2] ever Augustus:[3] to the most holy and blessed father of fathers[4] Silvester,[5] bishop and pope[6] of the city of Rome, and to all of his

---

7 Though the last campaign against the Sarmatians is the most famous (Eusebius, *Constantine* 4.320), Barnes (1976c), 149 deduces from the position of the epithet Sarmaticus in an inscription that a victory must have taken place within a year of Constantine's accession in 306. See further the Latin version of the *Advent of the Holy Cross* in this volume.

8 As many as four such victories can be verified from *Latin Panegyrics* 7(6).4.2, 6(7).10.2, 4(10).16.5 and other sources attested in Barnes (1976c).

1 Possibly an allusion to a campaign against the Picts which he undertook with his father Constantius: see *Latin Panegyrics* 6(7).7. When the title Britannicus appears in inscriptions of 315 and 318, however, Barnes (1976c), 153–54 suggests that it refers to small excursions later in his reign.

2 Only in the late fourth century did Roman emperors start to claim victories against this people; again our author may have borrowed the royal nomenclature of Theodosius the Great at *Latin Panegyrics* 2(12).11 and 2(12).32. Or – and this would be another testimony to his learning, if not his acumen – he may have been acquainted with the inaccurate tradition of the Byzantine life at Opitz (1934), 568. He may also have had in mind the frequent wars of Charlemagne against these foes: Einhard, *Life of Charlemagne* 13, *Annals of the Franks* for year 790 etc.

3 The title conferred by the Senate on Octavian, the founder of the Principate, in 27 BC. It was borne by subsequent emperors, and was more than a formality to Constantine, whose panegyrics frequently liken him to the first Augustus.

4 Implying that the bishop of Rome is the supreme patriarch, but avoiding that Greek term, which (notwithstanding Isidore of Seville, *Origins* 7.12.4 and the use of *patriarchium* by Pope Stephen at Mirbt and Aland (1967), 115) was seldom used in the west. This passage may be intended as a rebuttal of the pretensions of the bishop of Constantinople to be the 'oecumenical' (i.e. worldwide) patriarch. Cf. the expostulatory letter of Gregory the Great to John of Constantinople (595 AD) in Mirbt and Aland (1967), 244–45.

5 Bishop of Rome from 31 January 314 to 31 December 335, and thus the one whose tenure spans almost the entirety of the reign of Constantine. None the less, little is known of relations between him and the emperor, with the exception of the many endowments enumerated in the *Book of Pontiffs*, where the life of Silvester is the longest before the eighth century. Both Yarnold (1993), 96 and Fowden (1994b), 156–57 find the first evidence of Silvester's role in a homily by Jacob of Serug, written c. 500 and studied at length by Frothingham (1883). He appears as the minister of Constantine's baptism in *LP*, p. 75 Duchesne. This account can claim more verisimilitude than that which makes Eusebius of Rome the celebrant, since the latter's tenure of the Roman see ended at least four years before Constantine's conversion.

6 This word appears to derive from a colloquial Greek equivalent for patriarch, which was applied to bishops of a number of sees, especially Alexandria. In the west it is bestowed on a local bishop at *Passion of Perpetua* 13.3, on the bishop of Rome or Carthage by Tertullian, *On Decorum* 13, on Cyprian of Carthage by the antipope Novatian in the superscriptions to letters 30 and 31 of Cyprian's correspondence, and on Silvester himself in a somewhat barbed epistle from the prelates at the Council of Arles in 314 (Optatus, *Against the Donatists*, appendix 4).

successors,[1] who shall sit in the chair of Peter[2] up to the end of the age, and furthermore to all the most reverend[3] and God-beloved catholic[4] bishops who are subject to that same most holy Roman church throughout the whole earth according to this imperial constitution of ours,[5] established as they are for all foregoing times as well as for the present and for posterity. Grace, peace, love, joy, long-suffering and mercy[6] be with you all from God the Father Almighty, and Jesus Christ his Son, and the Holy Spirit.

2. As to the things that our Saviour and redeemer the Lord Jesus Christ, Son of the Most High Father, has done in his wondrous condescension, through his holy apostles Peter and Paul with the mediation of our father[7] Silvester,

1 Rome was the first bishopric to possess a list of successive incumbents from apostolic times: the one preserved by Irenaeus, *Against Heresies* 3.2, was preceded by that of Hegesippus and succeeded by others, culminating in the *Book of Pontiffs*. There is strong agreement between the lists, but not perfect unanimity, and there is even less agreement among modern scholars as to when Rome came to function as a monarchical episcopate, rather than as a synod with the 'bishop' as its chairman. See Brent (1995) on Roman governance; Molland (1950) on the nature of the succession; Turner (1916/17) on disparities between the pontifical lists.

2 At some time this became a physical artefact, according to Ruysschaert (1973), though we may be sure that it was not yet so in the reign of Constantine. Optatus, *Against the Donatists* 2.2 makes Peter a bishop, not merely the appointer of bishops as in Irenaeus, and speaks of his seat or *cathedra*.

3 As elsewhere, Migne reads *reverendissimis* where Mirbt and Aland (1967) regularly read *reverentissimis*.

4 First attested in Ignatius, *Smyrnaeans* 8.3, this term implies that certain rites and doctrines are common to the Church as a whole and cannot be ignored or contravened by any local congregation without incurring the charge of schism. Most of those who held this view inferred that it was the privilege and duty of the bishops to collaborate in preserving the rule of faith. Constantine's devotion to catholicity is attested (for example) by his letters in appendices 3 and 9 to Optatus, *Against the Donatists*.

5 The fact that this decree purports to create, or at least to ratify, the precedence of the Roman see would have made it unpalatable to the early bishops, such as Leo the Great, who held that Rome owed its precedence to its apostolic foundation. A similar scruple in the early middle ages led to the deletion of a reference to Constantine's decree in version (B) of the *Acts of Silvester*: Pohlkamp (1988), 444–45.

6 Grace and peace are the usual terms in Pauline salutations (Rom. 1.7, 1 Cor. 1.3, Gal. 1.3, Eph. 1.3, Phil. 1.2, Col. 1.1, 1 Thess. 1.1); 1 Tim. 1.3 adds mercy, but the nearest parallel to this roll of virtues is Gal. 5.22.

7 Cf. Philemon 10 and Gal. 4.19 for the notion that one who converts another is his spiritual father.

supreme pontiff[1] and universal pope – our most benign Serenity has taken pains to publish a clear account of these in the text of this imperial constitution[2] of ours, so that it may come to the knowledge of all people throughout the earth. First, for the instruction of all your minds we profess, and confess from the depths of the heart, our faith in which we have been schooled by the aforesaid Silvester, the universal pontiff and our own most blessed father and advocate,[3] and thereby we proclaim the mercy of God which has been shed upon us.

3. Our purpose is that you should know, as we revealed through that earlier holy and pragmatic[4] ordinance of ours, that we have turned away from the worship of idols, from images mute and deaf, the work of hands,[5] from diabolical inventions, and from all the mummery of Satan,[6] and have attained to the perfect faith of Christians, which is the true light and ever-lasting life.[7] Following the instruction of the same most bountiful pontiff Silvester, our supreme father and teacher, we believe in God the Father Almighty, maker of heaven and earth and of things visible and invisible; and

---

1 Throughout this text the bishop of Rome is styled the *pontifex*, and even *pontifex maximus*. Originally the *pontifices* were only one of four Roman priesthoods, but the title *pontifex maximus* ('great pontiff') was united to that of *princeps* by Augustus, and was retained by all the emperors, including Constantine, until it was formally renounced by Gratian. It had indeed been used as a designation of a leading western bishop in Tertullian's *On Modesty* (c. 216 AD), but evidently with insulting purpose. We do, however, find the title *religionis pontifex* in a letter of the Roman synod to Gratian and Valentinian I, so it is clear that as soon as the emperors laid it down the word began to lend its ancient dignity to the pretensions of the Roman bishopric. See Pohlkamp (1988), 474 n. 30; at Pohlkamp (1988), 483 n. 255 we find that the priests of the Capitol are called *pontifices* in the *Acts of Silvester*.

2 Hence the alternative title, *Constitutum Constantini*, used by Fuhrmann (1968).

3 As in Salvian, *Letter* 8, the word *orator* seems here to signify one who prays effectually for another.

4 For 'pragmatic' see below; royal ordinances are *sancta*, like those of the Senate, because the Latin verb *sancire* means to pass a law with due formality.

5 Of many Old Testament passages, the most similar in content are Ps. 115.4–7 (114.4–7 Vulgate) and 135.15–17 (134.15–17 Vulgate). Raymond Davis points out to me that the former was used regularly in Roman worship in the ninth century.

6 A phrase introduced into Christian parlance by Tertullian, *On Shows* 12 and 24, and also found in the *Acts of Silvester*: Pohlkamp (1988), 480 n. 246. The renunciation of Satan is part of the baptismal liturgy: Hippolytus, *Apostolic Tradition* 21.9.

7 Cf. John 1.4.

in Jesus Christ his only-begotten[1] Son, our Lord,[2] through whom all things were made; and in the Holy Spirit, the Lord, giver of life to all creation. These, the Father, Son and Holy Spirit, we confess in such a manner that in the Trinity there is the perfect fulness of divinity and unity of power. The Father is God, the Son is God and the Holy Spirit is God, and the three are one in Christ Jesus.[3] Thus there are three forms, but one power.[4]

4. For God who had always been wise[5] brought forth his Word from himself,[6] through whom it was always his plan to produce the temporal world.[7] And when he had formed the universal creation from nothing[8] by the agency of this same sole Word of his wisdom,[9] he was with him, arranging

1 But Mirbt and Aland (1967), 251 and Fuhrmann (1968), 60 read *unicus*, 'only', rather than *unigenitus*. The Greek term *monogenes* (John 1.18 etc.) could be rendered in Latin either as *unicus* ('unique') or as *unigenitus* ('only begotten'). The former is characteristic of the fourth century, and appears in the Apostles' Creed as cited by Kelly (1972), 369. Elsewhere *unicus* was generally superseded by *unigenitus* in the liturgy to make it proof against an Arian interpretation.

2 Mirbt and Aland (1967), 251 add the word *Deus*, 'God'.

3 Cf. verses 15 and 16 of the so-called Athanasian Creed at Heurtley (1911), 4; here there appears to be also a loose reminiscence of Col. 2.9. Brewer (1909), 16 traces the formula to the so-called *Faith of Damasus*, perhaps a Spanish forgery of the fifth century, but at 18–19 he notes that it occurs in a Veronese manuscript of the Athanasian Creed, and sees a forerunner at Ambrose, *On the Holy Spirit* 3.82 ('God the Father is adored in Christ').

4 This statement is unequal to the mystery of unity in trinity, but the author is in good company: cf. Athenagoras, *Embassy* 10 (second century); Origen, *Dialogue with Heraclides* 2.27 (third century); Ambrose, *On Luke* 2.66 (fourth century).

5 Cf. Jude 25. 'Constantine' seems to imagine a chronological beginning to the discrete or hypostatic existence of the creative Word. This was denied by Origen, *On First Principles* 1.2.1 as well as by many orthodox Christians after Nicaea, on the grounds that the Father was never without his wisdom. 'Constantine' here anticipates this objection by alluding to the distinction between the two meanings of the word *logos* and thus tacitly subscribing to the opinion of Tertullian (*Against Praxeas* 5) that Christ was eternally present to the Father as his *ratio* or reason, but then projected as his *sermo* or speech for the creation of the world.

6 That is, he is of the substance of God the Father, as the Nicene Creed of 325 affirmed, rather than a creation out of nothing, as Arius held (Theodoret, *Church History* 1.5), or a product of the Father's will, as Origen surmised: *First Principles* 4.4.1(28).

7 An answer to the question what God was doing before he created the world; cf. Augustine, *City of God* 12.4–5.

8 As May (1994) demonstrates, this had become an article of Christian faith by the end of the second century, as an antidote to the teaching of the 'Gnostics' that the world was made from pre-existent matter or from the divided substance of the Godhead.

9 Christ is the word or *logos* of God at John 1.1, and the subsequent text declares that he was the universal instrument of creation. This is the role assigned to Wisdom at Wis. 7.25–26, which is echoed in Heb. 1.3 and Col. 1.15. To authors such as Arius and Origen it was a natural

all hidden purposes by his own secret counsel.[1] Thus when the powers of heaven had been perfected, along with all the materials of the earth, by the pious bidding of his own wisdom, he fashioned the first human being from the mud of the earth in his own image and likeness,[2] and placed him in a paradise of pleasure. From the same joys this man was exiled by the ancient serpent,[3] his jealous enemy the devil,[4] through the most bitter taste of the forbidden tree; and, this man once expelled, the devil did not desist from shooting forth his envenomed darts in many ways,[5] so that, leading the human race astray from the path of truth, he could persuade it to serve the worship of idols, that is to say the creation rather than the Creator.[6] By this he ensured that those whom he was able to ensnare by his intrigues should burn along with him in eternal punishment.[7]

But our God, taking pity on his own handiwork,[8] sent his own holy prophets and through them announced the light of the future life,[9] that is the advent of his own Son, the Lord God and our Saviour Jesus Christ, and then sent that same only-begotten Son of his, who was also the Word of his wisdom. Descending from the heavens for our salvation, he was born from

---

inference to identify Christ with the Wisdom who accompanies God in Prov. 8.22, even though the translation in the Septuagint implies that she was created. Both the translation and the application of this passage were contested after Nicaea, but authority for entitling Christ the wisdom of God, insofar as he reveals God's secret counsel, can be found at 1 Cor. 1.19–24, if not at Luke 11.49.

1 The Latin word is *mysterium*; cf. Col. 1.26, 1 Cor. 2.7 etc. Wisdom declares that she was with God at the creation at Prov. 8.30, and the same is said of the Word at John 1.1–2. Raymond Davis observes that such texts inspired the antiphonal hymn *O Sapientia* ('Oh Wisdom') in the eight or ninth century.

2 Combining Gen. 1.26–27 with Gen. 2.7, ignoring both the apparent contradictions between the accounts and the possibility (hinted by Gen. 1.27 and taken up by Origen, *First Principles* 3.6.1) that the image was initially conferred without the likeness, which was to be perfected by the Holy Spirit (cf. Irenaeus, *Against Heresies* 5.6).

3 See Gen. 3.1, with Rev. 12.9 and 20.2, the only text in scripture where the serpent is identified as the devil.

4 Cf. 1 Pet. 5.8 on the enmity of the devil, and Wis. 2.24 on his jealousy.

5 Cf. Ps. 91.5–6 (90.6 Vulgate) for the coupling of arrows with the noonday demon.

6 Cf. Rom. 1.19–20, though here the devil is not blamed, as he was by Augustine and other ancient Christians.

7 Cf. Eph. 6.11; Matt. 25.41. On the devil's companions in perdition see Rev. 12.4.

8 Conflating the thought of verses such as Rom. 5.6–8 with the language of Plato, *Symposium* 191b.

9 Cf. Isa. 60.1 ('arise, shine, for thy light is come') and John 1.4: 'the light was the life of men'.

the Holy Spirit and the Virgin Mary,[1] and as the Word made flesh he made his home among us.[2] He did not relinquish what he had been, but he became what he had not been.[3] Through the preaching of our father Silvester, the supreme pontiff, we understand that he was perfect God and perfect man, working miracles as God and sustaining human passions as man,[4] at once a human word and the Word of God;[5] and thus we are in no doubt that he was both true God and true man. And having chosen twelve apostles, he shone among them by his miracles,[6] and among countless others of the popular multitude. We confess that the same Lord Jesus Christ fulfilled the law and the prophets,[7] that he suffered and was crucified according to the scriptures,[8] that he rose from the dead on the third day, was taken up into the heavens, and that, seated at the right hand of the Father, he will come from there to judge the living and the dead, and that his kingdom will have no end.[9]

1 The virgin birth is recorded in Matt. 1.18–24 and Luke 1.35. In the early second century it is part of the confession of Ignatius at Ephesians 7.2, but it does not occur in the Nicene Creed of 325, though a little earlier Bishop Alexander of Alexandria had seen fit to include it in his definition of faith: Theodoret, *Church History* 1.4; Kelly (1972), 188–89; Fr. 14 Opitz (1934). After 341, when it occurs in the apology of Marcellus of Ancyra, it becomes an indispensable clause in every creed, and was included in that version of the Nicene Creed which appears to have been endorsed in 381 at the Council of Constantinople and continues to be recited in Christian churches. See Heurtley (1911), 10, 12, 15, 21, together with Kinzig and Vinzent (1999), 551.

2 John 1.18.

3 An important caveat to all orthodox writers of antiquity, expressed with greater technical precision as clause 33 in the Athanasian Creed at Heurtley (1911), 44.

4 The standard Latin theology, as we meet it in Tertullian, *On the Flesh of Christ* 9–13, as well as in the *Tome to Flavian* of Leo the Great (*Letter* 128, 449 AD).

5 *Verbum hominem* and *verbum Dei*. Mirbt and Aland (1967), 253 and Fuhrmann (1968), 64 prefer a different reading, which states simply, with the Nicene Creed, that Christ was true God (*verum Deum*) and true man (*verum hominem*).

6 Cf. Matt. 4.16.

7 Cf. Matt. 5.17.

8 As we are told at Luke 24.27, Mark 14.21, and 1 Cor. 15.3, notwithstanding the absence of any prophecy of a suffering Messiah in the Old Testament. On the authority of Acts 8, most interpreters have looked to Isaiah 53, along with Hos. 6.2. Mirbt and Aland (1967), 253 punctuate the passage so that the resurrection rather than the crucifixion is said to take place according to the scriptures, thus making this text concur with the Nicene formula and with 1 Cor. 15.4.

9 See Heurtley (1911), 10, 12, 15, 21 for credal statements of this dogma, which, although it seems to contradict 1 Cor. 15.28, was even endorsed by Marcellus of Ancyra: Epiphanius, *Panarion* 72.2; Kinzig and Vinzent (1999), 551.

5. Yes, this is our catholic faith,[1] as it was vouchsafed to us by our most blessed father Silvester the supreme pontiff. For this cause we exhort every people, and the folk of the divers nations, to hold, cultivate and proclaim this faith, and to seek the grace of baptism in the name of the holy Trinity,[2] and with devout hearts to adore our Lord Jesus Christ, our Saviour, who with the Father and the Holy Spirit lives and reigns through unending ages, the one whom Silvester our most blessed father proclaims, being universal pontiff.

6. For this same Lord of ours,[3] having taken pity on me a sinner,[4] sent his holy apostles[5] to visit us, and infused into us the radiance of his splendour, so that I might rejoice in my rescue from the shadows and my arrival at the true light and the knowledge of the truth. For when a virulent and blighting leprosy possessed the whole flesh of my body,[6] and many doctors had

1 The Nicene Creed of 325 anathematizes errors in the name of the catholic church – Kelly (1972), 216 – and an interpolated passage in the *Apostolic Tradition* of Hippolytus 21 states that the neophyte will receive instruction in the catholic faith: see Dix and Chadwick (1968), 35–36. The sentence attributed here to Constantine, however, does not contain the word *catholica* in any of the MSS consulted by Fuhrmann (1968). It may have been inserted to echo the peroration of the so-called Athanasian Creed, composed in Latin and probably in Gaul some time after 400: see Heurtley (1911), 42 and 27, with Brewer (1909), 16 on the *Faith of Damasus,* a precursor of the Athanasian Creed which appears to have been quarried in other parts of the *Donation.*

2 As ordained by Christ, Matt. 28.19.

3 Fowden (1994b) conjectures that this story was concocted as an antidote to one put about by the pagan emperor Julian (*Caesars* 336a–b; *Against the Galilaeans*, Fr. 57), denied by the Christian Sozomen (*Church History* 1.5.1) and endorsed on the authority of Eunapius by the anti-Christian Zosimus (*New History* 2.29). According to this, it was only after Constantine had put his son to death on a specious charge in 326 that he was forced to turn to the bishops for the absolution that the pagan priests refused to grant him.

4 Cf Luke 17.13; 1 Tim. 1.13.

5 The term 'apostle' originally denoted those 'sent out' to proclaim the kingdom of God (Matt. 10.2 etc.). Peter was of the number, but Paul was not; nevertheless he declares himself an apostle at Gal. 1.1 and 1 Cor. 9.1, and Gal. 2.8 implies that he was acknowledged in Jerusalem as the apostle to the Gentiles. Raymond Davis reminds me that in Rome the term 'apostolic' was generally used with exclusive reference to Peter and Paul, the putative founders of the church there.

6 This story appears to have originated in the *Acts of the Blessed Silvester,* and is based partly, as Valla, *Donat.* 4.12 (p. 9 Schwahn) perceived, on the healing of Naaman the Syrian by Elisha at 2 Kings 5. The point is admitted in the *Acts of Silvester,* where the leprosy is defined as elephantiasis: see Pohlkamp (1988), 461 n. 248. Fowden (1994b) also compares the miraculous cure of King Abgar of Edessa by Christ himself at Eusebius, *HE* 1.13. We should also remember the cure of Uzziah at 2 Kgs 7.1–15, if only because Jerome offered an exposition of it to Pope Damasus at Letter 18.1.

gathered to apply their cures, yet we had not been rewarded with health by any of their cures,[1] the priests of the Capitol[2] came on this account, saying that a font ought to be made for me on the Capitol, that this should be filled with the blood of infants, and that when it ran warm I could be cleansed by washing in it. And in accordance with their assertions, I had collected a great many innocent infants,[3] and the sacrilegious priests of the pagans were intent on sacrificing them and filling the font with their blood; but our Serenity, perceiving the tears of their mothers, felt an immediate abhorrence of the crime. Taking pity on them,[4] we bade that their sons should be restored to them, and, having furnished vehicles and bestowed gifts, we let them go rejoicing to their own.

7. Thus that day passed, and once the silence of the night had fallen upon us, when the time of sleep had arrived,[5] the apostles St Peter and St Paul[6]

1 On the impotence of doctors cf. Mark 5.26; as Luke 4.23 reminds us, Christ is the true physician, both of body and of spirit. Pohlkamp (1988), 453–54 suggests that the episode is designed as a retort to the healing miracles reported of the god Asclepius, and at 454 n. 152 he quotes Paulinus of Nola, 19.45–56, where Peter and Paul are linked with Christ as instruments of healing.

2 The Capitol (Campidoglio), though by no means the highest eminence in Rome, housed the citadel and the temples of Jupiter, Juno and Minerva. At the temple of Jupiter Optimus Maximus (Best and Greatest) spoils were dedicated and sacrifices offered on behalf of the Roman state. We are therefore to understand that the priests will have represented the massacre of the little ones as a public duty, not merely as a private remedy. In a Byzantine life of Constantine, similar counsels are followed by Maxentius: chapter 11 at Lieu and Montserrat (1996), 117. Constantine himself rejects their overtures before the atrocity can be completed, and only then receives his vision: chapter 15 at Lieu and Montserrat (1996), 119–21.

3 Cf. *Acts of Silvester* at Pohlkamp (1988), 449 nn. 132, 135. Though different both in motive and in outcome, the project is reminiscent of Herod's massacre at Matt. 2.16. Pohlkamp (1988), 450 also sees an allusion to the *taurobolium*, or baptism in the blood of bulls, which was practised in the mysteries of Mithras and Cybele. At 483 n. 255 Pohlkamp notes that a slaughter of infants is attributed to the odious Elagabalus at *Augustan History, Elagabalus* 8 – a largely fictitious record, almost contemporary with the first version of the *Acts of Silvester*, and evincing strong hostility to Constantine. We may add that at Zosimus, *New History* 2.29, Constantine puts his wife Fausta to death by immersion in boiling water, and that this is one of the crimes for which he seeks to make amends by his conversion.

4 Showing the philanthropy already ascribed to God in Chapters 4 and 6.

5 This is the hour when dreams are true, as Horace reminds us at *Satires* 1.10.33, recounting the occasion when he was visited by the patron deity of pagan Rome.

6 The association of Peter and Paul with the church in Rome is ancient. Paul wrote a letter to the congregation, while one in Peter's name is often assumed to be referring to the city of persecution under the name of 'Babylon' (1 Pet. 5.13). Ignatius, *Romans* 4.3 already pairs the

presented themselves, saying to me: 'seeing that you have put an end to the atrocities and have shown abhorrence of shedding innocent blood, we have been sent from Christ our Lord and God, to give you advice on the recovery of your health. Hear therefore our admonitions, and do whatever we tell you: Silvester,[1] the bishop of the city,[2] has fled before your persecutions[3] to the Mount of Soracte,[4] and keeps to a hiding place[5] along with his clergy in the caves of the rock.[6] When you have had this man brought to you, he will show you the bathing-pool of piety, and when you have immersed yourself in this

---

two, as does Irenaeus, *Against Heresies* 3.2, where the first presbyter or bishop of the Roman church is said to have been appointed by their joint authority. As Pohlkamp (1988), 453–57 shows at length, they can also be regarded as the 'Christian Dioscuri', supplanting the glorified heroes Castor and Pollux who had hitherto been the guardians of the city and its armies. See especially the inscription of Damasus at Pohlkamp (1988), 457 n. 160.

1 One might suspect the author of a pun if we could be sure that he knew Pliny the Elder, *Natural History* 20.144, in which we are twice informed that a plant of the woods (*silvestris*) is a cure for elephantiasis.

2 The name of Rome is printed by Mirbt and Aland (1967), 254 and by Fuhrmann (1968), 70, but does not appear in Migne.

3 Constantine was a signatory to the palinode of Galerius in 311, which while it repealed the persecution did not cease to condone it (Eusebius, *Church History* 8.17.3). The *Acts of Silvester* states that he oppressed the Church at the instigation of Maximiana, his wife and the daughter of his predecessor and sometime colleague Maximian (see Duchesne at *LP* 1, cv; in fact the wife was Fausta, daughter of Maximian). This information is not to be despised, for it appears that the clergy of Africa suffered when Maximian returned to power in 308, a little before he made Constantine his son-in-law: see Edwards (1997), 16 and n. 68 on Optatus, *Against the Donatists* 1.17.

4 This peak is also mentioned in the *Acts of Silvester*, though Pohlkamp (1988), 451 n. 142 records numerous variants on the name, including Sarepta. In the *Book of Pontiffs* the name appears as Syraptim, and Fuhrmann (1968) also reads Sarepta. As this was the scene of one of Elijah's miracles (1 Kgs 17.9), it is possible that the author of the *Donation* substituted the biblical name for the one that he found in the *Acts of Silvester*, and that a later hand corrected him.

5 As David hid from Saul in 1 Sam. 22.1, and as the prophets hid from Jezebel in 1 Kgs 18.4. One purpose of this story may be to justify Silvester's reputation as a saint, which he may have enjoyed as early as 354 if we accept the (somewhat speculative) reasoning of Pohlkamp (1988), 422 n. 35. In the early church this honour was generally reserved for those who had suffered for their faith; the *Acts of Silvester*, which also record this flight, bestow on Silvester the title *confessor*, which normally denoted one who had been imprisoned during persecution: Pohlkamp (1988), 428.

6 The word *petrarum*, rather than the more classical *lapidum*, is employed, no doubt because it echoes the name of Peter (Matt. 16.18). Raymond Davis also notes the caverns of rock in the Vulgate of Isa. 7.18.

for the third time,[1] this leprous condition will leave you. When this has been accomplished, repay your Saviour for this change of fortune,[2] and let all churches throughout the world be restored by your command. Yourself too you must purify in this respect, and quitting all idolatrous superstition, and adore and worship the true and living God, who is both the sole and the true one, that you may attain to his will.'

8. Therefore I rose from sleep and straightway acted according to the admonitions that I had received from the apostles. And having summoned that same pre-eminent[3] father and illuminator of ours Silvester, the universal pope, I told him all the words that the holy apostles had enjoined upon me; and I asked him, who were these gods Peter and Paul?[4] His reply, however, was that they were not properly called gods, but the apostles of our Saviour, the Lord God Jesus Christ. And again we began to inquire of the same most blessed pope, whether he had an engraved portrait[5] of these apostles of his, so that we might learn from the picture that these were the ones of whom I had learned by revelation. Then the same reverend father bade that portraits of the same apostles should be displayed by his deacon;[6] and when I beheld them, and perceived that the faces that I had seen in sleep had been delineated in these very portraits, I testified with a great cry

1 Because that is the number of immersions required in baptism, in order that each of the persons in the Trinity may be confessed in turn. Tertullian, *Against Praxeas* 26 and Hippolytus, *Apostolic Tradition* 21, are the earliest witnesses to this stipulation, which, as Wiles (1999) observes, was generally regarded in the fourth century as a fulfilment of Matt. 28.19 and as a guarantee of orthodoxy against the Arians. Naaman, by contrast, bathed himself seven times (2 Kgs 5.14).

2 As the leper healed by Jesus was required to present his gift of thanks to God: Mark 1.43.

3 Mirbt and Aland (1967), 254 and Fuhrmann (1968), 73 add *almificus* ('benevolent').

4 A similar error was made by those who worshipped Paul and Barnabas at Lystra (Acts 14.12–15).

5 It was not in fact impossible that such pictures should be displayed in the early fourth century, as Eusebius, *Church History* 7.18.4 was not ashamed to have seen them in Palestine. The author has thus avoided a rank anachronism, though his purpose here is to rout the iconoclasts of his day. See my introduction on controversy between the Byzantine emperors and the pontiffs of the eighth century.

6 For the parallel in the *Acts of Silvester* see Pohlkamp (1988), 452 n. 144. See *LP* I, 499.27 for Hadrian I's representation of Peter's deliverance from prison; II, 9.29 for Leo III's depiction of the 'princes of the apostles'.

in the midst of all my satraps[1] that these were the ones that I had seen in sleep.

9. Thereupon the same most blessed Silvester, our father, bishop of the city of Rome, set for us a time of penance within our palace, the Lateran,[2] in a single hairshirt of penitence,[3] so that we might implore pardon from the Saviour our Lord God Jesus Christ for all that had been impiously done or unjustly administered by us, with vigils, fasting, tears also and prayers. Then, by way of the laying on of hands by the clergy, at last we reached the prelate himself. And there, renouncing Satan's mummery[4] with his works, and all idols made with hands, of my own free will in the presence of whole people I confessed[5] my belief in God the Father Almighty, maker of heaven and earth, of all things visible and invisible, and in Jesus Christ his only Son our Lord, who was conceived by the Holy Spirit and born of the Virgin Mary.[6]

1 Valla, *Donat.* 12.39 (p. 35 Schwahn) is right to mock the use of this term, which for Constantine could only have denoted the viceroys of the Persian king. It is, however, applied to rulers of other nations in the Septuagint and hence in the Latin Vulgate (Judg. 3.3 etc.), while in the *LP* I, 427.15 Duchesne we read of the satraps of a Lombard king. The scene depicted here is clearly a Germanic court, in which the king sits with his lords.

2 Pohlkamp (1988), 479 n. 244 observes that most of the edifices which bore the name *palatium* in later times remained pagan until the end of the fourth century. Nash (1976) identifies the building given by Constantine with the *domus Faustae in Laterano* where a synod under Miltiades passes judgment on the Carthaginian schism at Optatus, *Against the Donatists* 1.23. On the archaeology of the building see Pietri (1976), I, 4–11.

3 Penance was the usual prelude to baptism in the ancient church; for the stripping of all ornaments see Hippolytus, *Apostolic Tradition* 21.5. The *cilicium*, initially a military garment, became synonymous with penance because the word is used to render the Greek for 'sackcloth' at Luke 10.13.

4 As required, e.g in Hippolytus, *Apostolic Tradition* 21.9.

5 Constantine quotes not the Nicene Creed of 325 (reproduced in the present text of Hippolytus, *Apostolic Tradition* 21), but a conflation of the opening of this with the early clauses of a version of the Apostles' Creed, which was characterized by Kelly (1972), 369 as 'an elaborate variant of the Old Roman creed'. Though unknown in the east, this continued to be 'the Creed' *par excellence* to Rufinus, Augustine and Leo the Great and the one that became customary in the rite of baptism. The articles of the Creed were often elicited from the postulant in the form of a catechism.

6 Mirbt and Aland (1967), 253 and Fuhrmann (1968), 75 omit the word 'all' in the previous clause, and follow the Nicene Creed which states that Christ was born of the Holy Spirit and the Virgin Mary. The reading of the Migne text reproduces the Apostles' Creed, as at Kelly (1972), 369.

The font[1] was blessed, and there the water of salvation purified me with a triple immersion. And when I had been placed in the bosom of the font, I saw with my own eyes a hand from heaven touching me. And rising from it clean, I apprehended that I had been cleansed from the whole blight of leprosy. And once I had been raised from the holy font, and had put on white clothes, he applied to me the sealing of the sevenfold Holy Spirit[2] with the oil of the blessed chrism, and smeared the banner of the Holy Cross[3] on my forehead, saying, 'May God seal you with the seal of his faith, in the name of the Father and of the Son and of the Holy Spirit, in the sealing of faith.'[4] And the whole clergy replied 'Amen'; then the prelate added, 'Peace be with you'.

10. And thus on the first day after I had received the mystery of holy baptism, and after my body had been cured of the blight of leprosy, I apprehended that there was no other god but the Father, the Son and the Holy Spirit, whom blessed Silvester the pope proclaims, the Trinity in unity and unity in Trinity. For all the gods of the nations, whom I have worshipped up to this time, are clearly proved to be daemons, the work of human hands.[5] And furthermore, the reverend father explained to us most clearly what measure of power in heaven and earth that same Saviour of ours had conferred on his apostle the blessed Peter, when, finding that he showed faith in answering his question, he said, 'Thou art Peter, and upon this rock I shall build my church, and the gates of hell shall not prevail against it'.[6]

1 Not described either here or in the *Acts of Silvester*; the artefact of porphyry and precious metals described in the *Book of Pontiffs* was in fact the construction of Xystus III, according to Duchesne at *LP* I, 192. On the ancient baptistery see Pietri (1976) I, 11–14.

2 The seven gifts of the Spirit, according to the Septuagintal version of Isa. 11.2, are wisdom, insight, counsel, might, knowledge, fear and piety. This figure is already quoted by Augustine, *Sermon on the Mount* 1.4.11 but the 'sevenfold grace' almost certainly found its way into this document through the *Gelasian Sacramentary*, which enumerates all of them at the end of the baptismal liturgy. See Wilson (1894), 87 and Finn (1992), 106.

3 See Lampe (1951), 260–83 on the conjunction of anointing in the Spirit with the sign of the Cross, on the relative importance of the two ceremonies, and on the possibility that Christians in the patristic era wore a visible sign of the cross upon their foreheads.

4 The rite of confirmation, which then followed immediately on baptism, as at Hippolytus, *Apostolic Tradition* 22. On the seal of faith (*fides signata*) see Tertullian, *On Baptism* 6.

5 Two different understandings of the idol, but both attested e.g. by Paul at 1 Cor. 8.4–10 and 10.20–21.

6 Matt. 16.18 – a text which, as it came to be the cornerstone of Rome's claim to ecclesiastical primacy, ensured that Peter would overshadow Paul in her recollection. Ullmann (1960), 31 n. 2 remarks upon the 'scarcity of references to Matt. 16.18ff' in early asseverations

Take note, ye powerful, and attend with the ears of your heart, what the good master and Lord added, saying to his disciple, 'Whatever you have bound on earth shall be bound also in heaven'.[1] A marvellous thing indeed is this and a glorious one, to bind and loose on earth and have it bound and loosed in heaven.

11. And inasmuch as, learning these things from the preaching of the blessed Silvester, I also found that by the beneficence of the same blessed Peter I had been restored to perfect health:[2]

We have deemed it expedient, in company with all our satraps and the whole senate,[3] of my nobles[4] also, and furthermore the whole Roman populace which is subject to our imperial glory, that just as Saint Peter is seen[5] to have

---

of papal primacy; he argues (33ff.) that Leo I was the first pope who laid claim to a 'juridical succession' from Peter, although Damasus had styled himself the heir of the apostle, and some notion of succession was already on the lips of Stephen I in the mid-third century, to judge by Firmilian in Cyprian, Letter 75.

   1 Matt. 16.19, though part of this promise is also vouchsafed to the other apostles at Matt. 18.18 as well as at John 20.23. The previous and succeeding clauses of the verse from Matthew appear in Mirbt and Aland (1967), 253 and in Fuhrmann (1968), 79.

   2 Note c at Migne (1844), 573–74 indicates that in some versions the edict commences with a summary of the preceding narrative.

   3 The ruling body of Rome in the republican era, the right of participation being conferred by the censors with regard to property and the tenure of lower magistracies (especially that of *quaestor*). Although its powers became largely nominal under the later Empire, its members retained their hereditary wealth and local influence, and years continued to be dated by the names of its two leading magistrates or consuls, even when neither of these was the emperor. In this text, however, the term denotes an assembly of princes and nobles on the Germanic model, the Roman institution having become extinct in the late sixth century: see Stein (1968).

   4 The word is *optimates*, which, as Cicero, *In Defence of Sestius* 97–100 explains, was used of men who entered politics for the good of the state and not for their own aggrandizement, and who therefore maintained the dignity of the ancient constitution even when this gave offence to a venal and ignorant populace. As Valla, *Donat.* 12.40 (p. 35 Schwahn) notes, the use of the term to signify the nobility is not classical, but it appears in the *Book of Pontiffs* as a name for the acolytes of German kings and of the popes whom they protected: *LP* II, 406.5, 427.17 Duchesne etc. It also appears as a term for military officers in the decree of Pope Stephen II at Mirbt and Aland (1967), 115.5.

   5 The word *videtur* ('seems, is seen') is here employed redundantly for 'is', as is sometimes the case in classical Latin. I have rendered it fully here to convey the pompous tone of the decree, but the reader should remember that the pleonasm is more obtrusive in English than in Latin.

been established as the vicegerent of the Son of God on earth, so the pontiffs also who are vicegerents to this chief of the apostles, should receive by a grant from us and our dominion a power of primacy greater than the mildness of our imperial Serenity is seen to possess on earth; thus we choose this same chief and his vicegerents to be our steadfast advocates with God. And, as is the case with our imperial power on earth, so we have decreed that his sacred church in Rome is to be honoured with reverence, and that to a greater degree than our dominion and earthly throne the most sacred chair of the blessed Peter is to be exalted in glory; thus we assign to him power and glory, imperial in dignity, strength and honour.

12. And in this decree we ordain that he should possess a primacy above the four pre-eminent sees[1] of Antioch, Alexandria, Constantinople[2] and Jerusalem,[3] which he is likewise to have over all the churches of God throughout the whole world. As for him who before this time has been the pontiff of the sacred Roman Church, he is to be raised higher[4] to become head[5] of all priests in the entire world, and all that needs to be provided for the worship of God or the preservation of the faith of Christians is to be administered as he judges fit. Just it is indeed, that the place which supplies a head for the primacy of the sacred law should also be the place where the author of the sacred laws, our Saviour, bade the blessed Peter secure the seat of his apostolate. Here too it was that, bearing a capital penalty on the Cross, he

1 Although its bishop bore the title of pope in the time of Cyprian (251–258) Carthage was never recognized as a major see at ecumenical councils, and in any case the province was under Moslem rule when this text was composed. The proem to Justinian, *Novella* 109 enumerates the same patriarchates, except that Antioch is styled Theopolis.

2 Valla, *Donat.* 13.44 (p. 39 Schwahn) sneers at the presence of Constantinople here, because, as the document itself goes on to indicate, the city was not yet founded. Yet even the signatories to the Nicene Creed of 325 include the future president of the see, although it did not come into being until 330 (Gelasius of Cyzicus, *Church History* 2.28.13). The dignity of the bishopric was pronounced to be second only to that of Rome in the third decree of the council held there in 381; both here and in canon 28 of the Council of Chalcedon in 451, it was implied that political status was the measure of ecclesiastical eminence.

3 An anachronism, as Jerusalem became independent of Caesarea, its nominal metropolis, only at the council of Chalcedon in 451: see Bright (1882), 24.

4 As Pohlkamp (1988), 476 n. 235 observes, the first authentic edict to confirm the papal primacy throughout the Empire was that of Valentinian III in 445 AD, though in 378 Gratian had already extended the pontiff's jurisdiction beyond Italy and Illyricum (Croatia) to Africa, Britain and Gaul.

5 The name Cephas (1 Cor. 15.5 etc.) is traced here, by a false though common etymology, to the Greek word *kephalê* (head). Cf. Optatus, *Donatists* 2.2, with Edwards (1997), 32 n. 9.

drank the cup of a blessed death,[1] and proved to be an imitator[2] of his own Master and Lord. And let the nations bow their necks in confessing the name of Jesus Christ in the place where their teacher, the blessed apostle Paul, stretched forth his neck for Christ and was crowned with martyrdom.[3] Here to the end of time let them seek a teacher, where the teacher's holy body is at rest; and here, prostrate and humbled, let them minister in the service of the heavenly king, our God and Saviour Jesus Christ, where they were servants to the proud dominion of an earthly king.

13. In the meantime we desire the whole population of every race and nation throughout the earth to know that within our Lateran Palace,[4] to that same Lord God Jesus Christ our Saviour, we have built from the foundations a church[5] along with a baptistery;[6] and as to its foundations, know ye also that on our own shoulders we have carried extremely heavy baskets[7] of earth, equal to the number of the twelve apostles. This sacred church, as we determine, is to be named, honoured, venerated and proclaimed as the head and summit of all the churches throughout the whole world, just as we have determined through our other imperial decrees.[8] We have also built

1 For the metaphor cf. Matt. 20.23, 26.39 and parallels. For the crucifixion of Peter see *Acts of Peter* 38 at Elliot (1993), 425; at 392 Elliot assigns a second-century date to the Greek original.

2 As Christians are exhorted to be at John 13.14–15 etc.

3 On the beheading of Paul see *Acts of Paul* 11.5 at Elliot (1993), 387. At 356, Elliot cites Tertullian, *On Baptism* 17 and Origen, *First Principles* 1.2.3 to support a dating of the original text to the second century.

4 It is generally agreed that this was the house of Fausta mentioned in Optatus, *Against the Donatists* 1.23 as the scene of the Roman council against the Donatists under Silvester's predecessor Miltiades. Despite the doubts of Nash (1976), it is also widely believed that this Fausta was the daughter of Maximian and the wife of Constantine; if the author knows of this tradition, he has good reason to style the edifice a palace.

5 No such gift is attested in the *Acts of Silvester*, according to Pohlkamp (1988), 479 n. 244, although this text reports that after the inspection of the Lateran, Constantine pronounced that any pauper who became Christian would be clothed in royal vestments: Pohlkamp (1988), 482 n. 252.

6 Pohlkamp (1988), 480 n. 246 holds that the two great churches had distinct functions in late antiquity: the Lateran for baptism, the basilica of St Peter for the reconciliation of the lapsed.

7 An allusion, as Raymond Davis reminds me, to Matt. 14.20. The twelve baskets that were taken up after the feeding of the 5000 are here taken to represent the twelve apostles.

8 Huyghebaert (1979) and Pohlkamp (1988), 438–39 adduce this passage as evidence that one purpose of the *Donation* was to hallow both ends of the route from St Peter's to the Lateran, which was trodden by pilgrims in the Middle Ages.

churches[1] of the blessed Peter and Paul, the first of the apostles, and these we have adorned with gold and silver, and there with great honour we have also interred their most sacred bodies and have built resting-places for the same from electrum[2] (which yields in strength to none of the elements), and a cross of the finest gold with most precious gems in their respective resting-places, fastening them with golden studs. To furnish lights for these churches, we have conferred on them the estates of our possessions, we have enriched them with divers things, and through our sacred imperial command we have granted them through our munificence, both in the east and in the west, no less in the northern and in the southern zones, that is to say in Judaea, Greece, Asia, Thrace, Africa and Italy,[3] along with the divers islands, always on the understanding that all is to be administered through the hands of our most blessed father[4] Silvester the pontiff and of his successors.

14. Together with us therefore let the whole populace[5] rejoice, and the nations of races in all the lands of the world, and in our exhortation we bid

1 At *LP* I, 176.1–5 Duchesne we read that the Church of St Peter superseded a temple of Apollo, while at 178.12–15 the Church of Paul is said to have been built at Silvester's request. The number of churches attributed to Constantine and his contemporaries grew with the passage of the years: see Duchesne, *LP* I, 193–201 and Davis (1989), xix–xxvi on those attributed to him in the *Book of Pontiffs*. While few of these in their present form can be dated to the fourth century, Davis is of the opinion that many may originate as conversions of vacant property in the reign of Constantine. For St Peter's and St Paul's without the walls see Davis, xxi–xxii, where he admits that the second 'causes problems' and that the first cannot have received its endowment before 324, whereas he traces the Lateran church to 313 (see below).

2 A compound of gold and silver, according to Pliny the Elder, *Natural History* 9.139, 33.81 and 36.46. In these passages Pliny comments on its luminosity and its suitability for regal ornament.

3 Many of the provinces ruled by Constantine go unnamed here, including Gaul and Britain. All the named regions lay within the Byzantine Empire at its maximum extent, and thus the purpose of the document seems to be to make it clear that the popes have sovereignty, or at least the right to sovereignty, in this area without compromising the jurisdiction of the Frankish kings.

4 Cf. Philemon 10 and Gal. 4.19 for the notion that the one who converts another is his spiritual father.

5 The word *populus* seems to be used here, as elsewhere in the *Donation*, for those who regarded themselves as the Roman people, as distinct from the subject nations. After the *constitutio Antoniniana* of 215, which declared all freeborn persons in the Empire to be citizens, the difference, when alleged at all, was nominal. The text may contain a trace of the use of *populus* in the *Acts of Silvester* to denote the whole Christian laity: Pohlkamp (1988), 482 n. 252.

everyone give thanks without measure along with us to our God and Saviour[1] Jesus Christ, seeing that God himself in the heavens above, and in the earth beneath, visiting us through his own apostles has deemed us worthy to receive the sacred sacrament of baptism and health of body.[2] On this account we grant and at the present time hand over to those same holy apostles, my blessed lords Peter and Paul, and through them also to the blessed Silvester our father, the supreme pontiff and universal pope[3] of the city of Rome, and to all the pontiffs who shall be his successors and sit in the chair of the blessed Peter up to the end of the world, the palace of our dominion, the Lateran,[4] which is set above and excels all other palaces in all the lands of the world; and after that the diadem, that is the crown of our head,[5] and the Phrygian cap, that is the mitre,[6] not omitting the shoulder-piece, that is the collar which is wont to surround the imperial neck; and furthermore the purple mantle[7] and russet tunic,[8] and all the imperial

1 Cf. Tit. 2.13, though it is not clear from the Greek of that verse whether God and Christ the Saviour are a single subject.

2 Though Dölger (1913), 407 finds it remarkable that such an effect should be ascribed to baptism, Heb. 10.22 insists on the lustration of the body, while 1 Cor. 11.30 ascribes disease and death to the abuse of the eucharist.

3 The Latin rival to the Greek term 'ecumenical patriarch', as again in Chapter 17.

4 Often called simply the Constantinian basilica in the *Book of Pontiffs*, this is now the Church of S. Giovanni in Laterano. Davis (1989), xx opines that it was the earliest of all Constantine's ecclesiastical foundations. Pohlkamp (1988), 484 n. 258 finds a derisive echo in the mention of Elagabalus' *palatium* at *Augustan History, Elagabalus* 3.4

5 Mommsen (1996), 375 cites *Epitome on the Caesars* 41.1 to show that this item of headgear, hitherto reserved for women and deities, was introduced by Constantine himself to the royal wardrobe. On the diadem as an ornament of the Virgin in statuary, see *LP* II, 418.2 Duchesne

6 This clause is omitted as an editorial gloss in Mirbt and Aland (1967), 256 and in Fuhrmann (1968), 87. The word *mitra* in classical Latin denotes only a female ornament, or the affectation of an effeminate man. In Greek it has a wider and nobler range of senses, and its presence here would therefore be an argument for the Greek provenance of the text, were it not that the *mitra* appears in the Vulgate (Exod. 29.9) as an indispensable covering for the priesthood, and is even worn by monarchs in conjunction with a crown (Ecclus. 45.14; Zech. 6.11). The adjective 'mitred' (*mitratum*) is applied to the pope in the *Book of Pontiffs*, but only in the reign of Leo IX: *LP* II, 355.12 Duchesne. Ullmann (1958), 259 and 313 contends that even when the mitre was used for the coronation of a secular ruler in Ordo C of the Holy Roman Empire, it remained indistinguishable from the papal mitre of this epoch.

7 For the word *chlamys* cf. the *Acts of Silvester* at Pohlkamp (1988), 479 n. 245.

8 Valla, *Donat.* 16.52 (p. 46 Schwahn) mocks the apparent duplication of the costume, but he forgets that at Einhard, *Life of Charlemagne* 23 the emperor wore both *chlamys* and *tunica*, together with *calceamenta* and a *diadema* to honour the pontiffs Hadrian I and Leo III. See my

vestments;[1] and therewith too the honour of imperial horsemen for his retinue;[2] and with these we confer also the imperial sceptres, together with all the insignia,[3] the banners also and the divers imperial ornaments, the whole pageantry of the imperial eminence and the glory of our power.

15. As for the most reverend[4] men of the clergy who minister to that same sacred Roman church in their divers orders, we determine that they shall have, in its unparalleled power and precedence, that eminence whose glory is seen to bring honour to our most illustrious senate; that is, we proclaim that they are to be made patricians[5] and consuls,[6] and no less are they to be decorated with the other imperial dignities. And just as the imperial army[7] has its ornaments, so also we determine that the clergy of the sacred church of Rome shall have its ornaments; and just as the imperial power is adorned

---

introduction on the advantages that each of the parties reached from mutual deference; but note also that both Einhard and the *Donation* (though the purpose of the allusion remains obscure) appear to have in mind an attested variant of Matt. 27.28 which gives an equally tautological description of the purple robe of Christ.

1 At the corresponding point in the *Acts of Silvester*, Constantine divests himself of the 'albs': see Duchesne, *LP* I, cxii.

2 Following Pullan (1971), 10, except that I avoid the translation 'knights' because in classical usage this denotes citizens whose rank entitled them to administrative appointments. In this passage, of course, the mediaeval sense of *eques* (a man entitled to ride a horse in the service of his overlord) is assumed.

3 Reading *cuncta insignia*, with Migne. Mirbt and Aland (1967), 256 and Fuhrmann (1968), 88 have *conta et insignia*.

4 The reading *reverendissimis* makes more sense than the *reverentissimis* in Fuhrmann (1968). On the rule of preferring the *difficilior lectio*, this makes Fuhrmann's text superior, though I translate Migne here as everywhere else.

5 Under the republic, 'patrician' was a hereditary designation for those families which in ancient times had furnished all the members of the Senate. Constantine revived it as a title of distinction for those senators who had been advanced to the rank below that of consul: Jones (1964), II, 528. In the Carolingian period a patrician was often the steward of a particular territory or population; Ullmann (1958), 73 observes that Pepin had been granted the title 'patrician of the Romans' by the Roman see, which scrupled to acknowledge him as emperor.

6 The two officers elected annually to lead the armies of the Republic, and who even under the Empire continued to give their names to the year. Though Constantine was not so accustomed as his predecessors to take this title for himself, he certainly never granted it to a pope. See note at end on *clarissimus*.

7 Enlarging on the analogy between soldiering and faith that is already adumbrated at 1 Cor. 9.7, Eph. 6.11 etc. See also Tertullian, *Prescription of Heretics* 40 on the brand of Mithras, the soldier's god, which he sees as a parody of the Christian sealing with the Spirit. See also Augustine, *Sermon to Catechumens* 16 on the indelible brand of the Christian legionary.

with divers offices, namely those of the chamberlains,[1] the doorkeepers and all the domestic guards, so too we wish the sacred church of Rome to be decorated. And, in order that the glory of the pontiff may shine with the utmost splendour, this too we determine, that the horses of the clergy of that same sacred church of Rome are to be decorated with cloths and linen of the most brilliant hue,[2] and thus they are to ride. And just as our Senate wears shoes[3] with felt, shining with the most brilliant linen,[4] so too is the clergy to wear them, and thus are earthly things like heavenly ones to be decorated in praise of God.[5] Before all else, we assign this freedom to that same most holy father of ours Silvester, the bishop and pope of the city of Rome, and to all the most blessed pontiffs who shall stand in his succession for ever-lasting ages, for the honour of Christ our God, in that same catholic and apostolic[6] church of God: that by our express command,[7] if at his own will and pleasure he wishes to make someone a cleric[8] and to count him among

1 The *cubicularius* was the head of the servants in the imperial household, at least since the late first century (Suetonius, *Domitian* 17).

2 Cf. the equestrian spectacle described at *LP* I, 390.14–15 Duchesne.

3 The word is *calceamenta* rather than the more usual *calcei* of classical times (see next note), no doubt because the Vulgate ordains the *calceamentum* as the clerical shoe at Exod. 12.11 and makes the Baptist apply this term to the footwear of Christ at Mark 1.7 and parallels. It may be that Constantine was famous for his ostentatious footwear, since in the *Augustan History*, which professes to be written in his reign and is now generally suspected of satirical intent, the *calceamentum* is described as the mark of royalty (*Maximin* 28.8), and the jewelled *calceamenta* of Elagabalus (a mock Constantine in the view of many scholars) are singled out for mention at *Elagabalus* 4.4 and 23.4. On the possibility that our author was in possession of sources lost to us, see note above on the title Alamannicus.

4 Commenting on Cicero, *Philippics* 13.28, Shackleton-Bailey (1986), 343 n. 42 states that senators wore boots (*calcei*) with an ivory crescent at the tip. The consul Ausonius, *Daily Round* 2.1 bids a servant bring him his *calcei* and linen. White was a mark of senators in congress, as *Theodosian Code* 14.10.1 indicates by styling them the white order and making this attire compulsory.

5 Cf Heb. 8.5 and Exod. 25.40.

6 A coupling which is found first in the eighth canon of Nicaea at Jonkers (1954), 42, then in the fourth-century creeds of Epiphanius and the Council of Constantinople (381): see Heurtley (1911), 18 and 22. Kelly (1972), 187 reads it also in the so-called *Apostolical Constitutions* 7.41

7 Translating the *indicto* of Migne, rather than the *synclitu* of Mirbt and Aland (1967), 257, which would appear to be a transcription of the Greek word for the Senate.

8 Reading *clericare* for *clericali*, with Migne note c. Even so, the syntax is disordered, and the last clause may contain an accusative absolute, though this would have been ungrammatical in Latin and hardly more felicitous in Greek.

the number of the clergy in religion, no-one at all shall presume to act contumaciously.[1]

16. Herewith we have determined this also, that this same venerable father of ours Silvester the supreme pontiff, and all the pontiffs who succeed him, are to wear the diadem (that is the crown that we have granted him from our own head) made of gold and precious gems, and is to bear it on his head for the praise of God and the honour of the blessed Peter. Yet seeing that the most blessed pope himself refuses absolutely[2] to wear that golden crown on top of the crown of his clerical office, which he wears in honour of the blessed Peter: we with our own hands have placed upon his most sacred head the Phrygian[3] cap with its brilliant glow which symbolizes the splendid resurrection of our Lord;[4] and, holding the rein of his horse, out of reverence for the blessed Peter, we have shown him the office of a squire,[5] and have ordained that in processions all his successors are to enjoy sole use of that same Phrygian cap, in imitation of our dominion.[6]

17. Hence, in order that the pontifical majesty may not grow cheap, but may also be decorated with the power of glory,[7] and more richly than the dignity

1 Throughout the Middle Ages the popes contested the right of investiture both with lay powers and with other ecclesiastical dignitaries. For this period it may be relevant to notice the (alleged) decree of Hadrian I which appears at Hinschius (1863), 689, and asserts his right to appoint new prelates in Britain against the will of the incumbents.

2 Ullmann (1965), 61 writes: 'The forger's intention was to convey the idea that, since no-one had ever doubted that Constantine did wear a crown after reaching Constantinople, he wore it with the pope's agreement and acquiescence'. Verisimilitude may also have been a consideration: it was surely well known that pontiffs of the fourth century had affected a simplicity which in the eighth was thought to be unbecoming to the office.

3 Called the mitre above, and made from peacock feathers, according to the note at Migne (1844), 576 note e. Ullmann (1958), 312–13 identifies this with the *camelaucum* of *LP* I, 390.15 Duchesne, and deduces that until the eleventh century the popes wore only one piece of headgear. Eichmann (1951), 29–30 argues from the same evidence that two were worn. Although the noun *Phrygium/Frigium* does not occur in the *Book of Pontiffs*, one may compare the word *tyrea* (from Tyre) for purple cloths at *LP* I, 504.14ff.

4 For the association of light with the resurrection cf. Eph. 5.14.

5 See Huyghebaert (1979), 186 on the integrity of this passage, which recalls the prostration of Pepin before the pope in 754 (see introduction).

6 I follow here the punctuation of Migne, though, as Raymond Davis remarks to me, rulers did not wear the *mitra*, and Mirbt and Aland (1967), 257 therefore take this phrase with the following paragraph.

7 A pleonastic phrase, which may recall the conclusion of the Lord's Prayer as commonly recited in catholic churches (first attested at *Didache* 9.2).

of earthly dominion: behold, not only our palace, as was previously stated, but also the city of Rome and all the provinces of the whole of Italy and the western regions, their districts and cities, we grant and relinquish to that aforesaid pontiff of ours Silvester the universal pope; these, as we determine with our steadfast imperial judgment through this solemn[1] and pragmatic[2] constitution of ours, are to be administered by his power and authority and that of the pontiffs who shall succeed him, and we grant that they shall remain under the jurisdiction of the sacred church of Rome.

18. Hence we have also perceived it to be fitting that our dominion and imperial power should be transferred and changed to the regions of the east, in the best site in the province of Byzantium,[3] a city is to built in our name,[4] and our dominion is to be established there; the reason is that it is not just for the earthly emperor to hold power in the place where the primacy among priests and the headship of the Christian religion have been established by the heavenly emperor.[5]

19. All these things we have ordained and ratified through other solemn decrees, and we determine that they are to remain undiminished and unbroken until the end of the world. Wherefore in the presence of the living

---

1 The word *divalia* meant 'divine' in early Latin usage, but became almost obsolete until it was rescued for jurisprudence by Justinian, *Digest* 5.9 etc. At this point its meaning was 'sanctioned by God'. It occurs at *LP* I, 350.4, 354.16, 363.12, 366.9 and 368.17 Duchesne to denote the imperial letters received by the pope at his installation. In the first three instances the emperor is Constantine, but the ceremony of letters is not recorded in those lives which show the popes at loggerheads with the eastern throne. There is a clue to date, if not to authorship, in the fact (pointed out to me by Raymond Davis) that all uses of *divalia* in the *Book of Pontiffs* occur in lives 81–85, all of which are thought, on other grounds, to have been composed by the same eighth-century contributor.

2 A legal term for the ordinances of kings, unknown to the *Book of Pontiffs*, but already made current by Justinian, *Digest* 15.1 proem and *Theodosian Code* 11.1.36, 16.5.32.

3 As Valla, *Donat.* 19.62 (p. 55 Schwahn) points out, no such province existed, Byzantium being merely a city.

4 Constantinople was dedicated in 324, and was established in 330 as the seat of government for the richer half of the Empire, becoming the sole capital after the fall of the western realm in 476.

5 Therefore, though Byzantium has supplanted Rome, it cannot overshadow the papacy, and the pontiffs of the eighth century were right to defy the iconoclastic rulers of the east in matters spiritual even while they remained their loyal subjects in matters temporal. See my introduction on the historical circumstances of the forgery.

God,[1] and in the presence of his terrible judgment, we through this imperial constitution of ours adjure all the emperors who shall succeed us, and all our nobles and satraps, with the most illustrious senate and the whole population in all the lands of the world which is subject to us both now and in all ages to come, that in no way is it permitted to any of them, to break, infringe or in any way violate these grants which are made with our imperial sanction to the sacred church of Rome or to all its pontiffs. But if anyone (as we do not believe will happen), should prove to be so audacious or so overweening, let him be bound in subjection to eternal torments, and let him be aware that the holy chiefs[2] of the apostles, Peter and Paul, are his adversaries in this life and the next; and may he fall into consuming fire with the devil and all the impious in the lowest depths of hell.[3]

20. The page of this imperial decree of ours we have confirmed with our own hands, and have placed it upon the venerable body of the blessed Peter,[4] chief of the apostles, making a promise there to the same apostle of God that we shall preserve all these gifts without violation and leave to the emperors who succeed us a command that they are to be preserved, and we hand them over as an everlasting and happy possession to our blessed father Silvester, the supreme pontiff and universal pope, together with all the pontiffs[5] who shall succeed him, with the assent of the Lord God and our Saviour Jesus Christ.

1 Cf. Heb. 10.31 on the terror of falling into the hands of the living God.

2 The word is *principes* (singular: *princeps*), again perhaps punning on the likeness of the Greek word *kephalê* to Cephas, the original name of Peter; cf. Leo I, Letter 10.1. The formula *principes apostolorum* is frequent in the *Book of Pontiffs*, e.g. at II, 9.29 Duchesne (pontificate of Leo III).

3 Cf. Matt. 25.41, though 'Constantine' adds fallen mortals to the angelic rout.

4 Cf. *LP* I, 498.27, where Etherius lays Charlemagne's donation on the body of St Peter. 'Trophies' or memorials of Paul and Peter were known to a certain Gaius in the second century (Eusebius, *Church History* 2.25.7), and there is archaeological evidence that a monument was built by the catacombs on the Appian Way between 238 and 260: Chadwick (1957), 32. He notes (34–36) that the inscription of Damasus which records the translation of the apostles' relics to the Vatican is calculated to show that the 'Arian' east has lost its right to these Greek figures. He argues against Duchesne, *LP* I, civ–cvii, who maintains that an original deposition in the Vatican preceded the brief secretion of the relics on the Via Appia, and that these were returned to the Vatican under Constantine.

5 The words *per eum* ('through him'), which appear in Mirbt and Aland (1967), 258 and Fuhrmann (1968), 99, are not found in Migne.

And the imperial signature: May the Divinity[1] preserve you through many years, most holy and blessed fathers. Given at Rome, on the third day before the April Kalends,[2] the consuls being our lord Flavius Constantine Augustus for the fourth time[3] and Gallicanus,[4] both men of exalted rank.[5]

1 A fine stroke of verisimilitude: see L.J. Hall (1998) and my note to *Oration* 23.

2 That is 30 March, the Kalends being the first day and the reckoning inclusive.

3 In fact, as the edition of Migne (1844), 578 observes, the partner of Constantine in his fourth consulship (the year 315) was Licinius. The dating is of the standard form that can be found, for example, at the end of the genuine letter of Marcian after the Chalcedonian Council of 451: Hinschius (1863), 288.

4 Two Gallicani are attested as consuls, Ovinius with Bassus in 317, and Flavius with Symmachus in 330 (cf. *Theodosian Code* 16.2.7). The first is believed by Barnes (1982), 95 and 101n, and by Jones *et al.* (1971), 383 to be Constantine's co-benefactor commemorated at *LP* I,184.14 Duchesne. The second is often presumed to have been the one who was remembered as a saint; but Champlin (1982) contends that this is nothing but an inference from his date, and suggests that Ovinius is the one intended because the actions of a character of the same name in *Augustan History, Elagabalus* 48.1–6 can be read as a parody of his benefactions. In any case the shared consulship of Constantine and Gallicanus is imaginary. The author of the *Donation* no doubt assumed the identity of the saint and the benefactor, and 330 is perhaps the date implied, as this was also the year of Constantine's migration to the east.

5 The Latin *vir clarissimus* denoted in classical times a man with the right to bear the rank of consul, but from the late first century it was extended to everyone who was qualified to be a senator. While both the term and the consular rank were more widely distributed under the later Empire, it was still impossible to hold the consulship without being *clarissimus*: Jones (1964) II, 527–28.

BIBLIOGRAPHY

Classical literature. With the exceptions listed in the Primary Sources, these authors (Homer, Hesiod, Pindar, Herodotus, Thucydides, Antiphon, Plato, Theocritus, Cicero, Lucretius, Virgil, Horace, Ovid, Strabo, Seneca, Lucan, Pliny the Elder, Suetonius, Plutarch, Dio Chrysostom, Apuleius, Lucian, Diogenes Laertius, Philostratus, Plotinus, Julian, Ammianus Marcellinus, Nonnus) can be consulted in bilingual editions published by William Heinemann in the Loeb Classical Library (Cambridge, MA).

Christian literature. Apocryphal Christian gospels should be consulted in Elliot (1993), and Nag Hammadi texts in Robinson (1988). All Greek and Latin patristic literature, with the exception of works discovered after about 1830, is contained in the *Patrologia Latina* and *Patrologia Graeca*, compiled by J.-P. Migne (Paris). Many have been re-edited since in such series as Sources Chrétiennes (SC, Paris), Corpus Scriptorum Ecclesiasticorum Latinorum (CSEL, Vienna/Leipzig/Prague), Corpus Christianorum Scriptorum Latinorum (CCSL, Turnhout) and Griechische Christliche Schriftsteller (GCS, Berlin/Leipzig). Bilingual editions of the following are available in the Loeb Classical Library: Ignatius (under *Apostolic Fathers*), Clement of Alexandria (*Protrepticus, Schoolmaster, Rich Man's Salvation*); Tertullian (*On Spectacles, Apology*); Minucius Felix; Eusebius (*Church History*); Basil (letters and essay on reading Greek literature); Jerome (letters); Augustine (letters, *City of God* and *Confessions*); Prudentius.

With the exceptions listed in the Primary Sources, translations of ecclesiastical writers can be consulted in the Library of the Ante-Nicene Fathers, and the Library of the Nicene and Post-Nicene Fathers, published in the nineteenth century by T. and T. Clark (Edinburgh) and republished frequently in the twentieth century by W. Eerdmans (Grand Rapids). **Ante-Nicene Fathers** (**ANF**) include *Didache* (with Ignatius etc.), Ignatius, Justin Martyr, Athenagoras, Tatian, Minucius Felix, Theophilus of Antioch, Irenaeus, Clement of Alexandria, Tertullian, Hippolytus, Origen, Cyprian, Novatian, Methodius, Lactantius, Arnobius. **Nicene and Post-Nicene Fathers** (**NPNF**) include Eusebius, Athanasius, Basil of Caesarea, Gregory of Nazianzus,

John Chrysostom, Ephraem Syrus, Ambrose, Cyril of Alexandria, Rufinus, Jerome, Augustine, Socrates, Sozomen, Philostorgius, Theodoret.

Jewish writings. Canonical and Deuterocanonical texts (the latter including Wisdom, Ecclesiasticus, Greek portions of Daniel) are best consulted in the bilingual edition of the Septuagint by L.C.L. Brenton (London, 1851, often reprinted). Pseudepigraphic texts (*1Enoch, 2Enoch, Sibylline Oracles, Testaments of the Twelve Patriarchs*) should be consulted in H.F.D. Sparks, *The Apocryphal Old Testament* (Oxford, 1985). Philo and Josephus are edited with translation in Loeb editions.

Note on titles. The title given first in this list is the one used in the text. Usually this is an English title, except where a work is so obscure that no English title has come into common use.

PRIMARY SOURCES

Alcinous, *Isagoge*, ed. C.F. Hermann, *Plato*, vol. VI (Leipzig, 1874), 147–89; trans. with commentary by J. Dillon as *The Handbook of Platonism* (Oxford, 1993).

Alexander of Aphrodisias, *On Fate*, ed. and trans. R.W. Sharples (London, 1983).

Ambrose of Milan, Letters 16 and 17, ed. with related works of Symmachus and Prudentius in M. Lavarenne, *Prudence* III (Paris, 1948). This contains a French translation; these letters are translated with other relevant documents in B. Croke and J. Harries (eds), *Religious Conflict in Fourth-Century Rome. A Documentary Study* (Sydney, 1982).

Ammianus Marcellinus, *Histories*, ed. and trans. J.C. Rolfe (Loeb, Cambridge, MA, 1936–39).

Annals of the Franks, *Annales Regni Francorum*, ed. G.H. Pertz and F. Kurze (Hanover, 1895). I am not acquainted with any English translation of this text.

Arator, *Acts of the Apostles*, partially edited and translated in R. Hillier, *Arator on the Acts of the Apostles* (Oxford, 1993).

Aristides of Athens, *Apology*, ed. and trans. J. Armitage Robinson (Cambridge, 1891).

Augustan History, *Scriptores Historiae Augusti*, ed. and trans. D. Magie (Loeb, Cambridge, MA, 1922–32).

Aurelius Victor, *Caesars*, ed. F. Pichlmayr and R. Gruendel (Leipzig, 1966);

trans. H.W. Bird (Liverpool, 1994).

Book of Pontiffs, *Le Liber Pontificalis*, ed. P. Duchesne, vol. I (Paris, 1886), vol. II (Paris, 1892), supplementary vol. (Paris, 1957). When Duchesne's edition is cited, this is regularly abbreviated to *LP*; otherwise the name appears in English.

Chalcidius, *Commentary on the Timaeus of Plato*, ed. J.H. Waszink (Leiden, 1962).

Chaldaean Oracles. *Oracles Chaldaïques*, ed. with French translation by E. Des Places (Paris, 1971); trans. R. Majercik (Leiden, 1989).

Clement of Alexandria, *Excerpts from Theodotus*, ed. and trans. R.P. Casey (Cambridge, 1934).

Collation of Mosaic and Roman Laws, ed. and trans. M. Hyamson (London and New York, 1913).

Constantine, *Oration to the Saints* (*Orat.*). *Konstantins Rede an die Heilge Versammlung*, ed. I.A. Heikel, *Eusebius Werke* 1 (GCS, Leipzig, 1902), 149–92. Previous translation appears in NPNF edition of Eusebius.

Cyril of Alexandria, *Select Letters*, ed. and trans. L. Wickham (Oxford, 1983).

Donation of Constantine. *Edictum Constantini*, in J.-P. Migne, *Patrologia Latina* 8 (Paris, 1844), 567–79, and *Patrologia Latina* 130 (Paris, 1853), 245–52. Also as *Constitutum Constantini*, ed. H. Furhmann, *Fontes Iuris Germanici Antiqui* 10 (Hanover, 1968). Also found in Hinschius (1863), 248–54, Williams (1964) and Mirbt and Aland (1967), 107–12. The edict without preamble is contained in Valla (*Donat.*). A partial translation is supplied by Pullan (1971).

Egeria, *Pilgrimage*, ed. A. Franceschini and R. Weber (CCSL, Turnholt, 1965); trans. Wilkinson (1971).

Einhard, *Life of Charlemagne. Vita Karoli Magni*, ed. G.H. Pertz, G. Waitz and O. Holder-Egger (Hanover and Leipzig, 1911); reprinted with German translation by E.S. Coleman (Stuttgart, 1968); English translation by L. Thorpe (Harmondsworth, 1969).

Empedocles. Remains edited in H. Diels, revised by F. Kranz, *Fragmente der Vorsokratiker* (Berlin, 1951); partially translated by G.S. Kirk and J.E. Raven, *The Presocratic Philosophers* (2nd edn, Cambridge, 1983).

Epiphanius of Salamis, *Panarion,* ed. K. Holl (GCS, Berlin, 1913–15, completed 1980); trans. F. Williams (Leiden, 1987–94).

Eusebius, *Chronicle. Chronicon*, ed. J. Karst (GCS, Leipzig, 1911). I am not acquainted with any English translation of this text.

——, *Church History. Kirchengeschichte*, ed. E. Schwartz, 3 vols (GCS, Berlin, 1903–09). Translated in both NPNF and Loeb editions.

——, *Gospel Preparation. Praeparatio Evangelica*, ed. and trans. E.H. Gifford, 5 vols (Oxford, 1903).

——, *Life of Constantine. Das Leben Constantins*, ed. I.A. Heikel, *Eusebius Werke* 1 (GCS, Leipzig, 1902), 1–147. F. Winkelmann (ed.), *Eusebios, Über das Leben des Kaisers Konstantins* (GCS, Berlin, 1975, revised 1992); for translation and commentary see Cameron and Hall (1999).

——, *Onomasticon, Theophanie*, ed. E. Klostermann (GCS, Leipzig, 1904).

——, *Tricennial Oration. Tricennatsrede an Constantin*, ed. I.A. Heikel, *Eusebius Werke* 1 (GCS, Leipzig, 1902), 193–259; translated by H.A. Drake, under title *In Praise of Constantine* (Berkeley, 1976)

Eutropius, *Breviary. Breviarium*, ed. C. Santini (Stuttgart, 1992); trans. H.W. Bird (Liverpool, 1993).

Gelasius of Cyzicus, *Church History. Kirchengeschichte*, ed. G. Loeschke and M. Heinemann (GCS, Leipzig, 1918). I am not acquainted with an English translation of this text.

Hilary of Poitiers, *On the Mysteries. Traité des Mystères*, ed. with French translation by J.-P. Brisson (SC, Paris, 1947). I am not acquainted with any English translation of this text.

Hippolytus of Rome, *The Treatise on the Apostolic Tradition*, trans. Dix and Chadwick (1968).

Iamblichus of Chalcis, *On the Mysteries*, ed. with French translation by E. Des Places (Paris, 1966); English translation by Thomas Taylor (London, 1851, reprinted San Diego, 1994).

——, *On the Pythagorean Life*, ed. F. Dübner (Leipzig, 1957, 1975); trans. E.G. Clark (Liverpool, 1989).

Invention of the True Cross, *Inventio Sanctae Crucis*, ed. A. Holder (Leipzig, 1899).

Jerome, *Chronicle. Chronicon*, ed. R. Helm (GCS, Berlin, 1956).

——, *Commentary on Zechariah*, ed. M. Adriaen (CCSL, Turnhout, 1970). I am not acquainted with an English translation of this text.

Justinian, *Digest. Digesta*, ed. T. Mommsen and P. Krueger (1905); trans. A. Watson (Philadelphia, 1985).

Justinian, *Novellae*, ed. R. Scholl and W. Kroll (Leipzig, 1954).

Lactantius, *Divine Institutes (DI). Divinae Institutiones*, ed. S. Brandt, 2 vols (CSEL, Vienna/Leipzig/Prague, 1890–93); translation in ANF edition.

——, *On the Deaths of the Persecutors (Pers.)*, ed. and trans. J.L. Creed (Oxford, 1984).

Latin Panegyrics. *Panegyrici Latini*, ed. R.B. Mynors (Oxford, 1964);

translated as *In Praise of Later Roman Emperors* by L. Nixon and B.S. Rodgers (Berkeley and Oxford, 1994).

Leo the Great, *Letters*, trans. E. Hunt (Washington, DC, 1957); Letter 128 in W. Bright, *Select Sermons of Leo on the Incarnation* (London, 1886). See Migne, *Patrologia Latina* 54 for full edition of works.

Liber Pontificalis, see Book of Pontiffs.

Mark the Deacon, *Life of Porphyry of Gaza. Vie de Porphyre*, ed. with French translation by H. Grégoire and M. Kugener (Paris, 1930). I am not acquainted with any English translation of this text.

Melito of Sardis, *On the Pasch* and *Fragments*, ed. and trans. S.G. Hall (Oxford, 1979).

Nemesius of Emesa, *On the Nature of Man. De Natura Hominis*, ed. G. Verbeke and J. Moncho (Leipzig, 1975); trans.W. Telfer (London, 1955).

Numenius of Apamea, Fragments, ed. with French translation by E. Des Places (Paris, 1973). Excerpts appear in Eusebius, *Gospel Preparation*.

Optatus of Milevis, *Against the Donatists*, ed. J. Labrousse (SC, Paris, 1995–96); trans. Edwards (1997).

Origen, *Werke*, edited by several hands in GCS edition. Translations include:

——, *Against Celsus*, trans. H. Chadwick (Cambridge, 1953).

——, *Commentary on John*, 2 vols, trans. R.E. Heine (Washington, DC, 1989, 1993).

——, *First Principles*, trans. G.W. Butterworth (London, 1936, reprinted Gloucester, MA, 1973).

——, *Homilies on Genesis and Exodus*, trans. R.E. Heine (Washington, DC, 1982).

——, *On Prayer*, trans. R. Greer, *Origen* (London, 1979).

——, *Philokalia*, ed. and trans. J. Armitage Robinson (Oxford, 1893).

Passion of Perpetua, ed. and trans. in H. Musurillo, *Acts of the Christian Martyrs* (Oxford, 1972).

Paulinus of Nola, Letter 31, can be consulted in appendix to Holder, *Inventio*; see further the complete edition of the letters by G. Harkel (CSEL, Vienna/Leipzig/Prague, 1999); complete translation by P.G. Walsh (Westminster, MD, and London, 1967).

Philostorgius, *Church History. Kirchengeschichte*, ed. F. Winkelmann (GCS, Berlin, 1981); translated with Sozomen by E. Walford (London, 1855).

Porphyry of Tyre, *On Abstinence. De Abstinentia*, ed. A. Nauck in *Porphyrii Opuscula* (Leipzig, 1886); trans. E.G. Clark (London, 2000).

——, *Life of Pythagoras. Vita Pythagorae* in Nauck (above). I am not acquainted with any English translation of this text.

——, *Sententiae ad Intelligibilia Ducentes*, ed. E. Lamberz (Leipzig, 1975); translated as *Launching-Points to the Realm of Mind* by K. Guthrie (London, 1989).

——, *On Statues*, appendix to J. Bidez, *Vie de Porphyre* (Ghent, 1913); trans. Gifford as part of Eusebius, *Gospel Preparation*.

Rufinus, *Church History*, as supplement to Eusebius, *Die Kirchengeschichte*, ed. E. Schwartz and T. Mommsen (GCS, Berlin, 1908); translation in NPNF.

Salvian, Letters, in *Oeuvres*, vol. I, ed. G. Lagarrigue (SC, Paris, 1971); trans. F. Sullivan in *Works of Salvian the Presbyter* (Washington, DC, 1962).

Socrates, *Church History. Kirchengeschichte*, ed. G.C. Hansen (GCS, Berlin, 1995); translation in NPNF.

Sozomen, *Church History. Kirchengeschichte*, ed. J. Bidez and G.C. Hansen (GCS, Berlin, 1995); translation in NPNF.

Stobaeus, *Eclogae*, ed. O. Wachsmuth and O. Hense (Leipzig, 1884–1923); no complete translation is available.

Theodoret, *Church History. Kirchengeschichte*, ed. L. Parmentier, F. Scheidweiler and G.C. Hansen (GCS, 3rd edn, Berlin, 1998); translation in NPNF.

Theodosian Code. *Codex Theodosianus*, ed. T. Mommsen and P.M. Meyer (Berlin, 1905); trans. C. Pharr (New York, 1952).

Valla, L., *On the Donation of Constantine (Donat.). De Donatione Constantini*, ed. W. Schwahn (Leipzig, 1994).

Zonaras, *Epitome*, ed. B.G. Niebuhr (Bonn, 1841–44).

Zosimus of Panopolis, *Treatise on the Omega*, with other works and notes, in W.B. Scott, *Hermetica*, vol. IV (Oxford, 1936), 104–53.

Zosimus, *New History. Nouvelle Histoire*, ed. with French translation by F. Paschoud (Paris, 1971–89); English translation by R.T. Ridley (Canberra, 1982).

SECONDARY LITERATURE AND COMMENTARIES

Aldridge, R.E. (1999), 'The Two Ways', *Vigiliae Christianae* 53, 233–64.

Alföldi, A. (1948), *The Conversion of Constantine and Pagan Rome*, trans. H. Mattingly (Oxford).

Baldwin, B. (1976), 'Vergilius Graecus', *American Journal of Philology* 97, 361–68.

Barnes, T.D. (1973), 'Lactantius and Constantine', *Journal of Roman Studies* 63, 29–46.

Barnes, T.D. (1976a), 'The Emperor Constantine's Good Friday Sermon', *Journal of Theological Studies* 27, 414–23.

Barnes, T.D. (1976b), 'Imperial Campaigns, A.D. 285–311', *Phoenix* 30, 174–93.

Barnes, T.D. (1976c), 'The Victories of Constantine', *Zeitschrift für Papyrologie und Epigraphik* 20, 149–55.

Barnes, T.D. (1981), *Constantine and Eusebius* (Cambridge, MA).

Barnes, T.D. (1982), *The New Empire of Diocletian and Constantine* (Cambridge, MA).

Barnes, T.D. (1995), 'Statistics and the Conversion of the Roman Aristocracy', *Journal of Roman Studies* 85, 135–47.

Barnes, T.D. (2001), 'Constantine's Speech to the Assembly of the Saints: Place and Date of Delivery', *Journal of Theological Studies* 52, 26–36.

Baynes, N.H. (1931), *Constantine the Great and the Christian Church* (London).

Bleckmann, B. (1997), 'Ein Kaiser als Prediger: Zur datierung der konstantinischen Rede an die Versammlung der Heiligen', *Hermes* 125, 183–202.

Bolhuis, A. (1956), 'Die Rede Konstantins des Grossen an die Versammlung der Heiligen und Lactantius, *Divinae Institutiones*', *Vigiliae Christianae* 10, 25–32.

Borgehammar, S. (1991), *How the Holy Cross was Found* (Stockholm).

Bowersock, G. (1986), 'From Emperors to Bishops: The Self-Conscious Transformation of Political Power in the Fourth Century A.D.', *Classical Philology* 81, 298–307.

Bradbury, S. (1996), *Severus of Minorca. Letter on the Conversion of the Jews* (Oxford).

Brent, A. (1995), *Hippolytus and the Church of Rome at the End of the Second Century* (Leiden).

Brewer, H. (1909), *Das sogenannte Athanasianische glaubensbekenntnis ein Werk des heiligen Ambrosius* (Paderborn).

Bright, W. (1882), *Notes on the First Four Oecumenical Councils* (Oxford).

Burckhardt, J. (1880/1949), *Die Zeit Konstantins des Grossen*, trans. M. Hadas (New York).

Cameron, A. and S. Hall (1999), *Eusebius: Life of Constantine* (Oxford).

Chadwick, H. (1957), 'St Peter and St Paul in Rome', *Journal of Theological Studies* 8, 30–52.

Chadwick, H. (1958), 'Ossius of Cordova and the Council of Antioch, 324', *Journal of Theological Studies* 9, 292–304.

Champlin, E. (1982), 'Saint Gallicanus (consul 317)', *Phoenix* 36, 70–76.

Coakley, J.F. (1984), 'A Syriac Version of the Letter of Cyril of Jerusalem on the Vision of the Cross', *Analecta Bollandiana* 102, 71–84.

Coleman, R. (1977), *Virgil: Eclogues* (Cambridge).

Corcoran, S.P. (1996), *The Empire of the Tetrarchs* (Oxford).

Courcelle, P. (1957), 'Les exégèses chrétiennes de la quatrième éclogue', *Revue des Études Augustiniennes* 59, 294–317.

Cook, J. (1973), *The Troad* (Oxford).

Creed (1984), see Lactantius in Primary Sources.

Daniélou, J. (1961), *Message Évangelique et Culture Hellénistique* (Tournai).

Davies, P. (1989), 'Origin and Purpose of the Persecution of 303', *Journal of Theological Studies* 40, 66–94.

Davies, P. (1991), 'Constantine's Editor', *Journal of Theological Studies* 42, 610–18.

Davis, R. (1989), *The Book of Pontiffs (Liber Pontificalis)* (Liverpool).

Davis, R. (1992), *The Lives of the Eighth Century Popes (Liber Pontificalis)* (Liverpool).

De Decker, D. (1978), 'Le Discours a l'assemblée des saints attribué a Constantin et l'oeuvre de Lactance', in J. Fontane and M. Perrin (eds), *Lactance et son Temps. Recherches Actuelles* (Paris), 75–87.

Dillon, J. (1977), *The Middle Platonists* (London).

Dix, G. and Chadwick, H. (1968), *The Treatise on the Apostolic Tradition of Hippolytus of Rome* (London).

Dölger, F.J. (1913), 'Die Taufe Konstantins und ihre Probleme', in Dölger (ed.), *Konstantin der Grosse und seine Zeit* (Freiburg).

Drake, H.A. (1985a), 'Eusebius on the True Cross', *Journal of Ecclesiastical History* 36, 1–22.

Drake, H.A. (1985b), 'Suggestions of Date in Constantine's *Oration to the Saints*', *American Journal of Philology* 106, 335–49.

Drake, H.A. (1989), 'Policy and Belief in Constantine's *Oration to the Saints*', *Studia Patristica* 19, 43–51.

Drake, H.A. (2000), *Constantine and the Bishops. The Politics of Intolerance* (Baltimore).

Drijvers, H. and J.W. (1997), *The Finding of the True Cross. The Judas Kyriakos Legend in Syriac* (Louvain).

Drijvers, J.W. (1992), *Helena Augusta. The Mother of Constantine the Great and her Finding of the True Cross* (Leiden).

Drijvers, J.W. (1996), 'The *Protonike* legend and the *Doctrina Addai*', *Studia Patristica* 33, 517–23.

Dufraigne, P. (1997), *Adventus Augusti, Adventus Christi* (Paris).

Edwards, M.J. (1995), 'The Arian Controversy and the *Oration to the Saints*', *Vigiliae Christianae* 49, 379–87.

Edwards, M.J. (1997), *Optatus: Against the Donatists*, translated with notes and introduction (Liverpool).

Edwards, M.J. (1999a), 'The Flowering of Latin Apologetic: Lactantius and Arnobius', in M.J. Edwards, M.D. Goodman and S.R.F. Price (eds), *Apologetics in the Roman Empire* (Oxford), 197–222.

Edwards, M.J. (1999b), 'The Constantinian Circle and the *Oration to the Saints*', in M.J. Edwards, M.D. Goodman and S.R.F. Price (eds), *Apologetics in the Roman Empire* (Oxford), 251–76.

Ehrhardt, C. (1980), '"Maximus", "Invictus" und "Victor" als Datierungs-kriterien auf Inschriften Konstantins des Grossen', *Zeitschrift für Papyrologie und Epigraphik* 49, 177–81.

Eichmann, H. (1951), *Die Weihe und Kronung des Papstes im Mittelalter* (Tubingen).

Elliott, T.G. (1992), 'Constantine's Explanation of his Career', *Byzantion* 62, 212–34.

Elliott, J. (1993), *The Apocryphal New Testament* (Oxford).

Elsner, J. (1998), *Imperial Rome and Christian Triumph* (Oxford).

Elze, B. (1960), *Ordines Coronationum Imperatorum* (Fontes Iuris Germanici Antiqui 9) (Hanover).

Encyclopaedia Judaica (EJ), 16 vols (Jerusalem).

Finn, T.M. (1992), *Early Christian Baptism and the Catechumenate. Italy, North Africa and Egypt* (Collegeville, MN).

Folz, R. (1974), *The Coronation of Charlemagne*, trans. J.E. Anderson (London).

Fowden, G. (1991), 'Constantine's Porphyry Column: the Earliest Literary Allusion', *Journal of Roman Studies* 81, 119–31.

Fowden, G. (1993), *Empire to Commonwealth: Consequences of Monotheism in Late Antiquity* (Princeton).

Fowden, G. (1994a), 'Constantine, Silvester and the Church of S. Poly-euctus in Constantinople', *Journal of Roman Archaeology* 7, 274–84.

Fowden, G. (1994b), 'The Last Days of Constantine: Oppositional Versions and their Influence', *Journal of Roman Studies* 84, 146–70.

Frede, M. (1999), 'Eusebius' Apologetic Writings', in M.J. Edwards, M.D. Goodman and S.R.F Price (eds), *Apologetics in the Roman Empire* (Oxford), 223–50.

Frothingham, A.L. (1883), 'L'omelia di Giacomo di Serug sul battesimo di Costantino imperatore', *Atti delle Accademia dei Lincei* 8, 167–242.

Fuhrmann, H. (1959), 'Konstantinisches Schenkung und Silvesterlegende in neuer Sicht', *Deutscher Archiv für Erforschung des Mittelalter* 15, 523–40.

Fuhrmann (1968), see Donation of Constantine in Primary Sources.

Gibbon, E. (1929), *The History of the Decline and Fall of the Roman Empire*, ed. J.B. Bury, 6 vols, 2nd edition (London).

Ginzberg, L. (1920), *The Legends of the Jews*, vol. II (New York).

Grauert, H. (1882), 'Die Konstantinisches Schenkung', *Historisches Jahrbuch*, 3–29.

Gregorovius, F. (1971), *Rome and Medieval Culture. Selections from the History of the City of Rome in the Middle Ages*, ed. K.F. Morrison, trans. G.W. Hamilton (Chicago).

Grigg, R. (1977), 'Constantine the Great and the Cult without Images', *Viator* 8, 1–32.

Hall, L.J. (1998), 'Cicero's *instinctu divino* and Constantine's *instinctu divinitatis*: The Evidence of the Arch of Constantine for the Senatorial View of the Vision', *Journal of Early Christian Studies* 6, 647–71.

Hall, S.G. (1998), 'Some Constantinian Documents in the *Vita Constantini*', in S. Lieu and D. Montserrat (eds), *Constantine: History, Historiography and Legend* (London and New York), 86–103.

Halphen, L. (1977), *Charlemagne and the Carolingian Empire*, trans. G. de Nie (Amsterdam).

Hanson, R.P.C. (1973), 'The *Oratio ad Sanctos* attributed to the Emperor Constantine and the Oracle at Daphne', *Journal of Theological Studies* 24, 505–11.

Heath, T.L. (1913), *Aristarchus of Samos* (Oxford).

Heid, S. (1992), 'Zur frühe Protonike und Kyriakos legende', *Analecta Bollandiana* 109, 73–108.

Heine, R. (1998), 'The Christology of Callistus', *Journal of Theological Studies* 49, 56–91.

Herrin, J. (1987), *The Formation of Christendom* (Oxford).

Heurtley, C.A. (1911), *De Fide et Symbolo* (Oxford).

Hinschius, P. (1863), *Decretales Pseudo-Isidorianae et Capitula Angilramni* (Leipzig).

Horowitz, I. (1996), *The Generations of Adam* (London/Philadelphia).

Hunt, E.D. (1982), *Holy Land Pilgrimage in the Later Roman Empire A.D. 312–460* (Oxford).

Hunt, E.D. (1997), 'Constantine and Jerusalem', *Journal of Ecclesiastical History* 48, 405–24.

Huyghebaert, N. (1976), 'La Donation de Constantine ramenée à ses véritables dimensions. A propos de deux publications récentes', *Revue d'Histoire Ecclésiastique* 71, 45–69.

Huyghebaert, N. (1979), 'Une légende de fondation: le *Constitutum Constantini*', *Le Moyen Age* 85, 1177–209.

Ison, D. (1987), '*Pais Theou* in the Age of Constantine', *Journal of Theological Studies* 38, 412–16.

Jones, A.H.M. (1954), 'Notes on the Genuineness of the Constantinian Documents in Eusebius' *Life of Constantine*', *Journal of Ecclesiastical History* 5, 194–200.

Jones, A.H.M. (1964), *The Later Roman Empire. A Social, Administrative and Economic Survey*, 3 vols (Oxford).

Jones, A.H.M, J. Martindale and J. Morris (1971), *The Prosopography of the Later Roman Empire*, vol. I (Cambridge).

Jonkers, E.J. (1954), *Acta et Symbola Conciliorum quae Saeculo Quarto Habita sunt* (Leiden).

Kamesar, A. (1990), 'The Virgin of Isaiah 7.14: the Philological Argument from the Second to the Fifth Century', *Journal of Theological Studies* 41, 51–75.

Kazhdan, A. (1987), '"Constantin Imaginaire": Byzantine Legends in the Ninth Century about Constantine the Great', *Byzantion* 57, 196–250.

Kelly, J.N.D. (1972), *Early Christian Creeds* (London).

Kelly, J.N.D. (1975), *Jerome* (London).

Kinzig, W. and M. Vinzent (1999), 'Recent Research on the Origin of the Creed', *Journal of Theological Studies* 50, 535–59.

Kurfess, A. (1936), 'Die griechischen Übersetzer von Vergils vierter Ekloge in Kaiser Konstantins Rede an die Versammlung der Heiligen', *Zeitschrift für die Neutestamentliche Wissenschaft* 35, 97–100.

Lachower, F. and I. Tishby (1989), *The Wisdom of the Zohar*, vol. II (Oxford).

Lampe. G.W.H. (1951), *The Seal of the Spirit. A Study in the Doctrine of Baptism and Confirmation in the New Testament and in the Fathers* (London).

Lane Fox, R. (1986), *Pagans and Christians in the Mediterranean World from the Second Century to the Accession of Constantine* (Harmondsworth).

Lieu, S. and D. Montserrat (1996), *From Constantine to Julian* (London).

Loenertz, R.J. (1974), '*Constitutum Constantini*: destination, destinateurs, auteur, date', *Aevum* 48, 199–245.

Lovejoy, A.O. and G. Boas (1935), *Primitivism and Related Ideas in Antiquity* (Baltimore).

Luigi, G. (1904), 'Textes orientaux inédits du martyre de Judas Cyriaque, évêque de Jérusalem', *Revue de l'Orient Chrétien* 9, 79–95 and 310–22.

Luigi, G. (1906), 'Textes orientaux inédits du martyre de Judas Cyriaque, évêque de Jérusalem', *Revue de l' Orient Chrétien* 11, 337–51.

Maffei, D. (1964), *La Donazione di Costantino nei Giruisti Medievali* (Milan).

Markschies, C. (2000), *Alta Trinità Beata* (Tübingen).

May, G. (1994), *Creatio ex Nihilo. The Doctrine of 'Creation out of Nothing' in Early Christian Thought*, trans. A.S. Worall (Edinburgh).

Mazzarino, S. (1974), 'Antico, Tardantico ed Era Costantiniana 1', *Storia e Civilta* 13.

Merdinger, J. (1997), *Rome and the African Church in the Time of Augustine* (New Haven).

Millar, F. (1977), *The Emperor in the Roman World* (London).

Mirbt, C. and K. Aland (1967), *Quellen zur Geschichte des Papstums und der Romischen Katholizismus*, 6th edition, vol. I (Tübingen).

Mitchell, S. (1988), 'Maximin and the Christians in 312 A.D.: A New Latin Inscription', *Journal of Roman Studies* 78, 105–24.

Molland, E. (1950), 'Irenaeus of Lugdunum and the Apostolic Succession', *Journal of Ecclesiastical History* 1, 12–28.

Mommsen, T. (1996), *A History of Rome under the Emperors* (London).

Moraux, J. (1954), *Lactance: Les morts des persécuteurs*, 2 vols (Paris).

Nash, E.T. (1976), '*Convenerunt in domum Faustae in Laterano*: Optati Milevitani 1.23', *Romische Quartalschrift für Altertumskunde und für Kirchengeschichte* 71, 1–21.

Nestle, E. (1889), *De Sancta Cruce* (Stuttgart).

Nisbet, R.G. (1978), 'Virgil's Fourth Eclogue: Easterners and Westerners', *Bulletin of the Institute of Classical Studies* 27, 59–78.

Norden, E. (1924), *Das Gebürt des Kindes* (Leipzig).

Opitz, H.G. (1934), 'Die *Vita Constantini* des Codex Angelicus 22', *Byzantion* 9, 540–90.

Osborne, C. (1994), *Eros Unveiled. Plato and the God of Love* (Oxford).

Pegoulewsky, N. (1921), 'Le Martyre de S. Cyriaque de Jérusalem', *Revue de l'Orient Chrétien* 26, 305–49.

Pietri, C. (1981), *Roma Christiana*, 2 vols (Rome).

Piganiol, C. (1932), 'Dates Constantiniennes', *Revue d'Histoire et de Sciences Religeuses* 12, 360–72.

Pohlkamp, W. (1988), 'Privilegium Ecclesiae Romanae pontifici contulit: Zur Vorgeschichte der Konstantinischen Schenkung', in *Falschungen in Mittelalter. Internationaler Kongress der Monumenta Germaniae Historica, München, 16–19 September 1986, 2* (Hanover), 413–90

Pohlkamp, W. (1992), 'Textfassungen, literarische Formen und geschichtliche Funktionen der römischen Silvester-Akten', *Francia* 19, 115–96.

Preisendanz, K. (1973–74), *Papyri Graecae Magicae*, 2 vols (2nd edition, Stuttgart).

Price, S.R.F. (1999), 'Latin Christian Apologetics: Minucius Felix, Tertullian and Cyprian', in M.J. Edwards, M.D. Goodman and S.R.F. Price (eds), *Apologetics in the Roman Empire* (Oxford), 105–30.

Pullan, B. (1971), *Sources for the History of Medieval Europe* (Oxford).

Rapp. C. (1998), 'Imperial Ideology in the Making: Eusebius of Caesarea on Constantine as Bishop', *Journal of Theological Studies* 49, 684–95.

Rendel Harris, J. (1894), 'Kenyon on Greek Papyri in the British Museum', *Classical Review* 8, 45–49.

Rist, J.M. (1981), 'Basil's "Neoplatonism"', in J. Fedwick (ed.), *Basil of Caesarea. Christian, Humanist, Neoplatonist* (Toronto), 137–200.

Rives, J.B. (1995), 'Human Sacrifice among Pagans and Christians', *Journal of Roman Studies* 85, 65–85.

Rives, J.B. (1999), 'The Decree of Decius and the Religion of the Empire', *Journal of Roman Studies* 89, 235–54.

Robinson, J.M. (1988), *The Nag Hammadi Codices in English* (Leiden).

Ruysschaert, J. (1973), 'La légendaire "sedes pétrinienne" du Majer', *Rivista di archeologia cristiana* 49, 293–99.

Sallares, R. (1991), *The Ecology of the Ancient Greek World* (London).

Salzman, M. (1993), 'The Evidence for the Conversion of the Roman Empire to Christianity in the Theodosian Code', *Historia* 42, 362–78.

Sambursky, S. (1959), *Physics of the Stoics* (Westport, CT).

Samuel, A.E. (1972), *Greek and Roman Chronology* (Munich).

Schultze, V. (1894), 'Quellenuntersuchungen zur *Vita Constantini* des Eusebius', *Zeitschrift für Kirchengeschichte* 14, 503–55.

Schürer, E. (1986), *History of the Jewish People in the Age of Jesus Christ*, revised by M. Black, M. Goodman and G. Vermes, vol. III (Edinburgh).

Shackleton Bailey, D.S. (1986), *Cicero: Philippics* (Chapel Hill, NC).

Skarsaune, O. (1987), *The Proof from Prophecy* (Supplements to *Novum Testamentum* 56) (Leiden).

Smith, M.D. (1997), 'The Religion of Constantius I', *Greek, Roman and Byzantine Studies* 38, 187–209.

Staubinger, J. (1912), *Die Kreuzauffindungslegende. Untersuchungen über ihre altchristlichen Fassungen mit besonderen Berücksightigung der syrische Texte* (Paderborn).

Stein, E. (1968), 'La disparution du Sénat de Rome à la fin du Ve siècle', in E. Stein, *Opera Minora Selecta* (Amsterdam), 359–84.

Stemberger, G. (2000), *Jews and Christians in the Holy Land*, trans. R. Tuschling (Edinburgh).

Storch, R.H. (1970), 'The Trophy and the Cross', *Byzantion* 40, 105–17.

Tarn, W.W. (1932), 'Alexander Helios and the Golden Age', *Journal of Roman Studies* 22, 135–60.

Taylor, J.E. (1998), 'The Sites of Jesus' Crucifixion and Burial', *New Testament Studies* 44, 180–203.

Thümmel, H.G. (1992), *Die Frühgeschichte der Ostkirchlichen Bilderlehre* (Berlin).

Turner, C.H. (1916–17), 'The Episcopal Lists, III, IV', *Journal of Theological Studies* 18, 103–34.

Ullmann, W. (1958), *The Growth of Papal Government in the West* (London).

Ullmann, W. (1960), 'Leo I and the Theme of Papal Primacy', *Journal of Theological Studies* 11, 25–51.

Ullmann, W. (1965), *A History of Political Thought in the Middle Ages* (Harmondsworth).

Van Esbroeck, M. (1984), 'Jean II de Jérusalem et les cultes de S. Étienne, de la Sainte-Sion et de la Croix', *Analecta Bollandiana* 102, 99–134.

Van Unnik, W.C. (1962), 'The Christian's Freedom of Speech in the New Testament', *Bulletin of the John Rylands Library* 44, 466–88.

Van Winden, J.M.C. (1959), *Calcidius on Matter. His Doctrine and Sources* (Leiden).

Veyne, P. (1992), *Bread and Circuses*, trans. B. Pears (Harmondsworth).

Wallace-Hadrill, J.M. (1967), *The Barbarian West 400–1000* (London).

Walter, C. (1970), 'Papal Political Imagery in the Mediaeval Lateran Palace', *Cahiers Archéologiques* 20, 156–77.

Wigtil, D.M. (1980/81), 'Toward a Date for the Greek Fourth Eclogue', *Classical Journal* 76, 336–41.

Wiles, M.F. (1999), 'Triple and Single Immersion: Baptism in the Arian Controversy', *Studia Patristica*, 337–49.

Wilkinson, J. (1971), *Egeria's Travels* (London). Reprinted, with different arrangement of material, Warminster, 1999.

Williams, S. (1964), 'The Oldest Text of the *Constititum Constantini*', *Traditio* 20, 448–61.

Wilson, H.A. (1894), *The Gelasian Sacramentary* (Oxford).

Woods, D. (1997), 'Where Did Constantine I Die?', *Journal of Theological Studies* 48, 531–34.

Woods, D. (2001), 'Some Eunapiana', in K. McGroarty (ed.), *Ekloga. Studies in Honour of Thomas Finan and Gerard Watson* (Maynooth), 87–132.

Wright, D.F. (1991), 'Constantine and the Mother of God', *Studia Patristica* 24, 355–59.

Yarnold, E. (1993), 'The Baptism of Constantine', *Studia Patristica* 26, 95–101.

Young, F.M. (1999), 'Greek Apologists of the Second Century', in M.J. Edwards, M.D. Goodman and S.R.F. Price (eds), *Apologetics in the Roman Empire* (Oxford), 81–104.

MAPS

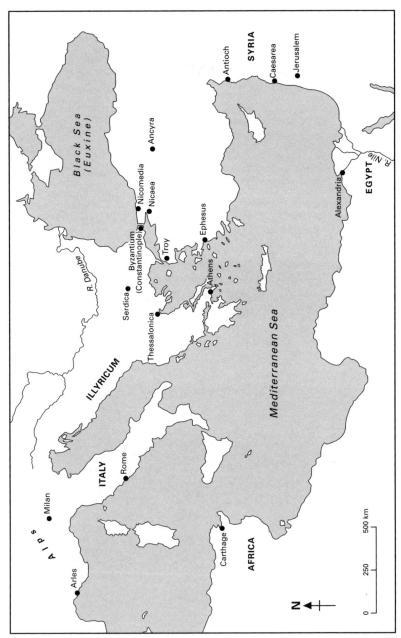

The Mediterranean World in the Age of Constantine

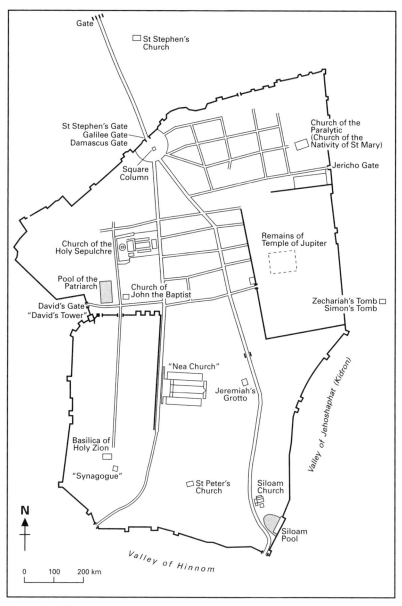

Gate

St Stephen's
Church

St Stephen's Gate
Galilee Gate
Damascus Gate

Church of the
Paralytic
(Church of the
Nativity of St Mary)

Square
Column

Jericho Gate

Church of the
Holy Sepulchre

Remains of
Temple of Jupiter

Pool of the
Patriarch

Church of
John the Baptist

David's Gate
"David's Tower"

Zechariah's Tomb
Simon's Tomb

"Nea Church"

Jeremiah's
Grotto

Valley of Jehoshaphat (Kidron)

Basilica of
Holy Zion

"Synagogue"

St Peter's
Church

Siloam
Church

Siloam
Pool

N

0   100   200 km

Valley of Hinnom

Byzantine Jerusalem

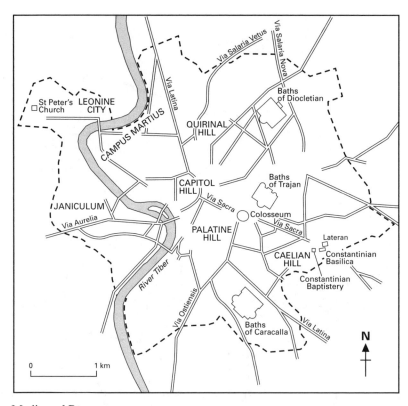

Mediaeval Rome

INDEX TO THE ORATION TO THE SAINTS

INDEX TO TEXTS ON THE DISCOVERY
OF THE CROSS

INDEX TO THE EDICT OF CONSTANTINE